coachbook

A Guide to
Organizational Coaching Strategies
& Practices

By

William Bergquist, Ph.D
and Agnes Mura, M.A. M.C.C.

ISBN: 1456562959
ISBN-13: 9781456562953
Library of Congress Control Number: 2011901131

Dedicated to
Dusi Mura, master coach

Table of Contents

CHAPTER 4 BEHAVIORAL COACHING

CHAPTER 5 DECISIONAL COACHING

Preface

The Twenty-First Century has brought with it not only the prospects of advancement in technology and human welfare, but also organizational challenges associated with complexity, unpredictability and turbulence.(Bergquist and Mura, 2005) Men and women who serve in leadership roles are most likely to face these exceptional challenges. This doesn't necessarily mean that these women and men are situated at the top of the organization. In many cases, these men and women are asked to convene a task force, provide timely advice, mentor a new hire, or initiate a project. They might not even think of themselves as "leaders." In fact, these men and women may not even be formally invited to accept a leadership role. They may simply be in the right place, at the right time, to influence the organization of which they are members.

Postmodernism and the World of Organizational Coaching

It may not be coincidental that the field called organizational coaching emerged at the same time (during the 1990s) as many organizational analysts began identifying and describing this postmodern world of complexity, unpredictability and turbulence.(Vaill, 1989; Wheatley, 1992, Stacey, 1996) To the extent that organizational coaching is about enhancing the processes of performing, making decisions and discovering deeply felt values and aspirations within a world of complexity, unpredictability and turbulence, then this field is particularly timely and its future is bright.

We propose that any employee in an organization who must engage in work under the challenging conditions of complexity, unpredictability and turbulence—but particularly those in a formal or informal leadership role - can benefit from the assistance of a knowledgeable and skillful organizational coach. *Complexity* demands a level of cognitive functioning that often leaves us, as Robert Kegan (1994) suggests, "in over our heads." We must be able to understand and grapple with complex issues that are often nested inside other complex issues or are juxtaposed with other challenging issues. In complex settings we are faced with an additional challenge: we must simultaneously be able to think about our own thinking and take actions. We must be able to learn from our mistakes and successes, as well as be aware of the particular settings in which we learn and in which we don't learn (often called meta-learning)

We are even more challenged when faced with *uncertainty*. Under conditions of uncertainty, obviously, we can't predict what will happen next. However, there is an additional challenge: we are continually faced with new information that comes from many different angles. We must continually accommodate to this new information while abandoning—at least temporarily—old assimilated models, assumptions, and social constructions of organizational reality (Berger and Luchman1967: Argyris and Schön, 1974; Argyris, 1989; Senge, 1990). Using Kurt Lewin's (1947) term: we are always unfreezing and never have a chance to settle in with our new learning and new accommodation.

Turbulence further compounds the challenge, given that we, as decision-makers, must live in a swirling "white water world" (Vaill, 1989) in which rapid change intermixes with patterned change, stagnation and chaos. Somehow in the midst of this turbulence—which is driven by ever-accelerating change—we must find our own personal (some would say "spiritual") core. We search for sanctuary from this turbulence and must always adjust to a world with new change-dynamics. At the end of the day, we can't even remember what happened to us at the start of the day—because we have had to make so many adjustments throughout the day!

We further propose that if we, as organizational coaches, can demonstrate in our daily work the value of the services we render as being directly aligned with, appreciative of, and effective in addressing the challenges of complexity, unpredictability and turbulence, then we can anticipate that the profession of organizational coaching will be sustained and become a mature discipline or inter-disciplinary domain. It will be a profession that plays a growing and increasingly important role in 21st Century organizational life. This book's purpose is to enable organizational coaches, internal and external, to deliver the highest efficacy to their dual clients: the organization and the person being coached.

Why 21ˢᵗ Century Leaders Seek Organizational Coaching

In their sometimes temporary and sometimes long-term leadership roles, 21ˢᵗ Century women and men face challenges of many different kinds, coming from many different sources. The system around them may have varying and often contradictory expectations regarding how this person is likely to *perform* as a leader, as well as how they would like this person to perform as a 21ˢᵗ Century leader. The leaders often find themselves making difficult *decisions* that impact not only on their lives, but also the lives of people about whom they care deeply. The leaders' fundamental *values* and the relationship between these values and those of their organization are always being called forth—and challenged. Are the leader's values and those of the organization aligned or does the leader repeatedly have to trade off what is most important in her life for that which the organization most values? Conversely, can the leader always consistently role model the noble values that make up the specific organizational culture in which he works?

In the flattened 21ˢᵗ Century organization, leaders often live in solitude, working in emotional *isolation* as performers, decision-makers, and people who must relate their own personal values with those of their organization. Even though these leaders may receive input from many sources, ultimately they alone must perform, make choices with unprecedented speed and align values and interests among dizzying numbers of stakeholders. These organizational responsibilities, often coupled with a need for confidentiality and support from equally over-extended peers and bosses, leave the leader with few, if any, outlets to share these burdens. We have noted with alarm that *burn out* occurs with great frequency among leaders at many different levels and in many different kinds of organizations—big and small, for profit and not for profit, high tech and low tech, manufacturing and service-oriented.

Our challenged leader might read an article about coaching or talk with a colleague about their successful use of a coach. Perhaps this will motivate the harried leader to contact a coach for help with her day-to-day work. She may use other words, but at the heart of the matter is a desire to break down the isolation. Increasingly, perceptive and strategic leaders and talent development professionals are learning to identify when a leader needs and deserves coaching. The coaching resources - external or internal – that are made available at that point hold the potential, if well prepared, of having a greater impact on the work life of the leader than any other single developmental activity that could be offered.

Certainly, sympathetic listening, a willingness to observe the leader in operation, and the skills needed to provide helpful feedback are essential in this situation, but these skills might not be at all sufficient. What does a planned, logical and sufficiently in-depth sequence of organizational coaching services look like if the leader is to be helped rather than harmed? This book will offer the reader a variety of suggestions regarding masterful organizational coaching strategies for today's leaders.

In many books these strategies are grouped under one heading, *executive coaching*. However, the term *executive* may not be appropriate, for the strategies we will describe and explore in this book encompass not only the coaching work with men and women who are in formal positions of leadership in an organization, but also the work with other members of an organization who seek out or find themselves in position of leadership under conditions of complexity, unpredictability and turbulence. Those who head committees on a local school board or who are Distinguished Engineers in a software company – with no direct authority over others—are leaders to whom people look up. A finance professional who takes the responsibility to raise attention about ethical conflicts is a leader, as is the supervisor who must inform a subordinate of his unsatisfactory performance. These people, along with formal titular leaders, must perform, make many decisions, and align values in meeting their civic or professional responsibilities. This book describes ways in which each of these leaders, formal and informal, can best be supported by organizational coaching. We will use the terms *executive, administrator* or *manager* when describing work with those in formal leadership positions, but will in most instances use the much more broadly-defined term *leader* (or *client*).

Another implication of the term executive coaching as it is used in the literature is that it describes a *triangular* relationship. In that sense, we agree that all organizational coaching has to satisfy both the interests of the sponsoring organization and those of the individual being coached. Numerous return-on-investment (ROI) studies (for example, Schlosser, *et al.*, 2007) are highlighting the impact of effective coaching on factors like performance, team climate, retention, innovation, strategic thinking and, ultimately, the financial bottom line. Such organizational benefits are corollaries to the personal development and growth experienced by the individual leader being coached. The three interlocking gears on our book cover are a reminder of this—one of the greatest challenges and distinctions in organizational coaching: the triangular stakeholder configuration. The number of stakeholders involved can even grow in certain cases, when boards, communities or public bodies are involved in the successful outcome of a coaching assignment.

An Overview of this Book

The first section of this book expands a practitioner's awareness and widens his horizon towards an appreciative, systemic and potentially transformational approach to coaching. The second section provides over thirty Coaching Resources – tools that are immediately usable by internal or external coaches with the colleagues or clients they are coaching. Future editions will build on the dialogue these tools and practices generate in the coaching community, as well as on the original future contributions of our readers.

In the first three chapters of this book, we set the stage for the full description of the various organizational coaching strategies.

In *Chapter One,* we distinguish among and suggest the relationship that exists between organizational coaching and two other ways of assisting members of organizations: counseling and consulting. We also offer a description of appreciation as a concept and strategy, and suggest three types of coaching issues that inform masterful coaching strategies.

We then turn in *Chapter Two* to the basic interpersonal tools needed by anyone who wishes to provide effective organizational coaching. These interpersonal tools are critical to any successful organizational coaching program and it's important to be reminded of these fundamental yet highly sophisticated elements in a helping relationship. With these caveats in mind, seasoned practitioners might quickly review Chapter Two—for some experienced coaches are already familiar with these tools and approaches.

In *Chapter Three,* we describe and differentiate between three different clusters of coaching models. One of these clusters focuses on the Behavioral challenges faced by a coaching client, while a second cluster focused on the Decision-making challenges faced by this client. The third cluster focuses on the Aspirational challenges faced by a coaching client.

We focus in detail on these three coaching clusters in the following three chapters of this book. Specifically, in *Chapter Four* we look at *Behavioral coaching,* which has to do with coaching leaders who wish to refine or transform their one-on-one interactions as well as team-based interactions. *Decisional coaching,* focusing on the choices and dilemmas in modern working life is described in *Chapter Five,* with attention being given to the processes of reflective coaching, instrumented coaching and observational coaching. *Chapter Six* concerns the cluster of models that relate to *Aspirational Coaching.*

We encourage all readers—whether novice or experienced—to return at some point to the first three chapters in order to better understand our own perspectives regarding the nature and purpose of organizational coaching and the conditions in which we find ourselves as members of 21st Century organizations. Ultimately, the frames of reference we use as authors and practitioners strongly influence the strategies and models that we offer. The overall coaching taxonomy we are introducing is summarized in Table One for quick (and frequent) reference.

The last section of the book includes a wide variety of Coaching Resources that can directly benefit the organizational coach who is implementing one or more of the strategies and models identified in the first part of the book. The resources we have selected have repeatedly proven useful and appropriate in many different and challenging coaching engagements, and we refer to them throughout the descriptive first section of the book.

Our Personal Expression of Appreciation

This is a book about appreciation. We suggest that the forces of appreciation are ultimately much stronger than the forces of criticism. In keeping with this belief, we wish to acknowledge the indispensable encouragement and support we received. Bill wishes to extend his appreciation to his colleague, Christopher Browne, and his four provosts who have served his graduate school (The Professional School of Psychology) over the past decade: Betsy Eubanks, Tom Smith, Suzan Guest and Robin Drotleff. He also wishes to acknowledge the inspiration and encouragement that have been offered by many coaching colleagues over the past two decades. Bill wants to point in particular to the sustained support offered by John Lazar, Linda Page, Richard Wale and April Chi. The greatest amount of love and deep gratitude go to Bill's three generations of family: Kathleen, Jason, Kate, Erik, Marybeth, Alicia, Julia, Miles, Dylan and Izaak.

Agnes wishes to acknowledge that she has had the good fortune of having in her mother, the late piano artist teacher Dusi Mura, the friend and inspirational role model that decisively guided her outlook on life and people. Prof. Mura nurtured many significant European pianists in the enormously difficult climate of Communist Romania, after which she built a second strong following in Southern California, where her magnetic chamber music master classes publicly demonstrated how she developed musicians… and people. Agnes also fondly acknowledges the most important boss and mentor in her life, Peter Ueberroth, president during the 1984 Los Angeles Olympics, Contrarian entrepreneur and civically engaged leader, who can count on Agnes' life-long friendship. Her most recent, warmly appreciated communities of learning and friendship have been the faculty team at Oliver Wyman Leadership Development and her colleagues at the International Consortium for

Coaching in Organizations. To her protector, nurturer and loving husband, John Heinritz, goes the ultimate recognition for enabling Agnes to work and live happily, every day.

William Bergquist
Harpswell, Maine

Agnes Mura
Santa Monica, California

Chapter One

An Appreciative Perspective

Many sources of learning exist for leaders. They learn from their successes and failures in addressing daily challenges, from formal training and education, and from informal conversations with colleagues. They also learn from their spouses, children, friends and relatives. They learn from professionals they seek out for personal support and assistance, as well as from the consultants they bring into their organization. (McCall, Lombardo, and Morrison, 1988)

In considering ways in which to foster significant learning, we differentiate between two forms of assistance. On the one hand, valuable support is provided by colleagues to one another on a frequent and informal basis, or as part of their organizationally-defined relationship. On the other hand, formal, professional services are provided to (and in) organizations by consultants, counselors and coaches. To anticipate the conclusion: The key factor that differentiates the first, informal from the second, formal kind of assistance is the time-limited nature of the second approach. Furthermore, the key factor that can distinguish organizational coaching from both consulting and counseling is *appreciation*.

We identify ways in which appreciative strategies can be employed to confront the complex challenges and opportunities facing leaders and conclude with a description of the more general appreciative perspective on organizational life that provides the foundation for the organizational coaching strategies proposed and described in this book.

The Three C's: Consulting, Counseling and Coaching

Consulting and counseling services are usually provided by professionals with expertise, academic degrees and licenses in specific fields or disciplines. A certified accountant, professor of business or organizational psychologist often engages in organizational consultation, while counseling is usually provided by a mental health professional. Coaching, on the other hand, can be provided by a trained professional and even by a wise and communication-savvy (though unlicensed and uncertified) colleague.

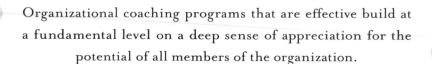

> Organizational coaching programs that are effective build at a fundamental level on a deep sense of appreciation for the potential of all members of the organization.

While clear distinctions may be drawn between the roles of counseling, consulting and coaching, in reality, these three roles often overlap. In some cases, we find that two or all three of these roles are blended in a single initiative. In other cases, the person who serves in a helping role will shift from one role to another depending on the needs and roles played by her client. The overlap in roles and functions is particularly common when one is assisting a formally-designated leader, for this person can benefit from all three types of service. Two of our colleagues, Sandra Hill and Joel Rothaizer, have recently made a particularly persuasive statement regarding the intimate relationship between organizational coaching and consulting (Hill and Rothaizer, 2007, Rothaizer and Hill, 2010) as has our colleague, Mary Beth O'Neill. (2007).

Coaching bridges the gap between friendship, on the one hand, and both consulting and counseling, on the other hand. Unlike either a consultant or counselor, a person providing coaching to someone could at least hypothetically switch roles (if both people wish) and become the recipient of the other person's coaching. Roles are flexible, and at times fluid. The primary role of the coach varies, given the needs and interests of his client. A coach might help his colleague expand the availability of valid and useful information. He might instead (or in addition) help his colleague gain a clearer sense of her personal intentions (often as related to the intentions of her organization) or help her generate and critically examine a variety of potential solutions to the complex issues she faces. Most importantly, a coach helps his client make informed decisions and take informed and sustained actions, based on intentions that she has reflected upon and therefore committed to and on viable options that have been generated and evaluated.

Members of organizations often face considerable stress and must frequently re-examine personal aspirations in highly complex situations. Counseling can be very helpful in these settings. The contemporary member of an organization also confronts critical and intricate systematic issuess that are best addressed with the assistance of a consultant. This person might need a safe and supportive setting and relationship in which to reflect on and learn more about her own behavior. Organizational coaching that is conducted from an appreciative perspective can meet these needs. Thus, in order to better understand the way in which one might best assist members of organizations, and the context in which organizational coaching should take place, we will briefly describe the functions of counseling, and consulting and contrast them with one another and with organizational coaching.

Consulting

The consultation process is a systematic process whereby a client requests and receives assistance from an expert who is not immediately involved in the ongoing operations of the organization in which the client works. As a result of this seeming objectivity or disinterested detachment, the consultant can diagnose issues and provide a viewpoint which insiders often are unable or unwilling to see.

The actual process of consultation takes on various forms. In some cases, the consultant primarily assists his client in better understanding the nature of the organizational challenges she faces and formulating an appropriate strategy to address these challenges. In other cases, the consultant actually conducts a change project for the client. In yet other cases, the consultant provides the client with resources or ideas so that the client can complete the change project herself or with others.

A consultant relationship is established with a specific client or small client group in the organization. This consultative relationship tends to be quite stable and the consultant/client relationship is rarely reversed. It would usually be considered inappropriate (even unethical) for a consultant to switch roles with one of his clients. As a rule, clients hold formal administrative positions in the organization. While they need not be at the top of the organization, they usually are in a place to initiate and fund a consultation and take action based on the recommendations made by the consultant. Consultative meetings usually take place in the client's office during work hours. The agenda is typically established by the consulting client—often with clarifying assistance from the consultant. The length of a meeting will vary depending upon the client's calendar.

Both the client and consultant must begin to trust one another's competence, intentions and perspectives if the consultation is to be successful. Nevertheless, meetings between the client and consultant usually focus upon the task before them. They are rarely diverted to more personal issues, like, for example, the client's personal concerns about the implementation of the ultimate recommendation or its impact on certain team relationships.

The role of the consultant is one of focusing upon the convening consultative task, while also building sufficient rapport and trust to ensure continuous mutual understanding and increasing the likelihood that the client will execute the resulting recommendations. While the relationship between client and consultant can be cordial, it is also somewhat detached insofar as it is focused on the project and organization at hand.

Fees for the consultation are often negotiated before beginning the process or intervention. Financial remuneration for the consultant service can be fixed (such as hourly, daily or total amount for the project) or variable (such as a percentage of the gross amount of money saved over a given time). Traditionally, the consultation relationship is terminated and financial obligations are settled once the consultative task or project is completed.

Counseling

Organizations have come to realize that an employee is a valuable asset and that its investment in that person needs to be sustained on an ongoing basis. Considering the cost to train and develop an employee, it is far better to help resolve an employee's personal issues than to terminate her and hire a new employee. Thus, there has been a significant rise in Employee Assistance Programs (EAPs) in recent years. EAPs assist referred employees with personal life issues that have negatively influenced their job performance. EAPs are often external counseling service agencies that are separate from the main or referring organization. They contract with a company for counseling services and are paid a capitation rate (a set amount per employee per month). Their task is to provide counseling to the employee (and occasionally to the employee's family) in order to allow the employee to function fully in her organizational role. EAPs primarily confront issues associated with stress-related disorders, drug and substance abuse disorders, and marital or financial challenges.

 Appreciation is about fuller understanding, not merging, with another person's problems or identity.

Counseling, or psychotherapy, has a focus that is directed toward the individual and how that person is functioning in the larger context of their lives. There is usually an exploration of the client's past life and the relationship between this past life and the feelings and issues that currently confront the client. (Wheeler, 1995, p. 50) The counselor is usually trained as a psychotherapist and licensed by a governmental agency to provide this type of professional service. The client (patient) presents a problem: This problem may be overt such as substance abuse, or covert such as a character disorder. In any presenting problem, it is the job of the counselor to work through the presenting problem with the client and restore a degree of mental health. This is often regarded as a medical model because the scope of the relationship is one of "healing" the client.

Counseling is often non-directive and the focus of the communication is on what is conveyed by the client. The counselor encourages the client to examine her own personal issues and work them through to a satisfactory conclusion. The work occurs in the counselor's office with a specific appointment hour and a specific time limit (usually 50 minutes). The counselor can assure the client confidentiality within the limits imposed by the law. Counseling can be short or long term depending on the issues presented and the manner in which the counselor proceeds.

The relationship established between the counselor and client is difficult to describe succinctly. The counselor must remain objective and distant, yet at the same time exhibit a quality of warmth and interest in the client. The counselor must demonstrate empathy toward the client and her issues. This is a general rule of counseling. Thus, the counselor must attempt to create an environment in which the client feels safe and free to express herself. The counselor will often employ different types of communication techniques at appropriate times during a counseling session. These techniques may involve reflecting emotionally laden material back to the client for clarification, probing or asking questions that may lead to greater insight for the client or perhaps confrontation when both client and counselor are aware of a true distortion presented by the client.

The responsibility for changing behavior rests primarily with the client. Optimally, with insight or training, the client will make satisfactory adjustments and the curative effect will have occurred. Client and counselor usually meet weekly unless the situation demands a more intensive intervention. Typically, the client, medical insurance company, or employer will reimburse fees for services rendered by the counselor. Usually the rate charged is by the appointment hour. The rules of the therapist prevail in providing this type of service. However, it should be noted that with the advent of managed care and health management organizations (HMOs), there is a current trend to set a limit on the number of counseling hours allowed or approved for an individual.

Len Sperry was among the first to differentiate between coaching and other forms of assistance offered by mental health professionals (Sperry, 1993, p.257). Like many other health professionals who work with organizational leaders, Sperry suggested that these men and women embrace high aspirations and, as a result, are vulnerable to dysfunctional behavior brought about by stress. Sperry characterized the healthy and successful leader as having a high need for power and being an active leader and risk-taker. This also means that the successful leader must be willing to tolerate high levels of stress.

The impaired or burned-out leader, by contrast, is at risk of substance abuse, marital difficulties and stress-related disorders. Furthermore, the impaired leader often doesn't fit the organization for reasons that may or may not be directly related to ability. Regardless of the reasons, an impaired leader may seek the assistance of a mental health professional. Sperry suggests that this person will benefit most from clinical treatment that is action oriented and focused on behavior change. Therapy for leaders usually should be time-limited and cognitively based. While counseling for today's leaders is typically pragmatic and outcome-oriented, it is also personal and focused on the impaired client's capacity to deal with the stresses of life. In general, counselors provide support and insight regarding personal matters, while a consultant often serves as a source of expertise for clients about their work-related issues.

Let's look with Sperry at coaching, as a distinct organizational intervention.

Coaching

There are many viable and (at least potentially) effective ways in which to improve the performance of someone about whom we care. Counseling and consulting are certainly of great value and often incorporate elements of the coaching process. Yet, organizational coaching offers several critical differences from the usual (as well as more informal) modes of coaching with which we are all acquainted.

Sperry states that *organizational coaching* clients often have three expectations that are not found when they seek out a counselor or therapist.

1. They expect that a coach will be "able to increase their effectiveness as both a manager and a person."

2. They expect that the coach will be able to "help them integrate information, providing not only perspectives and objectivity, but also a keen insight into problems with people."

3. They would like the coach to help them "grow personally and become more effective in meeting the scrutiny of more critical audiences."

Put much too simply, counseling is about the heart, consulting is about the head, and coaching is about the head, heart and guts in interaction. Stated with a bit more precision, we can differentiate between consulting, counseling and coaching by noting that feelings (heart) are often the focus of a counseling session, whereas consulting involves primarily the systematic reasoning through of an organizational issue based on rational analysis and review (head). Coaching issues inevitably address the interplay between feelings, reasoning and the resulting will to action. Using psychological terms, we might say that consulting is situated primarily in the domain of cognition (thinking). By contrast, counseling is situated primarily in the domain of affect (emotions). The third C, coaching, is situated at the intersection between cognition and affect, as well as in the domain of conation (behavior).

We are inherently involved in the interaction of cognition and affect when we confront the challenges of complexity, unpredictability and turbulence. How is this interaction treated in coaching? First, feelings are treated as important data during a coaching session but are not the focus of this session. If feelings were the focal point, then the person conducting the session would become a counselor or therapist. She would no longer be a coach. Unfortunately, some coaches—especially those doing so-called personal coaching—move in and out of therapeutic relationships with the people they are coaching, without making such shifting explicit. This has, in turn, led to considerable controversy regarding the field of coaching and, in particular, over-generalized condemnation of (and heavy-handed attempts to regulate) this emergent field.

Confusion also exists about the relationship between consulting and coaching. A coaching session is not just about arriving at a reasonable solution to a difficult organizational problem. If it were, then the coach would have become a consultant. Coaching is always about the process as well as the short-term and long-term outcomes of decision-making. The coach and decision-maker being coached are always moving beyond the specific issue to be solved in order to expand the leader's ability to cognitively and emotionally apply present learning for the future and, as a result, create lasting behavioral change or even personal transformation.

Appreciative Coaching

We propose that coaching is most clearly differentiated from counseling and consulting when conducted in an appreciative manner. A short-term focus and a mechanistic, deficit-based view of performance development cause some organizations to utilize coaching primarily to "fix" perceived performance and behavioral deficits. Organizational coaching programs that are effective build instead at a fundamental level on a deep sense of appreciation for the potential of all members of the organization. We suggest that such an appreciative perspective must undergird any organizational coaching program and holds the key to masterful and effective organizational coaching. Thus, this book is devoted primarily to the description of this approach and to the identification of strategies and models needed to design and conduct this type of program. (Please also see the Coaching Resource entitled "The Forms of an Appreciative Approach to Coaching").

> The coach who fully appreciates her client has raised the client's value by seeing him in ways that neither he himself nor his associates nor the organization might have seen him before.

What is the nature of such a perspective? *In essence, an appreciative perspective concerns a willingness to engage with another person from an assumption of mutual respect, in a mutual search for discovery of distinctive competencies and strengths, with a view to helping them fulfill their aspirations and their potential.* This simple statement might at first seem to be rather naive and idealistic, but at its core it holds the promise of helping committed and empowered staff to generate extraordinary organizational results. As we trace out its implications, a series of profound insights and realistic strategies emerge. (Srivestva, Cooperider and Associates, 1990)

Understanding Another Person

The term appreciation itself has several different meanings that tend to build on one another; however, as a foundation for coaching, *appreciation refers first to a clearer understanding of another person's perspective.* We come to appreciate the point of view being offered by our colleague or the challenges which the other person faces. This appreciation, in turn, comes not from some detached observation, but rather from direct engagement. One gains knowledge from an appreciative perspective by "identifying with the observed." (Harmon, 1990, p. 43)

Empathy is critical. One cares about the matter being studied and about those people one is assisting. Neutrality is inappropriate in such a setting, though compassion implies neither a loss of discipline nor a loss of boundaries between one's own problems and perspectives and those of the other person. Appreciation, in other words, is about fuller understanding, not merging, with another person's problems or identity.

Valuing Another Person

Appreciation also refers to an increase in worth or value. A painting or stock portfolio appreciates in value. Van Gogh looked at a vase of sunflowers and in appreciating (painting) these flowers, he increased their value for everyone. Van Gogh similarly appreciated and brought new value to his friends through his friendship: "Van Gogh did not merely articulate admiration for his friend: He created new values and new ways of seeing the world through the very act of valuing." (Cooperrider, 1990, p. 123)

Peter Vaill recounts a scene from the movie Lawrence of Arabia in which Lawrence tells a British Colonel that his job at the Arab camp was to "appreciate the situation." (Vaill, 1990, p. 323) By appreciating the situation, Lawrence assessed and helped add credibility to the Arab cause, much as a knowledgeable jeweler or art appraiser can increase the value of a diamond or painting through nothing more than thoughtful appraisal. Lawrence's appreciation of the Arab situation, in turn, helped to produce a new level of courage and ambition on the part of the Arab communities with which Lawrence was associated. The coach who fully appreciates her client has raised the client's value by seeing him in ways that neither he himself nor his associates nor the organization might have seen him before, thus opening new vistas for his growth.

Recognizing the Contributions of Another Person

From yet another perspective, the process of appreciation concerns our recognition of the contributions that have been made by another person: "I appreciate the efforts you have made in getting this project off the ground." Sometimes this sense of appreciation is reflected in the special recognition we give people for a particularly successful project or in the bouquet of flowers or thank you note we leave with an assistant.. This form of appreciation, however, when it is the only kind provided, typically leads only to praise inflation, praise addiction and the tendency to keep people who report to us permanently in a needy and, therefore (ironically), one-down position (Kanter, 1977).

Appreciation can instead be exhibited in a more constructive manner through the daily interaction between an administrator and her associates. It involves mutual respect and active engagement, accompanied by a natural flow of feedback, and an exchange of ideas. More specifically, appreciation is evident in attitudes regarding the nature and purpose of work. If the administrator "sees work as the means whereby a person creates oneself (that is, one's identity and personality) and creates community (that is, social relations), then the accountability structure becomes one of nurturing and mentoring." (Cummings and Anton, 1990, p. 259)

These are the three most common uses of the term appreciation. We appreciate other people through seeking to understand them, through valuing them, and through being attentive and thoughtful in acknowledging their ongoing contributions to the organization. The term appreciation is now being used in organizational settings in three additional ways that are distinctive—yet closely related to the first three.

Establishing a Positive Organizational Image of the Future

Appreciation can refer to the establishment of a positive image of the future within an organization. We grow to appreciate an organization by investing it with optimism. We invest it with a sense of hope about its own future and the valuable role potentially it plays in our society. "Organization-wide affirmation of the positive future is the single most important act that a system can engage in if its real aim is to bring to fruition a new and better future." (Cooperrider, 1990, p. 119) Effective leaders, therefore, must be "not only concerned with what is but also with what might be." (Frost and Egri, 1990, p. 305)

We come to appreciate our own role and that of other people in the organization with regard to the contributions we make jointly in helping the organization realize these images, purposes and values. An appreciative perspective is always *leaning into the future*. While we appreciate that which has been successful in the past, we don't dwell with nostalgia on the past, but instead continually trace out the implications of acquired wisdom and past successes regarding our vision of the future.

Recognizing Distinctive Strengths and Competencies

Appreciation in an organizational setting also refers to recognition of the distinctive strengths and potentials of people working within the organization. An appreciative culture is forged when an emphasis is placed on the realization of inherent potential and the uncovering of latent strengths rather than on the identification of weaknesses or deficits. People and organizations "do not need to be fixed. They need constant reaffirmation." (Cooperrider, 1990, p. 120)

> People are least likely to change if they are being asked to change and are most likely to change when they have received positive regard—what we would identify as appreciation.

Even in a context of competition, appreciation transforms envy into learning, and personal achievement into a sense of overall purpose and value. The remarkable essayist Roger Rosenblatt (1997, p. 23) reveals just such a process in candidly describing his sense of competition with other writers. He suggests that the sense of admiration for the work of other writers can play a critical role in his own life:

> Part of the satisfaction in becoming an admirer of the competition is that it allows you to wonder how someone else did something well, so that you might imitate it—steal it, to be blunt. But the best part is that it shows you that there are things you will never learn to do, skills and tricks that are out of your range, an entire imagination that is out of your range. The news may be disappointing on a personal level, but in terms of the cosmos, it is strangely gratifying. One sits among the works of one's contemporaries as in a planetarium, head all the way back, eyes gazing up at heavenly matter that is all the more beautiful for being unreachable. Am I growing up?

Paradoxically, at the point that someone is fully appreciated and reaffirmed, they will tend to live up to their newly acclaimed talents and drive, just as they will live down to their depreciated sense of self if constantly criticized and undervalued. Carl Rogers suggested many years ago that people are least likely to change if they are being asked to change and are most likely to change when they have received positive regard—what we would identify as appreciation.

Acknowledging the Value of Diversity

A final mode of appreciation is evident in an organization when efforts are made to form complementary relationships and recognize the mutual benefits that can be derived from the cooperation of differing constituencies. A culture of appreciating differences actually provides organizational integration (the glue that holds an organization together) while the organization is growing and differentiating into many distinctive units of responsibility (division of labor) and geography. (Durkheim, 1933; Lawrence and Lorsch, 1969) The appreciative perspective is particularly important in the era of globalization, when there are significant differences in vision, values or culture among members or regions of an organization or between independent division or organizations that are seeking to work together. (Rosinski, 2010)

As many surprising cooperative endeavors have demonstrated in recent years, from open-source software development to the explosion of Wikipedia and its unexpectedly high-quality content, what lies beyond the era of information and sheer competition is an era of collaboration. (Bergquist, Betwee and Meuel, 1995) Businesses are learning to *connect versus create,* to borrow, duplicate ("the highest form of flattery"), create alliances and networks instead of focusing on the organizational gigantism popular at the end of the last century. Appreciative competition, we might call it.

The Window of Strengths

As we journey outward as coaches in learning to appreciate other people and situations we also begin to understand and appreciate ourselves in new ways. We come back full circle to ourselves and to self-understanding—a necessity for the coach who has to role-model a superior level of self-awareness and inner alignment. The *appreciative window of strength* offers one way in which to comprehend the self-insight to be gained from an appreciative perspective, and becomes a fundamental tool for the organizational coach.

There are essentially two ways in which both we and our coaching clients come to appreciate our own distinctive strengths: through self-perception and through the perceptions of other people. Our self-perceptions of strengths are based on the processes of reflection upon our own impact on the world in which we live and work, and comparisons we draw with other people who are also having an impact on this world. The perceptions of other people are made known to us through direct or indirect feedback. In some cases we know of our strengths. In other cases we do not. Similarly, in some cases other people know of our distinctive strengths. In other cases they do not.

Given this scheme, there are four views of our strengths, as the much used Johari Window (Luft, 1969, 1984) has popularized:

1. First, some of our strengths can be known both to ourselves and to other people. These are *publicly recognized strengths;* if well-used, they will have been a big part of our success strategy. The coach will celebrate these strengths with her client, and also be alert to over-use.

2. Second, we might personally be aware of other strengths that we posses; however, other people might not be aware of these strengths. These are our *private strengths*. We may be aware of them, but they are rarely of much value to us, given that others never see them being used, like the poetry one may be writing in one's mind. Evoking such private strengths from our clients by listening attentively to their stories of past successes gives us a chance to encourage them to experiment and apply the lessons learned from these past successes to currently challenging situations.

3. The third possibility is one in which we are not fully aware of a distinctive strength we possess, whereas other people are aware. These are *obscure strengths*. These strengths are also of little value to us until we have become fully acquainted with them and know how to put them to work. When a promotion feels undeserved and/ or intimidating to a manager, it is often because he doesn't see his own strengths as clearly as his colleagues and superiors do.

4. Finally, there are strengths we possess that have never been acknowledged by any-one—including ourselves. These are *potential strengths*. They represent the farthest edge of our growth and development.

The process of appreciation, in which the coach plays a central role, expands the size of the *public window* by providing an opportunity - through feedback - to learn more about our observed strengths. It also provides people with an opportunity to reflect on the nature of their strengths. The *private window* becomes smaller in an organizational culture that is appreciative: We begin to feel more comfortable in sharing personal insights based on our distinctive strengths and talents. The *obscure window* also shrinks with appreciation: We have access to clearer information regarding our distinctive strengths when the climate allows people to feel comfortable in providing one another with such observations.

Finally, with both the private and obscure windows shrinking in size, the *potential strength* window grows smaller and feeds into the public one: Potential strengths are recognized for the first time both by the coaching client and his colleagues. Organizational coaching relates directly to this process of expansion of the public domain of our acknowledged strengths. This appreciative process provides the coach with a framework and the client with resources and processes to reflect on her own strengths and receive feedback from other people regarding the strengths that they most want to leverage for their own growth and the accomplishment of organizational goals.

Coaching Issues as Puzzles, Problems, Dilemmas and Mysteries

There is yet another way in which to differentiate coaching from both consulting and counseling, which also assists in the differentiation between coaching and friendly advice-giving. This distinction focuses on the nature of the issue(s) being addressed by the person who seeks coaching assistance. We propose that there are four kinds of issues being addressed in not only coaching, but also most human service engagements: *puzzles, problems, dilemmas* and *mysteries.*

Puzzles

Puzzles are the everyday issues that anyone working in an organization must face. Puzzles have answers. They are uni-dimensional, in that they can be clearly defined and can readily be quantified or at least measured. Puzzles concern such things as changing a production schedule to accommodate a major new order or determining the appropriate fee for a new, longer training program. Puzzles also concern changes in organizational policies to accommodate new federal laws, or re-arranging an office floor plan or a parking space distribution. With a puzzle, the parameters are clear. The desired outcome of a puzzle-solution process can readily be identified and is often important to (and can be decided by) a relatively small number of organization members. It is the sort of issue rightly passed to the lowest level of responsibility where the necessary information is available.

> Problems can be differentiated from puzzles because there are multiple perspectives that can be applied when analyzing a problem.

Researchers who study complex systems use the metaphor of landscapes to distinguish a complex challenge from other types of simpler challenges being faced in various systems, including organizations, (for example, Miller & Page, 2007). They point to the image of a single, dominant mountain peak when describing one type of landscape. Often volcanic in origin, these imposing mountains are clearly the highest point within sight. For those living in or visiting the Western United States, we can point to Mt. Rainer (in western Washington) or Mt. Shasta (in northern California). Mt. Fuji in Japan also exemplifies this type of landscape. You know when you have reached the highest point in the region and there is no doubt regaining the prominence of this peak. Similarly, in the case of puzzles, one knows when a satisfactory solution has been identified and one can stand triumphantly at the top of the mountain/puzzle, knowing that one has succeeded and can look back down to the path followed in reaching the solution/peak. As we shall see shortly, there are other landscapes that are much more challenging—and these are the primary domains of coaching.

Problems

There is a second type of issue that a 21st Century leader faces. We identify these issues as problems. Problems can be differentiated from puzzles because there are multiple perspectives that can be applied when analyzing a problem, several possible solutions associated with any one problem and multiple criteria that can be applied to the evaluation of the potential effectiveness of any one solution.

There are many more cognitive demands being placed on us when we confront problems than when we confront puzzles—given that problems do not have simple or single solutions. Problems are multi-dimensional and inter-disciplinary in nature. They are inevitably complicated in that they involve many elements (Miller and Page, 2007). Any one problem can be viewed from many different points of view—thus it is unclear when they have been successfully resolved. For example, we find a technical solution and realize that the problem has financial implications. We address the financial implications and soon find that there are a whole host of managerial concerns associated with the problem.

Problems that exist in contemporary organizations often concern such things as personnel policies (that are not forced by new government regulations), compensation systems (that are not just annual inflation-driven wage increases but incentivize certain behaviors), productivity, morale, creativity, risk-taking, flexibility—and trust. Because the outcome of the problem-solution process itself is of significant interest to multiple stakeholders, often the most important and difficult discussions revolve around agreeing on the criteria for solving a problem or even evaluating when solutions are successful.

Researchers and theorists who are seeking to understand complicated problems often describe the settings in which problems emerge as "rugged landscapes." (Miller and Page, 2007, p. 216) This type of landscape is filled with many mountains of about the same height (think of the majestic mountain range called the Grand Tetons or the front range of the Rocky Mountains that citizens of Denver Colorado see every day), as compared with a landscape in which one mountain peak dominates (think of Mount Rainier). In a rugged landscape that is complicated, one finds many competing viewpoints about which mountain is higher or which vista is more beautiful. A similar case can be made regarding the challenging problems facing the 21st Century leader and the 21st Century coach who is working with this leader.

Dilemmas

When certain issues that managers face appear impervious to a definitive solution, it becomes useful to classify them as dilemmas. While dilemmas like problems are complicated, they are also complex, in that each of the many elements embedded in the dilemmas is connected to each (or most) of the other elements (Miller and Page, 2007). We may view the problem from one perspective and take action to alleviate one part of the problem, and we immediately confront another part of the problem, often represented by an opposing stakeholder group: We tighten up our policies regarding new product development and find that creativity is dropping off. We increase the price of a service that we deliver in order to increase revenues and find that we are losing customers, thereby losing revenues. Coaches and their clients may not always recognize a dilemma for what it is. New coaches and consultants tend to see problems and dilemmas in a limited or simplistic way, and attempt to deal with them as if they are puzzles. When that happens, clients dig themselves deeper and deeper into the complexity, seriousness, and paradox of the "mess." (Schön, 1983)

At times we find that the issue is a set of nested dilemmas. One set of conflicting priorities exists within another set of conflicting priorities. For instance, we want to pay one employee a bonus, but are concerned that if we do so other employees who find out about it will be resentful and less likely to collaborate with their bonused colleague. This dilemma, in turn, rests inside an even bigger dilemma: we want to increase salary and benefits to all our employees, yet also are trying to keep down costs because the market in which our product is being sold is highly competitive. These are complex dilemmas - not readily solved puzzles.

As organizational coaches, we are likely to often confront the challenge of helping our clients work with dilemmas and even nested dilemmas. As in the case of problems, dilemmas can be described as "rugged landscapes." (Miller and Page, 2007) However, because dilemmas involve multiple elements that are intimately interlinked, they are far more than a cluster or range of mountain peaks of similar size. This type of complex landscape is filled not only with many mountains of about the same height, but also with river valleys, forested plains and many communities (think of the Appalachian Mountains), as compared with a landscape in which one mountain peak dominates or in which a series of mountains dominate. In a complex, rugged landscape, one finds not only many competing viewpoints but also an intricate and often paradoxical interweaving of these differing viewpoints. The dilemma-filled challenges that the 21st Century leader faces makes the role played by a 21st Century coach even more important (perhaps even imperative).

> Whenever multiple stakeholders with unique interests are involved, it is safe to expect a dilemma to present itself for the leader who intersects with it.

Dilemmas confront us in complex rugged landscapes with the need to balance or manage two or more opposed, yet equally valid, interests or *polarities.* Whenever multiple stakeholders with unique interests are involved, it is safe to expect a dilemma to present itself for the leader who intersects with it. Barry Johnson, the "dean" of *polarity management,* suggests as a first step for handling everyday dilemmas that leaders identify the *two legitimate but opposite forces* at work in the dilemma, and then analyze each side's benefits and disadvantages. Organizationally, the two opposing forces are often embodied in "camps." For example, the comptroller's interest in minimizing expenses is pitted against the marketing department's need to invest in consumer research. A centralized corporation has the need to standardize its offerings, but the offices in other states or provinces need flexibility in running their daily affairs. Neither position is "wrong." A coach who understands polarity management will regularly encourage her client to bring both parties to the table and facilitate a mutual understanding of the respective benefits and possible negative consequences of holding either position *to the exclusion of the other.* Aspirational coaches can even invite individuals or groups to take the role that is opposite to their usual one, and describe the pros and cons from that unfamiliar perspective. Enormous understanding and empathy result from this first step alone.

Once the strengths and risks of the two sides are understood, the discussion is directed by the leader-as-coach to what happens when we try to *maximize* the benefits of either side (if we simply centralized everything, if we basically slept at the office and ignored our family, or if as managers we always sided with our people's needs or always drove them for maximum efficiency). It turns out that such unilateral bias to one side of a paradox or dilemma soon causes the downsides of that same force to manifest: Our nights at the office eventually lead to divorce, just as a 24/7 romance at the exclusion of work would likely lead to destitution. Total centralization causes the incapacity to customize, but totally giving way to the local interests of a subsidiary would drive up the cost to uncompetitive levels.

Therefore, Barry Johnson warns us as coaches and leaders that we not try to maximize but rather carefully *optimize* the degree to which the parties incline toward one side or the other and for how long. Optimizing means that we must find a reasonable and perhaps flexible set-point as we take action in favor of one side or another. Finding these acceptable optimum responses and redefining them again and again is the key to polarity management; and it requires a constant process of vigilance, negotiation and adjustments. We want our client to continuously seek and refine a dynamic, flexible balance so that each side's beneficial contribution can be enjoyed, without engendering serious negative consequences.

It is wise to encourage our coaching client to consult regularly with the other side of a polarity in order to evaluate to what degree, with what intensity or for what time period both sides can reap the benefits of one side. This is particularly important given the interconnected nature of complex dilemmas. If life-work balance were the issue, our client would listen to their family's feedback so as not to overshoot their dedication to work. If our CEO client cared about balancing her company's financial health with investments for growth, we would encourage our client to make sure that she regularly brought her conservative CFO as well as her expansionist, visionary head of global marketing to the table, agreeing on trade-offs, measurable goals and milestones for evaluating results.

As a safeguard against overshooting toward either side, it is prudent to build in alarm systems that warn us when we may be trying to maximize one side, and are on the verge of triggering the negative reactions. One of our clients tells us that his alarm signal for overworking and traveling too intensely was putting on ten pounds over his average weight. At such time, he would reduce his travels and dedicate even more specific attention to his health. The alarm signal implicit in America's current handling of the paradox of freedom versus security would be, on the security side, clearly, another attack on this soil. The alarm metric for safeguarding freedom is less clearly defined.

> Clearly, when a world of complexity collides with a world of uncertainty and a world of turbulence, the landscape begins to dance and we, as organizational coaches, learn how to dance with our clients.

The sign of a leading mind is that it can hold opposing views without flinching. The sign of a viable organization is that it can live with and manage its dilemmas and paradoxes in real time, without questioning its identity at every turn in the road, whip-lashing its strategies, tearing and rebuilding it structures reactively, or scapegoating its people. In the words of the British management expert Charles Handy (1994): "Successful firms live with paradoxes, or what they call 'dilemmas.' Those firms have to be planned, yet flexible; be differentiated and integrated at the same time, be mass marketers while catering to niches; they must find ways to produce variety and quality, all at low cost; in short, they have to reconcile what used to be opposites, instead of choosing between them."

As organizational coaches, we may already be finding (or soon will find) that polarity management, while significantly more sophisticated an approach than straight-line problem-solving, is not always sufficient, for the polarities and the conditions underlying polarities are themselves changing. To return to our landscape metaphor, we may find as coaches that our clients are living not just in a complex rugged landscape but in what Miller and Page (2007) call a "dancing landscape." Priorities are not only interconnected, they are constantly shifting, and new alliances between old competing polarities are being forged. Clearly, when a world of complexity collides with a world of uncertainty and a world of turbulence, the landscape begins to dance and we, as organizational coaches, learn how to dance with our clients. Both we (as coaches) and the leaders we are coaching are increasingly challenged to develop superlative strategic thinking and communication skills as participants in that ongoing dance.

Mysteries

As we begin to address the challenges associated with our clients' dancing landscapes, we enter a domain in which problems and dilemmas seem to merge into mysteries. *Mysteries* operate at a different level than puzzles, problems and dilemmas. Mysteries are too complex to understand and are ultimately unknowable. A specific mystery is *profound* (desired outcomes are elusive but of great importance to many stakeholders) and *awe-inspiring* or just *awe-ful*. A mystery is in many ways *theological* or teleological in nature. It is inevitably viewed from many different perspectives that are systematic and deeply rooted in culture and tradition. Mysteries have no boundaries, and all aspects are interrelated.

Mysteries are beyond rational comprehension and resolution, and they are viewed with respect. Depending on one's perspective, they are the things "we take to God" or are the unpredictable and profound events that we "take to heart"—and that Taleb (2010) described as "black swans." Some mysteries relate to traumatic and devastating events: Why did I get out of the World Trade Center while my desk mate perished? Why is there evil in the world? Why did lightning strike our freighter but not the one next to it? Why did my child die before me? Mysteries also encompass many positive events and moments of reflection: How did I deserve all these talents? What is my destiny? Why have I been so blessed in my professional life? Why did I fall in love with this person? Why did this remarkable person fall in love with me? How did I ever raise such an exceptional child? How did I earn so much affection from these people at my retirement party? In coaching conversations, such privileged discussions may occur and not lead to an "outcome." They often serve as perspective-raising instants, a way to view life and the world from a vantage point less tethered to the weeds of daily issues.

Locus of Control

We perceive mysteries as taking place outside our sphere of control or influence. Psychologists call this an *external locus of control* and note that some people are inclined to view most issues as outside their control (that is, as mysteries). By contrast, puzzles are usually perceived as being under our control. Psychologists identify this perspective as an *internal locus of control* and note that some people are likely to view all issues as being under their control (that is, as puzzles).

Problems and dilemmas are usually complex mixtures of controllable and uncontrollable elements. To successfully address a problem or dilemma, one typically needs a balanced perspective with regard to internal and external loci of control—a distinction coaches have to frequently help their clients make. One of the most helpful inquiries when confronting problems, dilemmas and (in particular) nested dilemmas is to identify what is and what is not under a client's control, and to do that from a perspective that challenges the client's immediate perceptions. A problem or dilemma that is embedded in a rugged landscape is more likely to have components that are under at least the partial control of a client than is a problem or dilemma that is embedded in a dancing landscape. Often, *obscure* or *potential strengths* (see The Window of Strengths) can come to light when a leader realizes how much broader her span of control is in actuality, when compared to her self-limiting awareness—in other words, when she expands the scope of her internal locus of control.

The Challenges

There are myriad challenges associated with the role of a coach in helping clients identify and address these four different kinds of issues. First, coaching clients typically want their issues to be puzzles they can control or perhaps mysteries for which they have no responsibility. Puzzles can be solved and we know when we have solved them. Mysteries are outside our control, so we don't have to feel responsible for resolving them. But problems and dilemmas—these are much more difficult to address. We have to determine which aspects of the problem or dilemma are under our control and which aspects are not. This confusing mixture of internal and external control is inherent in problems and dilemmas, and so is the balancing of competing but valid interests represented by different stakeholders. That's what makes them so difficult to address—and makes them ripe for organizational coaching assistance.

A second challenge concerns the values inherent in a coaching assignment. Coaches are often considered much more successful, in terms of both fortunes and fame, if they can "solve problems"—often by approaching them as puzzles. The beginner coach feels a great deal of satisfaction when he successfully helps a client analyze a situation, look at optional solutions and successfully implement a chosen set of actions. This is a proficiency that can help many clients who initially feel stuck or unsure of a course of action. Even very experienced and highly competent coaches will be tempted by organizations that are highly focused on a return on their coaching investment to "guarantee" certain outcomes in exchange for an attractive fee, as if a "puzzle" just needed to be put together correctly.

 Coaches are often considered much more successful, in terms of both fortunes and fame, if they can "solve problems"—often by approaching them as puzzles.

Ethically, however, a coach who is confident of his competency and is willing to embrace maximum accountability can at best hold out that the client will be close to "the top of her game" at the end of the assignment. What the coach cannot guarantee or "own" is the client's ultimate performance, long-term. Neither can she guarantee that the client's level "best" will satisfy all the organization's needs and expectations. There is an additional challenge: in order not to reduce complex problems and dilemmas to simpler puzzles, there has to remain room for qualitative (rather than just quantitative) measurements. Much subtler changes are inevitably involved in this client's performance—the kind of changes that may actually have lasting, long-term impact beyond currently measurable results. Return-on-Investment analyses are not a simple matter when assessing the benefits to be derived from coaching services.

Furthermore, we must wonder about the inherent paradox associated with a contract in which the coach's fee is tied to a specific result. What is going through the mind of the recipient of puzzle-based coaching, i.e. coaching where the coach has "guaranteed" certain outcomes? The recipient might be entertaining some of the following thoughts:

> The coach gets paid if I'm more successful. This puts great pressure on me. What did I do wrong? But the organization is willing to invest $50,000 in me. I wonder if I'm worth $50,000. I feel guilty—or is it anger?—that my performance is being judged so poorly that I am costing the organization $50,000. Or should I feel honored? What should I think about this coach? Does he really care about me or is he only motivated by the money? I could sure mess things up for him by performing better but not at the level that triggers his payment—and I would save the company $50,000! Why don't they just give me this money as an incentive and I will perform at any level they want!

There is a related challenge associated with the distinction we have drawn. While coaches may be judged most successful if they always address measurable and relatively-simply puzzles, rather than complex problems, it is challenging problems and dilemmas embedded in rugged and dancing landscapes that clients tend to actually bring to the coaching session. These problems and dilemmas caused by complexity, unpredictability and turbulence tend to be most amenable to the coaching process—particularly to an appreciative approach to coaching. A masterful organizational coach is uniquely positioned to hear out, help a client reflect on, and bring new perspectives to a challenging issue. Conversely, puzzles tend to be most successfully addressed by someone operating in a consulting or trainer role. Mysteries tend to be most successfully addressed by someone operating in the role of counselor (or, in a religious setting, a pastor). It is important, therefore, for the distinction to be made between these four types of issues, so that one might make an appropriate decision concerning the type of assistance they wish to receive.

Looking Ahead

Later, in Chapter Three, we propose three strategies under which we cluster different organizational coaching models that respond to the challenges and opportunities described in this first chapter and build on an appreciative perspective. But before proceeding to the description and analysis of these strategies we must attend to more fundamental matters.

First, in this next Chapter Two, we turn to the central interpersonal skills and methods that should underlie any effective organizational coaching process, regardless of the strategy being employed. We are particularly indebted to our colleague, Steve Phillips, for his insights in this area.

Five Distinctive Coaching Skills

We open this chapter with a brief coaching scenario, as context for our discussion of a number of essential coaching skills:

Robert first met with Karl in the cafeteria of the high-tech company where both Robert and Karl work. Karl had been referred to Robert as a peer coach by a member of their company's Human Resource Development department —an HRD specialist who had enough experience with coaching to know that some of the concerns expressed to him by Karl could be addressed best by a peer coach rather than a counselor. Robert, in his coach role, asked Karl to join him in the cafeteria partly in order to clearly differentiate his work as a coach from counseling. This was going to be different.

As Karl and his coach Robert decided during a preliminary phone call, they were going to focus on how Karl was dealing with the high tech project he had started two years ago, given that it was now being run by several "managers" who are not technological visionaries, like himself.

Karl was also aware when he first met with his coach that Robert didn't intend to be a "consultant" to his department. Karl's department already had several consultants who were helping to resolve several specific difficulties concerning the overall functioning of the department. Robert would probably never meet other members of Karl's department. But in the interest of the department, Robert's attention would be directed at the way in which Karl wanted to "be" and therefore behave with regard to the project in which he was so deeply invested.

So Robert and Karl met. It soon became obvious that they were both unclear about the primary focus of their dialogue. Karl wanted initially to talk about everything: his initial dreams for the project, the reactions of other "old-time" members of his project team to the growing power of the new members, and his very demanding working hours and responsibilities. Coaching often begins this way. A participant in the coaching process often initially cherishes (and makes full use of) the freedom to talk about anything. Everything feels relevant.

Robert, as coach, sat quietly for at least fifteen minutes, mostly listening to Karl and asking a few clarifying questions. In order to zero in more specifically on the issue(s) that Karl wanted to focus on, Robert then began to ask Karl some "tougher" questions—such as why he had never considered confronting these new members of his project team or moving on to a new project where his technical competencies might be more effectively employed. Coach Robert briefly shared his own experiences five years ago of being ambivalent about whether or not to sell a business he owned. Encouraged by Robert's disclosure, Karl began to focus on his own ambivalence—he wanted to move on to a new project, but didn't want to be known as a quitter. This ambivalence became the central coaching subject for the two colleagues.

In that context, there were financial matters to be considered (as there often are in coaching). If he stays in his current job for another year and helps orient the new members of his project team, then the company will benefit and probably give him a bonus. On the other hand, Karl can't imagine staying on the job just to get this bonus: "I hate the idea of tolerating this living hell for one more year—just to make a few more bucks!" Unless Karl found a way of having a productive relationship with the current project team, so that both he and the team could come out winners, he suspected that he was neither doing himself nor the company full justice.

Karl displayed great courage several times during the hour and a half meeting in the cafeteria. When he did, Robert saluted him by offering a "toast" in his honor (with Decaf Coffee). They both laughed, but Robert knew that Karl "appreciated" his "appreciation"—for Karl learned during this meeting that Robert too had once run a project that had "gotten away" from him.

By the end of this initial session, Karl and Robert had forged a distinctive charter for their work together: Karl would use their time together to take into consideration all of the forces impinging on his life (work load, personal and professional aspirations, degree of commitment to the team and the company, financial considerations, interpersonal relations and so forth). Robert would help him make sense of these forces as they interact with one another and would ask challenging questions that would encourage Karl to push deeper and wider in the exploration of his decisions about the next steps. Karl and his coach Robert set up a second meeting (at a nearby coffee shop) in three weeks and ended their first meeting together with a warm handshake.

While no organizational coaching session is ever "typical," this meeting between Robert and Karl exemplifies many of the basic strategies of this distinctive form of human service. It was *appreciative* in that Robert, the coach, began with the assumption that Karl was competent and in control (otherwise Robert would have never met with him in the cafeteria). Furthermore, Robert assumed that Karl had sufficient "ego strength" (to use a psychological term) to tolerate, and even welcome, the "hard" questions and challenges that Robert offered.

This coaching vignette also exemplifies five skills that set apart an effective coach in helping another person address complex, contradictory and chaotic challenges. Of course, coaches use many fundamental techniques like active and deep listening (see Coaching Resources "Active Listening" and "Empathic Listening"), mindfulness, perspicacious questioning, setting intentions, visualization, etc. Here, we wish to underscore in particular the skill sets that take the coaching work beyond the basics: (1) freeing (vs. binding) communication, (2) contextual knowing, (3) feeling through action, (4) reflective inquiry and (5) unique forms of coaching leadership. We know that many of these skill sets are obscure or laden with jargon. Each is also the cumulative result of a number of different coaching tactics. We will try to clear some of this up by saying something about each skill set with its tactics, facets and uses—and relating each skill set to Robert's initial work with Karl.

(1) Freeing Communication

This particular skill set is fundamental. In essence, freeing communication refers to the intensely attentive engagement of the coach in the narrative being offered by her client. A coach does not just sit back and nod politely as her colleague drones on. Rather she is asking open-ended, diverging questions not primarily for the benefit of her own understanding but in order to expand the client's vista and encourage exploration. The coach, in essence, asks questions and makes comments that must *free the client rather than bind* him. This is a critical concept.

A coach can never be the infallible expert—rather she is someone who has the maturity, experience and empathy to fully appreciate the difficult position in which the client sometimes finds himself.

For example, being overly and uncritically enthusiastic about another person's ideas—a reaction many coaches associate with being "appreciative" - is not necessarily freeing. It is often binding because the receiver of this support may not judge it as honest. He may also feel like he is placed in the awkward and distracting position of having to find something "nice" to say in return. Uncritically enthusiastic praise can also lock the client into a position about which he may have just been loosely brainstorming.

Freeing support for an idea often takes the truly appreciative form of *expansion or linkage*: the coach helps the client see additional advantages inherent in the idea, or to link the idea to related concepts or to previous ideas that were on the table. Similarly, as useful as mirroring back and paraphrasing can sometimes be, a rather mechanical repetition back to one's client of what he just said can be very binding—for the client hardly learns anything about how his statement has really been taken in by his coach. Since no statement remains un-interpreted by the listener, freeing communication requires the kind of paraphrasing through which the listening *coach owns and expresses the way(s) in which she has interpreted* what her client just said.

The coach is also able to use paraphrase in order to *expand on, test out or reframe the statement* of her client so that he can become even clearer about and/or can more fully appreciate his own ideas. Sometimes the client will disagree with the coach's paraphrase. This is excellent! It is in bumping up against alternative interpretations of one's statements that greater clarity occurs and more assurance is gained regarding the meaning and importance of the statement.

Freeing communication also involves the occasional *purposeful conveying of information or experience* from the coach to the client. In order for most of the talking to be done by the client, the coach is neither casual nor lavish with her input, nor remains mute. Robert briefly and purposefully talked about his own difficult experience in helping to design and manage a project. Without taking the focus away from Karl's issues, Robert's story did open a two-way conversation. Robert built trust by disclosing something of his own fallibility. A coach can never be the infallible expert—rather she is someone who has the maturity, experience and empathy to fully appreciate the difficult position in which the client sometimes finds himself, without the arrogance of thinking she "know exactly" what the client is dealing with.

Other instances of purposeful informing include sharing of principles, methods or models the coach may have studied and road tested, or direct suggestions based on the coach's prior experiences. Provided such information is then jointly submitted to the same intellectual scrutiny as any other good idea. It can move the action forward. In that vein, Robert, as the coach, might start a conversation around a method he finds appropriate: "Management by walking around is a method we have both heard of, and it may be useful in the way you want to build stronger bonds with your team. How well does it suit you? ...What would be the pros and cons of trying it? … How does it fit with your department's people and culture? … Is it then something you feel you could successfully experiment with?"

For even greater freedom and transparency in the communication, it is particularly appropriate for the coach to model the *description of emotions*, rather than the acting out or expression of emotions. Sadly, many people who find themselves in very challenging positions in their organization haven't developed the level of emotional intelligence truly needed for their success. Lacking self-awareness, they are not very clear about how they are actually feeling at any time, hence are unable to reflect on how these feelings influence their work. Alternatively, they have access to their feelings but are hesitant to describe, let alone express, these feelings in an organizational culture that emphasizes technical rationality (Schön, 1971). Developing a linguistic repertoire of feeling words is often a first step in helping build a manager's ability to recognize - first in himself and then in others – and then actually work with the emotions that form the undercurrent of so much organizational life. The sad alternative is that emotions like anger, envy, sadness or fear get manifested in myriad ways, while the surface discourse denies their existence. After Robert was able to name and articulate his own ambivalent feelings about stepping back from the business he owns, Karl felt more comfortable and competent in talking about his ambivalence about the future, and would likely call out a co-worker's ambivalence when he saw it.

(2) Contextual Knowing

Leaders of organizations during the past century—most of whom were male—placed great emphasis on the capacity to think logically and abstractly, applying general principles to the resolution of issues they faced. While this dominant way of knowing has proven to be of great value in the establishment and maintenance of our powerful industrial society, it has also gotten in the way—especially when leaders face complex, contradictory and chaotic conditions (when they confront problems and dilemmas rather than puzzles) and fast paced change.

There is an alternative mode of knowing that is more commonly found and valued in non-western cultures and among many women in western cultures. This way of knowing is often called *contextual knowing* and has received greatest attention in the writings of Carol Gilligan (1982), Mary Belenky (Belenky and Associates, 1996; Belenky and Stanton, 2000) and in the writings of their colleagues at the Stone Center (Wellesley Massachusetts). Contextual knowing involves the process of learning about a specific situation and inventing processes and principles that are specifically appropriate to this unique situation. An organizational coach is much more likely to be successful if he engages with his client in the processes of contextual knowledge than if he seeks primarily to help his client identify and apply abstract principles. Typically, the hard-pressed client already has a drawer full of principles, as well as a manual full of organizational policies and procedures at his disposal. Many leaders are usually theory-rich—having participated in many training programs. What they lack is the capacity to act fittingly, appropriately (let alone consistently) in response to the complex, contradictory and chaotic issues and potentials they now face. These problems and dilemmas were rarely covered very nicely within the training.

A masterful coach offers her client a unique opportunity to reflect on a specific issue within its unique context. Masterful coaches rarely offer general advice ("you first have to be clear about your goals") or worn out aphorisms ("follow your bliss") that may insult their clients' intelligence. Rather they invite their client to *tell their story*, encouraging them to *highlight what is distinctive about the challenge*. The appreciative coach and client then explore *past lessons learned* by the client when confronting similar challenges. An appropriate strategy often flows out of such insights, taking into account both the lessons learned in the past and the unique features of the current challenge. In listening to themselves and being listened to receptively, people discover the arch of their own journeys, of their exploits and of their learnings. Such contextual learning is not values-free or recklessly relativistic. Instead, it ensures that *the coach continues to learn with her client* about the complex and unique situation that faces the client, so that he may apply his values in full recognition of all facts and implications.

Robert is particularly skillful as a coach in focusing on non-linear context rather than abstractions. While it was tempting for Robert to label Karl's dilemma as the "typical" problem of high tech managers who possess technical but not managerial skills, he set this framework aside as he listened intently to Karl's story and asked Karl numerous questions to help him gain insight into his uniqueness. Sure enough, Karl's story did not fit into any "typical" model. He is not another unilaterally developed technology professional. Karl is a great salesman and a solid manager—he is not just a "techie nerd." Karl fully supported his boss's suggestion that some new folks come in to revitalize and introduce new processes into the department. Karl supported this suggestion not because he couldn't himself help manage the project, but because his greatest strength resides in his inventiveness and his ability to sell an idea to other technologically sophisticated men and women.

> Men have expressed feelings in modes other than words for many centuries in Western culture, and virtually all other cultures in the world.

This makes his current dilemma even more difficult, for Karl knows that he could move to a new company and apply his managerial as well as technical skills. But the same set of problems might exist: he would still have to choose between helping to run projects and being creative. Or is there another option? Could Karl find a way in his current company or in a new company to leverage his unique skills of communicating about complex technologies internally and externally and moving people into action? This alternative question became a major focus for Robert and Karl in their ongoing coaching sessions. There is the thread of a new story-line. This coach and client would never have arrived at this third option if Robert hadn't heard - and helped Karl hear - how his own unique set of skills unfolded in a distinct context.

On a very moving occasion, an executive coach recently encouraged the founder of a 15 year old firm to tell the founder story of the company as an opening introduction to a strategic planning session with her senior team, whose composition had recently changed. Throughout the day, there were moments when the executives referred to their historical context as a source of guidance for choices and decisions. No linear, analytical knowing would have achieved the same impact as the nascent contextual knowing that emerged from the shared history.

(3) Feeling through Action

In our society, it is the men's way which tends to prevail when it comes to *knowing* and it is the women's way that tends to be dominant with regard to *feeling*. Specifically: the so-called women's way of feeling is manifest as the clear articulation of feelings through the use of *words*. Women in our society have been socialized to share their feelings with other people through talking about these feelings. By contrast, men have traditionally been socialized to not speak about their feelings, nor to show these feelings directly in public. "Real men" aren't supposed to cry, be too exuberant or be too "touchy-feely."

On the other hand, what great coaches note is that men have expressed feelings in modes other than words for many centuries in Western culture, and virtually all other cultures in the world. Many men (and women) have used rituals, ceremony, gift-giving, symbolic gestures, and other physical modes to express their feelings. They bring flowers as an expression of love, engage in chants, face-painting and cheers to express their enthusiastic support for a sports team, go fishing (silently) as a manifestation of friendship and look forward to the expression of family devotion at the Sunday evening dinner each week. They choke up at the playing of the national anthem and care deeply about the special evening at the movies each Friday night with their spouse. Repetition, tradition and tangible evidence of support and commitment are at the heart of the matter. Men's ways of feeling begin with the assumption that one's *feelings are most believed when they translate into action*. This alternative mode of expressing feelings can be distilled into one phrase: "show me."

Several implications can be drawn from this analysis with regard to coaching. First, coaches should be sensitive to the *gestures they are articulating, the patterns they are forming*, in setting up and maintaining the coaching relationship. To the extent that organizational coaches don't always meet with clients at their office or at the office of the client, it is important to select an appropriate setting in which to meet. Robert and Karl decided to meet in the cafeteria and later at a coffee shop. Karl knew that he was more likely to speak candidly ("from the heart") when eating food or drinking coffee. This represents a long-term pattern of behavior for Karl—it goes back to Friday evening meals with his family. Robert respected this "tradition" in Karl's life by meeting with him in a comparable setting of Karl's choice. Robert also consistently made use of several *action-based modes of expressing feelings*. He shook hands with Karl at the end of each coaching session, looking Robert straight in the eyes and offering a brief statement of support and encouragement. He saluted Karl's courage by offering a decaf coffee "toast." These physical actions became an important part of the unique ritual that was forged by Robert and Karl in their peer coaching relationship.

Robert and Karl also began to create their own unique set of labels for several of the themes in Karl's life. These labels were always a bit humorous and certainly poignant. A pattern of confronting external authority was labeled "Uncle Bob" (in "honor" of a favorite uncle who was always complaining about his bosses). When Karl failed to look after his own personal interests and allowed himself to be "run over" by other people, both Karl and Robert would indicate that "I [Karl] should have listened to Beth." Beth is Karl's wife and she is always reminding him to stand up for himself.

> Coaches can question whether the fears identified by their client may be dated, whether unthinkable options may in fact be thinkable, and those "worst case scenarios" not too likely nor lethal.

Such *emblematic short-cuts*, especially when humorous, usefully replace for many men the need to elaborate on their insights or acknowledge vulnerabilities out loud.

Female coaches may have to resist the need of requiring their clients to verbally confirm and extensively acknowledge every shift or decision. *Allowing the male client to "speak through their actions"* is an appreciative way of acknowledging how men move forward and how they keep score. Male coaches often help female clients by challenging them to translate words into resolute action. At the same time, they often have to consciously linger in discovery mode longer than they might be primed to do, and resist the temptation of premature action planning. In our international work, the action vs. discussion preference often shows up culturally as well. An appreciative approach to a Spanish client – typically fast-talking and impatient to act - will differ from one with a French person, who delights in exploring more of the philosophical, social and even historical implications of many issues.

(4) Reflective Inquiry

Virtually all forms of coaching require a form of thinking that has only recently been identified as distinctive and essential in confronting complex, contradictory and chaotic problems and dilemmas. Sometimes called "post-formal thought" and at other times known as "meta-cognition" or "transformational learning" (Mezirow and Associates, 2000), the processes of reflective inquiry are based on the assumption that any skillful practice—be it playing golf, designing a new software program, or making a decision—requires an ongoing review of these practices and a testing out of alternative approaches.

Every skillful practitioner, in other words, is a *researcher who performs and ponders the results of various mini-research projects*: "what would happen if I more openly expressed my feelings of discontent when I meet with him at our weekly meeting?" "I wonder if I would be more successful if I held this training program at the start of our fiscal year rather than four months into the year." "Let me see…how did the fact that I put this information items at the end of the meeting rather than at the beginning impact the flow of the discussion?" "Shall I speak up first on this issue or last?" We propose that reflective inquiry can often be effectively engaged through deployment of the following three step process.

1. A masterful organizational coach assists his client in designing and conducting empirical mini research projects. Initially, a coach can help his client *identify the researchable questions to be addressed in this "project."* It is not enough to ask whether or not a training program will be more or less successful when given at a particular time of the year. One must also identify what success means in this instance. Does success refer to the number of people attending the workshop? To the achievement of certain learning goals? To the revenues generated by the workshop? It is also not sufficient to ask "what would happen if . . ." or "what if . . . ." Some time should be spent identifying alternative expectations and what one will be looking for when trying out a new approach. "When I try to be more open about my feelings, should I look for shifts in our ability to solve problems or in the way I feel about myself by the end of the meeting—or both?" "What was I most trying to achieve in moving the information items to the end of the meeting?"

2. The second step in the reflective inquiry process involves *implementation of the mini project.* Often this is best accomplished by letting other involved people know that this is an experiment, that this is being done for a specific purpose, and that you would like their reactions after this mini-project is complete. "Jim, I haven't been very pleased with the way in which we have worked together over the past three months in our weekly meetings. I want to try something out to see if we can improve the situation and would like your feedback when we are done." "I have rescheduled this training program because many of the participants in the past seemed to be very busy and distracted when the program was held in November. I would love to gather your opinions when this program is completed." "I am trying out something new. The information items for this meeting have been moved to the end of the meeting. I am doing this because we never seem to be able to get to the important action items. I look forward to hearing what you think of this change at the end of the meeting."

3. Third, the coach meets with his client to *reflect on the outcomes of the mini-project and to extract important lessons from this experiment that can serve as guides for future*

practices. "How did the meeting go and did it accomplish more than previous meetings?" "What have you learned and how could you do it even better next time?" "Which of your expectations were fulfilled and what surprised you?" "How might you change your assumptions about [this person, this group of people, this organization]?" It is at this point in the reflective inquiry process that a coach is often of greatest value, for we can usually benefit from a second party when reflecting on lessons learned from a complex social interaction.

An appreciative approach is important at this juncture. A masterful coach will particularly encourage his client to focus on what went right in the experiment and what is to be taken forward that can be of benefit in future engagements. It is not unusual for reflective mini-projects to be a mixture of success and failure—and it very tempting for mature, accomplished adults to abandon these experiments if they are not totally successful. It is always much easier to engage the old ways of doing things than new, untested ways—even if the old ways yield nothing but pain and suffering. Better to live with the failure that we already know than with a new failure. Better to live with long-term frustration than with new-found embarrassment.

 A dedicated coach can neither hijack the client's vision nor co-opt it unquestioningly, no matter her personal enthusiasm for the direction.

We all need encouragement when we are trying something new and a coach can play this indispensable role. This doesn't mean being uncritical about the outcomes of a failed experiment, nor does it mean being Pollyannaish about the difficulties inherent in trying out something new. Appreciation does mean *focusing on what worked and what can be replicated in future settings.* It also means helping the client move beyond knee-jerk lessons ("I'll never do that again!") to more thoughtful lessons ("Next time, I need to give each of the group members five minutes at the start of the meeting, but can still move the other information items to the end of the meeting.")

Regarding our case study on coaching, we clearly see the coaching role played by Robert in testing out several of Karl's assumptions. Even at the first meeting, Robert asked Karl why he had never considered leaving the company in order to become involved with a new project in his current company or in a new company—a project that he himself could help start and manage. This is a very strategic question and an answer to this question requires Karl to reflect on his own motives, resources and long-term vision. This question could readily lead to a mini research project. For instance, Karl might quietly inquire into potential new projects in his current organization, as well as check on the local job market. He might meet informally with several of the other members of his project team to brainstorm ways in which their department might more fully respect their long term contributions and make use of their extensive project experience. How does the manager of their department honor his older employees while also making use of the new ideas being offered by recently hired employees? Either of these mini research projects could yield rich information and insights for Karl that he could in turn use in making a decision about next steps in his life and career.

The ultimate "lab setting" available to every human being for endless reflective experimentation is, of course, one's *own self.* Before a leader (or a coach) can offer expert guidance to a colleague, it is most helpful for her to have first lived herself, viscerally, through a change project similar to the one she is recommending. For example, an executive who struggles with being excessively talkative, thus hampering or discouraging her associates' input, knows that such a compulsion or habit is hard to break. With a coach's encouragement, she might first start *experimenting with a self-awareness and mindfulness practice* that allows her to hear herself. She might then also use objects to remind herself of breaking the pattern: perhaps a miniature talking stick which she keeps close in order to remember to give the word to someone else. A trusted colleague might commit to a hand-signal that alerts her to a needed time-out. Once she has successfully changed her own behavior with such intimate – often secret – experiments in her own "personal lab," the executive gains the authority and competence to coach another colleague around a similar challenge, and do it authentically, empathically and appreciatively.

(5) Coaching Leadership: Learner, Risk-Partner, Servant

For Robert to be successful as a coach in working with Karl, he must provide leadership. This is not, however, the usual type of leadership that we have read about for many years in countless books on this complex subject. The contemporary leadership model that the coach role-models and inspires in her clients is much broader. We are no longer talking about the wise leader who has all the answers. Rather we are talking about the wise *leader who continues to be a learner* and views the coaching process as a vehicle for his own learning, as well as the learning of his colleague. Neither are we talking about the brave leader who rallies the troops in order to defeat some powerful enemy. Rather we are talking about a brave leader who recognizes that the most powerful and pernicious enemy usually resides within ourselves. The greatest acts of bravery often come in the form of taking a personal risk and of being willing to appear unskilled or even foolish in front of our coaching clients or associates. Neither does this new model assign the role of visionary to the leader in a solitary personal sense—rather the visionary leader is someone who helps to clarify, make visible, support and sustain the visions of other people. The leader as coach and coach as leader becomes the servant of his clients and the organization's vision rather than being its creator.

These new forms of leadership are appropriate for anyone to consider who is seeking to serve in a coaching role in any contemporary organization. How exactly do these new leadership roles and associated skill-sets manifest themselves in coaching? We turn briefly to each of these roles and illustrate their use in terms of the relationship between Robert and Karl.

Learner

As a client, Karl was a learner. So was his peer coach, Robert. Robert learned more about the unique problems associated with working in a high tech company. Some of the lessons to be learned by Karl from the coaching sessions can also be directly applied by Robert to his own situation. Other lessons are unique to high tech firms. The latter set of lessons will be of great value to Robert when he is providing coaching to other members of this high tech company. Given that Robert works in the same company as Karl, these lessons might also help Robert better perform his own day-to-day job. He now knows more about the operations in another part of the company and can more fully appreciate the challenges faced by the "techies" in his company. Robert has observed that he learns more from a successful coaching project than he does from any book he has read or any workshop he has attended. This is one of the reasons why Robert always tries to balance off his regular job inside the company with several peer-based coaching assignments.

Professional coaches routinely admit that they learn hugely from their clients, and the masterful ones clearly let their clients know that, as part of their appreciative relationship. When a coach becomes a co-learner with his client, this does not mean that he "dumbs" himself down. It is very appropriate for a coach to share his knowledge with a client and for a coach to offer informed advice when requested by a client. Unlike the counselor or therapist, the coach speaks with his client directly about work-related matters, so it is advantageous for a coach to have experience in his client's organization, industry, or culture. However, the problems that clients bring to a coaching session usually require something more than expert knowledge.

It is a key coaching skill to *narrow down the specific aspects of the problem or dilemma* that the client needs help with, and not waste energy with *redundant conversations* about matters the client knows well. Less experienced coaches, as the joke goes, look for the lost keys under the street lamp, because it's easier than looking in the dark near where they had actually dropped their keys. Being drawn to one's own areas of expertise, instead of curiously exploring where the client needs to go can give coaching conversations the reputation of being wasteful. Karl didn't need Robert to tell him about the nature of high tech businesses or even about ways in which to begin a new project in the context of 21st Century technology. Rather, he turned to Robert because he wanted to explore how his own ambivalence might be resolved in the context of a continuing commitment to his current company and an accompanying interest in operating with greater freedom on a new project.

A masterful coach helps her client identify the lessons to be learned from seeming failures as well as clear successes, and expands the options that are available when her client seeks to move in new directions.

Clients like Karl and coaches like Robert usually approach the issues that the client brings to the coaching session with shared appreciation for their complexity and newness. They recognize that many contemporary challenges involve contradiction, uncertainty, paradox and even mystery. Karl's issue certainly is filled with contradiction and uncertainty—and perhaps some paradox and mystery. Karl and Robert learn together about how to approach these challenging conditions. Successful coaching sessions inevitably involve *shared learning*. Both the masterful coach and his client leave their session together having gained new insights not only about the problem(s) or dilemma(s) they have addressed, but also about themselves as learners—especially if the activities of reflective inquiry are engaged in this learning process.

Risk-Partner

A colleague was recently coaching the senior faculty of a major American medical school. These men and women all had medical degrees, were fully tenured, had ample salaries and were in most instances at a place in their lives where they faced minimal financial pressures. Typically, their children were grown up, their home mortgage was almost paid off, and they were married to someone who was working full-time and earning a decent salary. Yet, these highly success medical educators felt powerless. Managed care and shifting funding priorities had left them unable to enact necessary changes in the curriculum of their medical school. This seeming lack of power was very perplexing to our colleague. What in the world were these men and women worried about? Why did they look to their younger, untenured colleagues for new ideas, given that these younger men and women had everything to lose from trying something new in ways they themselves didn't? It is up to the older generation to take the risks or at least partner with their younger colleagues in taking a risk—they have nothing to lose!

As the senior members of the medical faculty began to confront their own fears, they began to realize that these fears were "out-of-date" and no longer relevant given their more stable and protected state as tenured professionals with strong financial bases. These middle-aged men and women faced the negative scenarios: "What would they do to us if we said *no*? "What would they do to us if we simply went ahead without their approval?" They discovered that there wasn't much that could be done to them. So they decided to take action. They began to talk about the things that they could do to reclaim the power they had so willingly given over to the administration and, in particular, to the managed care systems with which they were now partnering at the medical school.

Coaches are uniquely situated to provide a similar type of challenge and encouragement to the clients they are seeking to help. Coaches can question whether the fears identified by their client may be dated, whether unthinkable options may in fact be thinkable, and those "worst case scenarios" not too likely nor lethal. This often means that the coach herself takes a risk in the coaching setting—both to model risk-taking behavior and to "practice what she preaches." It means that the coach becomes vulnerable as she tries out something new in the coaching setting. Robert took the risk of asking Karl for written feedback regarding his performance as a coach. Furthermore, he asked Karl to make an oral presentation regarding Robert's work with him at a monthly meeting of the peer-based coaches in their high-tech company. Robert didn't want Karl to talk about the content of their coaching sessions—this would be a violation of their confidentiality agreement. Rather he wanted Karl to talk about the process of coaching from the client's own perspective and about what Robert has done that has been of greatest benefit.

An appropriately risk-partnering coach, such as Robert, might suggest to his client that they jointly try out a new coaching procedure. We offer several different models of coaching precisely because effective coaching often involves the joint movement of the coach and client from one strategy to another. Furthermore, both coach and client will benefit from the new insights and perspectives gained from a shift.

Servant

The lyricist of a popular song of the 1990s wrote appreciatively of someone who was "the wind beneath my wings." This statement offers a wonderfully poetic image of the role played by a masterful coach as servant to the dreams, visions and aspirations of the person she is coaching. A coach can provide the "wind" beneath the wings of her client by first committing fully to the partnership, and then offering encouragement during difficult times. A banking executive who searched for her next career years ago still speaks fondly of her "anxious quest," and of the day her coach told her he would not "abandon her until she had reached the next trapeze."

A dedicated coach can neither hijack the client's vision nor co-opt it unquestioningly, no matter her personal enthusiasm for the direction. While a coach may prod and provoke, she never takes over the client's vision nor inserts her own alternative vision. There is yet another caution to keep in mind (and heart). Coaches can easily get caught up in the client's initial statement of his dream, vision or aspiration and soon acquire a sense of personal commitment to (and even shared ownership) of this dream, vision or aspiration. As a coach, the value we bring is to encourage ongoing reflection on the part of our client regarding whether or not this is the best direction to take. We repeatedly participate with our client in the process of discernment—determining if the internal and external evidence that seems to be pointing our client in a certain direction comes from a place that is compatible with our client's long-term welfare and growth. There is perhaps no more important role to play as a masterful coach than to help the client make the tough choices between the very obvious and not so obvious, between the short-term and long-term, and, in particular, between the expedient way of life and the way of personal integrity.

A masterful coach also helps her client identify the lessons to be learned from seeming failures as well as clear successes, and expands the options that are available when her client seeks to move (fly) in new directions. These are all sources of support (wind) as her colleague soars to new heights—or even sustains his current altitude under new, challenging circumstances. The client owns his successes (and bloopers) - the "wind" just supports him and provides the healthy friction needed for a change in direction.

Three Strategies of Organizational Coaching

Organizational Coaching comes in many forms and is called many names. We propose that three strategies and more than a dozen specific models of organizational coaching have been found to be most effective in addressing the challenges of 21st Century organizations. Thoughtful discussions about organizational coaching and research projects that focus on the outcomes of coaching must begin with clarity regarding terms being used and differing assumptions underlying the use of specific terms.

We wish to contribute to this process of clarification by offering our own taxonomy of organizational coaching practices (see Table One). We propose that one of the three strategies and three of the coaching models relate specifically to a client's performance-engendering behavior. (cf. Goldsmith, 2000; Whitmore, 2009) We have labeled this strategy *"Behavioral coaching"* and the three specific models pertaining to this strategy: *engagement, empowerment,* and *opportunity* coaching.

A second strategy and three of the models relate specifically to the decision-making processes in which the client engages. (cf. Freas, 2000; Goss, 1996) We have labeled this strategy *"Decisional coaching."* The three models associated with this strategy are: *reflective, instrumented* and *observational coaching.*

A third strategy, *"Aspirational coaching,"* relates to the personal values and aspirations that are held by the person being coached. This form of organizational coaching is typically engaged through one or more of four models: *philosophical coaching, ethics-oriented coaching, career coaching,* and *spiritual coaching.*

Cognition, Affect and Conation

Placed in a psychological context, the three strategies—Behavioral, Decisional, and Aspirational coaching—can be differentiated from one another by the predominance in each strategy of one of psychology's three domains of attention: *cognition* (thinking), *affect* (feeling) and *conation* (behavior). While Behavioral coaching tends to focus on the behavioral (conation) aspects of the client's life and work, Decisional coaching focuses on the decisions (integration of cognition and affect) that underlie this behavior. Similarly, Aspirational coaching focuses on the relationship between the actions taken (conation) and values (affect) held by the client. Each of these strategies will ultimately generate integrated action outcomes that serve the organization and the individual learner. This phase of the coaching process will relate the client's explicit goals and objectives (cognition) and the steps to be taken on behalf of these goals and objectives (conation).

We provide a summary of the three organizational coaching strategies in Table One, as well as offering a brief description of the models associated with each of the three strategies in the following sections of this chapter. While we will refer to "the Behavioral Coach," "the Decisional coach" or "the Aspirational coach" throughout the chapter, the three strategies will, in actuality, weave through a coaching assignment as needed, at different times. A coach, for example, who is working with an executive for the first 90 days of having taken on a new global function, will wear these different coaching strategy hats along the way. He might be a Behavioral coach when discussing how to forge key relationships and how to pull together a unified team - and do both while braving the physical distances among his far-flung team members and stakeholders. He will have Decisional coaching sessions when his client evaluates, for example, how to trade off resources between competing interests, or make a call on the projects that need to be discontinued in the face of resistance by their owners, or re-examine his leadership self-concept when faced with a change management challenge. Along the way, more profoundly personal lines of Aspirational inquiry may be called for, as when the client encounters a values conflict with or among his peers or team members, when he evaluates whether to make a courageous but unpopular ethical stand, or when he momentarily doubts his career calling when faced with a seemingly disastrous set-back. It is critical for the coach to be conscious of which "coaching strategy hat" he is wearing at different times, in order to utilize the full range of methods available to him.

Table One: Organizational Coaching Taxonomy

Organizational Coaching Strategy	Behavioral Coaching	Decisional Coaching	Aspirational Coaching
Focus of Coaching	*Behavior*	*Decision-Making, involving both Thoughts and Feelings*	*Fundamental Beliefs, Values, Purpose*
Nature of Issue Being Addressed	**Puzzle:** Uni-dimensional, quantifiable, internal locus of control **Problem:** Multi-dimensional, complex ("messy"), mixture of internal and external locus of control	**Dilemma:** Two or more equally valid but opposed polarities; can be managed but never solved **Problem:** Multi-dimensional, complex ("messy"), mixture of internal and external locus of control	**Mystery:** Unfathomable, unpredictable, external locus of control
Examples of Issues Being Addressed	Providing a subordinate with feedback Running effective meetings Preparing presentations for board Mentoring talent for succession Developing a high performing remote team	Lateral collaboration with powerful peers Managing control vs. flexibility with a team Managing multiple stakeholder communities Making go/no-go/stop decisions Adapting leadership style to group dynamics and to market events Navigating the corporate matrix structure Making an impact on culture	Identifying specific ethical and appropriate actions to take Examining the alignment between one's own and an organization's values. Role modeling, promoting values in a team Clarifying one's own values and purpose with regard to career advancement and personal autonomy
Coaching Models	**I.a. Engagement:** Preparing for difficult and important interaction with another person **I.b. Empowerment:** Preparing for difficult and important work in a group setting **I.c. Opportunity:** Preparing for a major event in one's life	**II.a. Reflective:** Deliberating about options, assumptions, beliefs **II.b. Instrumented:** Learning about one's own and others' preferences and strengths **II.c. Observational:** Gaining greater insight into one's own actions and their impact on the environment	**III.a. Spiritual:** Discerning spiritual directions **III.b. Philosophical:** Critically examining fundamental frames of reference **III.c. Ethics:** Identifying and consistently acting upon one's own values and ethics **III.d. Career:** Identifying and acting on broad life and career preferences

An Overview of Coaching Strategy I: Behavioral Coaching

We will begin with the three models that relate specifically to an employee's *behavior:* engagement, empowerment and opportunity coaching.

I. a. Engagement Coaching

This form of Behavioral coaching focuses on the complex and often quite subtle processes involved in any interpersonal relationship. As the name implies, this form of coaching is most useful with issues around *important interpersonal relationships* in which much is at stake. This relationship might involve a subordinate, a superior (boss), a colleague, a board member or a customer. The engagement coach typically works with her client on one or more of three communication approaches: *disclosure, feedback and helping.* First, the coach will ensure an assessment of the client's own preferred modes of interpersonal relationship. Second, the coach will engender introspection and reflection. Third, with the coach's assistance, the client will try out (rehearse) a specific interpersonal engagement. The coach may do some teaching and/or modeling in supporting this performance.

I. b. Empowerment Coaching

While engagement coaching focuses on the one-on-one relationships in a client's work life, empowerment coaching focuses on the *relationships between a client and the groups* in which she participates as a leader, facilitator or member. The term empowerment is employed to emphasize the role of this type of Behavioral coaching in helping both a client and the group of which the client is a member be not only more effective, but also more influential in determining their own mode of operation and their own destination. This second mode of Behavioral coaching often involves reflection with a client about her way of operating in the group and examination regarding how she relates to her own power and voice. The coaching session might also include assessment of the client's preferred roles and modes of interacting in a group. Occasionally, the coach will observe a client's work in the actual group setting.

I. c. Opportunity Coaching

The third type of Behavioral coaching concerns *preparation for special events in the professional life* of the client. A client may be preparing for a major presentation, interviewing for a new job, or facing a particularly difficult and stressful encounter with a critical stakeholder. The challenge may concern a licensing examination or mounting a major new project. There is an opportunity for success and long-term benefit for the client. There is also the opportunity that the outcome will be detrimental or even devastating for the client. Opportunity coaching typically involves three interrelated elements. First, the coach helps her client prepare substantively for the event. Second, the coach helps the client prepare emotionally for the event. Third, the coach helps her client design or at least influence the design of the setting in which the event will take place—so that this setting will be skilling rather than de-skilling.

An Overview of Coaching Strategy II: Decisional Coaching

We turn now to the three models that relate specifically to the *decision-making* (Decisional) processes in which the client engages. We focus on the decision-making process in a manner that is aligned with the way in which the "executive function" operates in the human brain. This executive function involves not just the so-called rational section of the brain (the prefrontal cortex), but also the so-called emotional section of the brain (the limbic system). As Johan Lehrer (2009) has so persuasively argued, effective decision-making inevitably involves the acknowledgement and integration of these seemingly contradictory and competing sections of the human brain. Given the powerful analyses of cortical and sub-cortical processes being offered by Lehrer and many of his colleagues in the cognitive and neurosciences, we propose that Decisional coaching is effective if it incorporates both the *rational and irrational, the cognitive and affective, the thoughtful and the intuitive*. Keeping this dynamic image of decision-making processes in mind, we turn to a brief description of three models of Decisional coaching that can be effectively used when a professional coach wishes to assist her client in making better decisions within a complex, unpredictable and turbulent organizational environment.

II. a. Reflective Coaching

When engaged in reflective coaching, a Decisional coach "walks" with his colleague through job related dilemmas, helping his client identify and test out basic frames of reference and specific assumptions regarding his or her own ways of working with problems and issues. The reflective coach helps his client reframe, manage, live with or resolve the messes, paradoxes and paradigm shifts that inevitably confront contemporary leaders on a daily basis. When using a reflective coaching model, the Decisional coach also helps his colleague reflect on critical issues in her work life: when it is an appropriate time to disassemble things (chaos) and when is it better to keep things together (order). A Decisional coach assists his client to reflect on and learn about herself—her styles of interpersonal relationships, learning, leading, managing people, making decisions and managing conflict.

> The three strategies will, in actuality, weave through a coaching assignment as needed, at different times.

One's client is the primary source of information for this model of coaching, so it is the least complex with regard to the need for resources or people other than the coach and client. It is the most demanding of the three models, however, with regard to the complexity of thought that is required for the client to benefit from this reflection.

II. b. Instrumented Coaching

Decisional coaching benefits from a flow of rich and varied sets of information, facilitated by questionnaires, assessments, inventories and interviews – all instruments of data gathering. First, the Decisional coach administers one or more *self-assessments* to a client: question-naires that help this client identify, learn about, learn through and expand her repertoire of executive behaviors. Moving beyond the information contained in the self-assessment, comparable *assessments are provided by other people* with whom his client works, so that the client may compare and interpret the broader perspectives. The self-referential perspective is thus expanded by including the expectations of the colleagues (and thus of the organi-zation) and their view of how the person can succeed. Using the instrumented coaching model, the Decisional coach then helps his client assess the interplay between her personal styles, values and attitudes and the *environment and culture* in which she works. With this information in hand, the coach reflects with his client on ways in which her styles, values and attitudes are manifest in the challenges she faces every day in his working environ-ment. Together they discover or invent ways in which to further enhance the use of her strengths and ensure the presence of conditions in the workplace that are conducive to the use of these strengths, for the benefit of the individual and the organization in which she is embedded.

II. c. Observational Coaching

The Decisional coach provides a systematic, reality-based and structured process of self-discovery for his client through the use of observational coaching. This process enables his client to identify her distinctive strengths as observed by the coach under *actual working conditions*. Using the observational coaching model, the Decisional coach collects information from his colleague regarding her own perceptions of personal strengths and then compares this with personal observation and occasionally audio or video-recordings of his client's work.

> It is critical for the coach to be conscious of which "coaching strategy hat" he is wearing at different times, in order to utilize the full range of methods available to him.

Increasingly, leaders invite coaches to shadow them in real time, by attending meetings or listening into conference calls, in order for the coach to gain the most unadulterated view of how the person operates in their real life, often stressful, surroundings. The observations are then fed back thoughtfully to the client, allowing the coach and the manager to collaboratively reflect on the meaning and implications of the findings.

An Overview of Coaching Strategy III: Aspirational Coaching

While we firmly believe that Aspirational coaching should be a central component of any masterful and comprehensive organizational coaching system, it is a strategy that is open to a wide range of approaches that may or may not be perceived as fitting certain organizational cultures. This third organizational coaching strategy is typically engaged through one of four models that relate specifically to the values and aspirations of the person being coached.

III. a. Philosophical Coaching

The philosophical coach encourages and assists her coaching client to probe deeply into his *underlying assumptions and beliefs*, and to reflect on how these underlying assumptions and beliefs relate to and impact on his perceptions and actions in all aspects of life. Much like the reflective coach, the Aspirational coach who takes a philosophical stance will inquire into the ways in which her client approaches, interprets and acts on the challenges she faces in an organizational setting. The philosophical coach, however, probes at a much deeply conceptual level than does the reflective coach—often asking him what specific words mean to him or what meaning resides behind a story that he often recounts to other people inside and outside his organization.

As employees express a growing thirst for meaning, story-telling has become one of the most recognized leadership tools. The client who has had a chance to reflect on the philosophical underpinnings of his beliefs and actions (even if the word philosophy is never used as such in the coaching conversation) will often move hearts and minds with greater ease and be able to point to a "bigger picture."

III. b. Ethics-Oriented Coaching

The ethics-oriented coach is in the business of helping her client address fundamental challenges concerning the identification and application of a specific set of values to the decisions being made in and actions being taken by her client's organization. This type of coaching is likely to become more prevalent as internationally-based and internationally-oriented organizations confront differing cultures, social norms and value systems, while trying to establish, monitor and reinforce consistent policies and procedures. Typically, the ethics oriented coach is involved not only in assisting leaders with the preparation of formal policies and procedures, but also in working with individual clients who must deal on a daily basis with ambiguous and complex situations where there does not appear to be a single "right" or "just" answer. When a certain deterioration of corporate ethics begins to take hold, coaches may be confronted with discussing the personal dilemmas of potential "whistleblowers."

III. c. Career Coaching

This fourth model of Aspirational coaching overlaps with personal coaching and is probably the most common and diverse of the four. What distinguishes this form of coaching from the other three and from personal coaching? The key factor concerns the breadth of the life review process. At critical inflection points in a person's trajectory, career coaching embraces the entire life-experience of the colleague. Broad and enduring life and career patterns are examined by the client, with the assistance of his coach. (Sheerer, 1999; Fortgang, 2005) Financial issues might interplay with issues concerned with friendships, the use of leisure time, the identification of alternative career paths, or establishing a legacy. (Whitworth, Kimse-House and Sandahl, 1998)

III. d. Spiritual Coaching

Building on of a long tradition in many cultures, spiritual coaching primarily concerns the reflective inquiry into and appreciation of the major transcendent forces that: (1) call on us to improve the quality of our lives, our community and our society, (2) provide meaning and context for our complex and often unfathomable life experiences, and (3) provide an institutional base or set of ceremonial activities that enable us to express our deepest purpose, longings and life-joys. A spiritual purpose that reaches beyond the self is often the most powerful motivator for people to make difficult and lasting changes. Such changes are a common coaching agenda, and progress is often facilitated by this type of coaching conversation.

Conclusions

With the completion of this brief tour through these organizational coaching strategies, all of which an accomplished organizational coach can call up during a complex coaching relationship, we turn in the following chapters of this book to a more detailed analysis of ways in which each of these diverse strategies and their associated coaching models can be deployed in a masterful manner.

Chapter Four

Behavioral Coaching

In this chapter we focus on three models of Behavioral coaching: *engagement, empowerment* and *opportunity* coaching. We provide a description of each model in this chapter and offer many Behavioral Coaching tools in the Resources section of this book.

Engagement Coaching

This first model of Behavioral coaching is all about relationships and, in particular, about communication between two people. A masterful organizational coach who offers engagement coaching will assist his client in making sense of the complex and often perplexing processes involved in interpersonal relationships. A client might wish to work with her coach on a particularly difficult supervisory relationship in which she is involved, either as subordinate or superior. Or, engagement coaching might focus on a colleague, a board member or a customer. The client might be encouraged by her own boss to participate in engagement coaching because of feedback she has received from a performance appraisal or 360 Degree Feedback she has received (Bergquist,2003). The incentive might also come from the client's own dissatisfaction with her interpersonal relationships in the workplace or from complaints she has received indirectly from people with whom she works on a regular basis.

Once the initial data have been gathered regarding the engagement problem, the engagement coach typically focuses on specific communication issues. Communication, after all, is at the heart of all interpersonal relationships. Employees in 21st Century organizations typically spend most of their time and generate most of their value communicating with other employees. Usually, they don't get into trouble when they are working alone—and if they do get into trouble on their own, then coaching is not the answer: They need more technical training, training in problem solving, or a basic course about reasoning.

Effective Listening: Active and Empathic

In providing Behavioral coaching to a client, it is often fundamental for the coach to focus first on the basic elements of effective interpersonal engagement: active and empathic listening. These two elements can either create or eliminate many of the barriers that we set up when interacting with other people.

For each of us there is likely to be a twinge of recognition when we review each of the following listener responses which often cause speakers to stop communicating, because they are not being listened to.

First, we can *order, direct* or *command*: "You've got to do this." "You cannot do this." "Stop it."

Second we can *warn, admonish* or *threaten*: "You had better do this or else." "If you don't do this, then…" "You better not try that." "I warn you, if you do that…"

Third, we block communication when we are *moralizing, preaching* or *imploring*: "You should do this." "You ought to try it." "It is your responsibility to do this."

Fourth, communication is blocked through heavy *advising*, giving many *suggestions* and quickly offering *solutions*: "What I think you should do is…" "Let me suggest…" "Why not take a different approach…" "The best solution is…"

There is a fifth rather subtle way in which communication is blocked. We throw up a barricade when we try to *persuade exclusively with logic*, by *lecturing*, and by *heavily arguing* for a specific position: "Do you realize that…" "What makes sense is this:…" "It stands to reason that…"

A sixth barrier is created when we are *judgmental, criticizing, constantly disagreeing* or *blaming*: "You're acting foolishly…" "You're not thinking straight…" "You didn't do it right…" "You're wrong…" "How could you do that?" Ironically, a similar barrier is created when we do the opposite—when we are always praising, always agreeing, always evaluating and coming to the same positive conclusion, and, in particular when we are "buttering up" or exaggerating: "You always have good judgment…" "If anybody in this company can do it, a go-getter like you can."

In working as a Behavioral coach, it is also important that we notice a seventh group of potential barriers to effective communication on the part of our client (or of an inexperienced coach). Barriers are set up when we engage in *name-calling, ridicule* or other actions that may *engender shame* in the person with whom we wish to interaction: "You're thinking like an engineer..." "You really goofed on this one." "I can't believe you're talking like this." "Here goes Miss Congeniality." While we may intend these comments, at some level, as humor, they often are "stinging" for the person we are kidding about and may create major barriers to future effective communications.

> We can model effective interpersonal engagement by being aware
> of our own use of communication strategies that build barriers
> between ourselves and our clients.

The eighth barrier is people's habit of attributing meaning to others' actions: a heavy and indiscriminant use of *interpretation, analysis* and *diagnosis*: "You're just saying this because you're angry." "You're just jealous" "What you really need is..." "You're being a bit paranoid." We try to be "junior shrinks" and place ourselves in a "one-up" role that is inappropriate. Furthermore, we end up making untested assumptions about the other person's motives or feeling state that is harmful to the relationship and creates mistrust. Once again, the opposite type of statement can also create barriers. We spend all of our time reassuring the other person, sympathizing, consoling and offering patronizing support: "You'll feel different tomorrow." "Things will get better..." "Don't worry so much about it. It's not that bad." When making these statements we may not only be minimizing the feelings and concerns of the other person, but also tending to set ourselves up as somehow superior to or wiser than the other person.

We wish to identify two other barriers that are often unacknowledged, yet can be very destructive when our client is trying to enhance his interpersonal relationships. One of these barriers -the ninth one- is the extensive (over-)use of *probing, questions* and *interrogating*: "Why did you do that?... How long have you felt this way?... What have you done to try and solve it?" While, on the one hand, questioning can signal our interest in the other person (and is a fundamental tool of effective coaching), excessive, serial questioning can also backfire, leading our colleague to assume we don't believe them, we think they are ignorant, we have the solution to their problem (but are hiding this solution behind our questioning), are attempting to lead them in a certain direction or are actually disguising a scolding as a questions.

Similarly, we are likely to create a tenth barrier when our interactions with other people are *distracting, diverting* or filled with other kinds of dismissive behavior (including excessive *kidding*): "I bet you didn't see that coming!" "Think about the silver lining…" "Let's have lunch and forget about it." "Hey, no big deal!"

When serving as Behavioral coaches we can provide invaluable service to our client by pointing to these barriers when we observe or analyze their dialogues—whether they be overt or subtle. We also can model effective interpersonal engagement by being aware of our own use of communication strategies that build barriers between ourselves and our clients.

Coaching the Relationship between Two People

Much of the work in Behavioral coaching focuses on a single manager and his strengths and opportunities—as he perceives them. It is, however, also very effective when used to support the relationship between two or more people, particularly if they often work together and wish to improve their working relationship. The participants should view this process not as one of solving a dysfunctional relationship. This is better handled by an organizational consultant. Rather the process is one of fully appreciating, further enhancing and leveraging an important potentially high-functioning relationship.

When coaching a client with respect to her relationship with another specific person, a coach typically inquires about the underlying work context, their goals and deliverables. Organizations often (intentionally or unintentionally) set up real conflicts of interest between managers, through the ways in which they define their goals and how the managers get compensated. At other times, technological or systems problems create justifiable friction between individuals. While it may be tempting for coaches to focus on behavioral issues, they may first need to attend to the very real and understandable conflicts that exist between individuals. These objective differences have to be addressed first, before they are (often) exacerbated by personality differences or a weakness in the colleagues' communication skills, creating havoc in the department.

Along with a look at the objective aspects of the working relationship, the coach focuses on the process of communication between the individuals concerned. Many of the central elements in conflicts between members of an organization involve communication. Many years ago, Watzlawick, Bavelas and Jackson (1967) suggested five axioms of communication. Each of these axioms still holds true and can be applied by a coach and client in understanding why most relationships break down:

1. the impossibility of not communicating

2. the importance of both the content and relationship levels of communication

3. the punctuation of the sequences of events in a relationship

4. the important role played by different types of communication (digital and analogical)

5. the important differences between symmetrical and complementary interactions among partners.

We believe that these five axioms are critical in conducting engagement coaching and so we briefly examine each axiom as it relates to the processes of coaching with regard to the working relationships between clients.

Axiom 1: It is Impossible Not to Communicate

This first axiom suggests that no matter how hard one tries, one cannot avoid communicating. All activity or inactivity by the individual influences another in his presence: "words or silence all have message value: they influence others and these others, in turn, can't not-respond to these communications and are thus themselves communicating." (Watzlawick, Bavelas and Jackson, 1967)

Take, for example, Heath and Martin, who are both partners in a major service organization. They fully recognize the communicative power of silence and address it before it gets out of hand. Martin puts it this way: "I sometimes harbor things. You know this is the 'manly' thing to do! Heath is better about getting stuff out in the open. But we always end up talking about it." After some encouragement from their coach, Heath adds his observations:

> Yeah, we always do. If Martin gets quiet, after a while I'll ask: "Are you all right?" And he'll say, "No, I'm not." And then we talk about it. We play this stupid game of Martin being silent for awhile. I know right away that something's going on but that seems to work for us. I give him a bit of time to be silent. It works for me to talk about it right away and I think that it would be better for Martin if he'd talk about it right away too, but he thinks about it for a while in silence; that is probably better for him.

Martin chimes in: "And he flies off the handle more, which is probably better for him!" These two men have forged a complementary relationship. The coaching process enabled them to recognize complementarities and to more fully appreciate the problematic role that is played by unacknowledged and unaddressed silence.

Virtually all the people we have coached acknowledge that they communicate only a small portion of their messages through words.

Virtually all the people we have coached acknowledge that they communicate only a small portion of their messages through words. In general, the longer people have worked together, the greater the percentage of total communication that seems to come through nonverbally. People who work closely together simply can't shut off their communication with one another. As much as they might like to, they continue to communicate. Move to another room to get away from one's colleague, and this communicates something. Find a few moments to get away from everything, and our partner gets a message (be it accurate or inaccurate). Pat someone on the back for a job well done, and we also communicate something to them and others without having to say anything.

Axiom 2: Both Content and Relationship Matter in Communication

The second axiom is closely related to the first. In addition to transmitting content, any communication implies a commitment (of some form) to a relationship and thereby defines the relationship. Communication is used by all animals (including humans) not only to transmit information but also to influence the behavior of other members of the same species. Gregory Bateson (1961, pp.116-122) refers to these two aspects of communication as "report and command functions." Bateson uses a neurophysiologic analogy in defining these two critical functions. He describes the linear firing of three neurons in the brain. According to Bateson, the firing of the second neuron is both a report that the first neuron has fired and a command that the third neuron also fire.

In the case of Dave and Kathy, who have worked together for many years, there was more communication going on between them than their coach could decipher. This is certainly more the rule than the exception with people we have coached who had worked together for many years. These people are particularly inclined to find the engagement coaching process of great value, for they have often lost their independent, critical ability to reflect on their own relationship and its rich complexity.

While they were being coached, Dave would often turn toward Kathy before answering any question directed to him. When Kathy responded, however, she never looked in the direction of Dave. While both Dave and Kathy are successful managers, Dave seemed to be always seeking Kathy's approval and direction before commenting. Kathy seemed to be playing the central role at these points in their relationship, though she exhibited this dominance not through words or even overt action but rather through her subtle nonverbal messages to Dave. The response (verbal or nonverbal) of Dave to Kathy's initial comments provides an indication (report) that Dave had in fact heard her. Dave's response also indicates that he is concerned enough about his relationship with Kathy to respond to her statement. Furthermore, his response is an inducement (command) for Kathy to respond, in turn, to him either verbally or nonverbally. As Dave and Kathy reflected on these two functions in their own relationship, with the assistance of their engagement coach, the dynamics of their relationship began to change and the quality of their relationship improved.

In their commitment to one another, Dave and Kathy use effective as well as ineffective ways of communicating. This was identified during the coaching process. When they are effective, Dave and Kathy can communicate about something outside their relationship, for example, their work, their career interests, or their avocations. They can also, however, communicate about their own relationship and, in particular, about their processes of communication. This ability to communicate about one's own processes of communication is called meta-communication. This ability to meta-communicate lies at the heart of the engagement coaching process. This ability is based, in turn, on the concept of any relationship as a third entity: person A (entity one), person B (entity two), and the relationship between A and B (entity three). Once two colleagues recognize that this third entity exists, they can discuss their relationship as an identifiable and changeable entity.

In the case of Kathy and Dave, we found out that Kathy has assumed a very passive, secondary role in most of her previous working relationships. In her relationship with Dave, Kathy has assumed a much more dominant and controlling role. During their engagement coaching session, Dave and Kathy came to recognize that this is one of the things that Kathy found appealing about working with Dave in the first place. As in the case of most engagement coaching processes, Dave and Kathy gained their own insights about their relationship. The coach did nothing more than pose questions and help to establish a safe environment in which Dave and Kathy could discuss the non-discussable (namely the nature of their long-term relationship).

This ability to communicate about one's own processes of communication is called meta-communication. This ability to meta-communicate lies at the heart of the engagement coaching process.

With their coach's assistance Dave and Kathy came to realize that they communicate about many different things; however, the relational aspects of their communication is mostly about Kathy's need for influence in the relationship. For this pattern to change, Kathy and Dave must be willing to meta-communicate. They must be willing to talk about this need for influence, but also the times when this influence is misused, resulting in Kathy's inappropriate pattern of control and dominance and Dave's inappropriate submissiveness. With these insights, Dave and Kathy began to consider the establishment and careful mutual monitoring of an alternative pattern of communication, a challenging and rewarding direction.

Axiom 3: How We Punctuate Events Changes their Meaning

Punctuation refers to the assignment of a "time-stamped" one-way causality to a sequence of events or behaviors. When we are assigning blame in a two or three person situation, we typically assume that the other person(s) did or did not do something that caused us to feel or act in a certain way. The other person(s) in this conflict-filled relationship is likely to identify a different event or behavior that led to the current conflict. What person X perceives to be their justifiable response to a stimulus evoked by person Y may just as accurately be perceived by Y as a stimulus for their own subsequent response—resulting in a spiraling chain of events.

We turn to the example of Dolores and Brenda to illustrate this phenomenon. They have worked together for several years in a large insurance company and are located in adjacent offices. Punctuation plays an important role in ongoing conflicts regarding Dolores's dramatic outbursts. During their engagement coaching session Dolores and Brenda agreed that Dolores tends toward the volatile. She is often loud and demonstrative. Her feelings are very much on the surface. By contrast, Brenda appears to be more reflective and quiet. Her emotions are not so visible.

Both attribute their current styles to their early family settings. Dolores had more or less adopted her family style, which she sees as loud and exuberant, but at the same time warm and loving. Brenda, on the other hand, remembers her family as smoldering with unspoken hostility. When conflict was expressed, it was unleashed in a torrent of rage. In response, Brenda places importance on the ability to disagree, but to do so in a reasoned, calm and quiet fashion. Their conflicts often center on these varying styles and how these two women interpret each other's behavior. These insights about the origins of one's interpretations of experiences and feelings are often central to the engagement coaching process. This focus on interpretation and the assumption that underlie our interpretation of another person's behavior or, in particular, another person's use of language is often closely associated with the ontological coaching process of Julio Olalla and his colleagues at the Newfield Team (Olalla, 2008) Neither Dolores nor Brenda need personal counseling to address their so-called problem. They are both doing fine in the organization and have no serious emotional problems. Their success in rising to a managerial level speaks to their emotional stability and competency.

Engagement coaching is not for dysfunctional people; however, Dolores and Brenda do sometimes clash with one another and would like their work relationship to improve. This neither requires nor justifies the expenditure of funds for a high-priced external coach. Rather, Dolores and Brenda benefited from the assistance of a colleague who had received training as a peer coach. After first asking questions that encouraged Dolores and Brenda to sketch out the origins of their interpretations of Dolores' emotional outbreaks, the coach asked them to illustrate these interpretations in terms of their current relationship. Dolores indicated that "when I'm angry, you [Brenda] tend to take it personally and you shouldn't." Brenda agreed:

> Yeah, I do, because like I say, I think it goes back to earlier days when people had those feelings, usually they were expressing feelings they had about one another, and not just a momentary personal disagreement . . . I interpret the yelling and the screaming and the slamming of things as not just a casual comment like: "This is how I'm feeling right now . . . just leave me alone," but as more of a deep-seated moodiness . . . or anger about me."

Dolores and Brenda worked hard during two coaching sessions to overcome these differences in interpretations of Dolores' anger. Dolores suggested that Brenda was getting better at understanding her anger:

> Dolores: . . . like, the other day, when I was trying to finish that damned monthly financial report and I was growling and you just. . .
>
> Brenda: I just watched her do her thing and made some suggestions . . .
>
> Dolores: I think you're getting better at dealing with that.
>
> Brenda: Well, sometimes it seems a little less personal. It seems a little less directed at me. That was something that was very obviously directed at the process of preparing a report that no one will probably read, but you appeared to be very angry at me.

Dolores: That's something you do . . . tend to do . . . quite a bit, is when I'm angry around you . . .

Brenda: I take it personally . . .

Dolores: You take it personally and you shouldn't.

Brenda: I've come to understand that is the way you communicate . . .

Dolores: But I've taken on some of your style too. Like when I go home and I'm around my mother and my sister. They seem so loud . . .

Brenda: But you have always said that you were as loud or louder . . . years ago you were spunkier than both of them combined.

Though Dolores's anger was not actually directed at Brenda, Brenda first framed it in a very personal manner (in part because anger in her own family was often personal, disguised and expressed indirectly). Brenda reacted to this situation by becoming defensive and often sarcastic. This, in turn, used to provoke Dolores toward further anger, this time truly directed at Brenda. The conflict escalated. Each saw the other as being responsible for starting and fueling the fire. Neither was to blame. Additional human relations training would be of little value, since this process tends to be triggered specifically with one another rather than with other people in their lives. Personal counseling would also have been inappropriate, as would organizational consulting (since this had specifically to do with these two people). Engagement coaching was appropriate.

> A masterful empowerment coach is in the business of helping his client identify the *structures, processes* and *attitudes* in her own organization that can most effectively contribute to these new, empowering ways in which members of her own team can work together.

Dolores and Brenda were able to escape their angry interactions in part because they have developed the ability through engagement coaching to communicate with one another *about* their communication. This ability has been difficult to acquire. Early in their working relationship, Dolores and Brenda's differing backgrounds and styles of communication caused them some major discomfort. Dolores recollected that:

Especially when we were first assigned desks next to one another and given several projects to work on together, we used to just go to opposite ends of the spectrum. Brenda would just completely clam up and say, "I'm fine, everything is fine" and I'd be just screaming my head off, saying "No, it's not!" Over the last year and a half we learned how to work together and to enjoy each other's company. Still, things weren't always right. Sometimes we still got into kind of a crisis situation, where we were just fighting all the time for a week or two. One day I heard about the Decisional coaching program and I came to work one day and said, I think we should get involved in this coaching thing.... it couldn't hurt and it might help us enjoy each other's company more and work together without killing each other!

The coaching process only works when all parties respect and appreciate one another. If Dolores and Brenda were at such a crisis point that their work together was dysfunctional (unproductive or counter-productive) or their conflict was spilling over into other organizational operations, a consultation or mediation would have been more appropriate than engagement coaching. This was not the case with these two colleagues. Dolores and Brenda often worked effectively together and they had become good friends. Yet, they wanted to improve their relationship and hopefully improve their individual and collective productivity in their organization. So they asked their colleague who had been trained in engagement coaching to lend a hand.

At this point, the coaching process began, and Dolores and Brenda went through their own process of reflecting on and meta-communicating about their engagement. They met with the coach twice a month. The first time they met for one hour and the second time for two hours. They continue to go back to see their coach when they feel they need a 'tune-up'. They have had three additional, one half-hour sessions. The coaching experience has helped them both learn how to more effectively talk about how they communicate and how their personal styles of communication shaped their interactions with one another (and other people in their lives).

Dolores and Brenda learned to step outside the invisible constraints of their interaction when they began to recognize and talk about their respective styles. They learned to break an escalating chain of events by taking time out when either person requests it in order to pursue their discussion after emotions have calmed. They are no longer ruled by unspoken assumptions nor by emotions. Dolores and Brenda have begun to communicate (and often meta-communicate) in a more mutually satisfying manner. Brenda has now herself become trained as a coach and is providing assistance to other employees who want to improve the quality of their working relationships.

Axiom 4: Digital and Analogical Messages Color Each Other

Humans have two ways of communicating. They can define things precisely in terms of yes/no, good/bad, right/wrong, 0/1 and other dichotomous categories. Much of the content of communication is conveyed in what might be called a *digital* mode: "It's cold today." "You should wear your gloves if you're going out in this weather." "We shouldn't go out to lunch with Fred and Tamara today, given that it's so cold outside and we both have so much work to do on this project." These are digital statements that speak to facts in the world. Typically, digital statements are verbal, verifiable (you said so and so, didn't you?) and subject to confirmation (is it really cold outside and should this influence my decisions regarding gloves or lunchtime activities?)

A second type of communication is much subtler. Meaning is conveyed through tone of voice, gestures, facial expressions, posture and various symbolic modes. These statements usually concern the relationship itself rather than the content of the communication. This *analogical* mode of communication occurs in ranges of "more-or-less," rather than distinct (digital) notions about what is or is not the case. We speak a little louder to add emphasis to a statement. A loud declaration, "It is cold today!" "I have got a mountain of work to do today!" is quite different from a statement made in a matter-of-fact manner that "It is cold today" or "I have a lot of work to do." Similarly, my request that you wear your gloves today can be made as a casual recommendation or as a forceful command solely as a result of the tone of voice and related nonverbal cues.

Coaching processes are seemingly conducted in a digital, verbal medium. We have quoted the words spoken by participants in coaching processes and only occasionally comment on the tone of voice or gestures that accompany these words. This is certainly not the full story. In the case of Kathy and Dave, the coach felt that Kathy's voice was very demanding and often seemed quite whiny, whereas Dave conveyed a clear sense of resignation with an underlying expression of exasperation and strained patience. Do Kathy and Dave hear these messages in each other's voices? Have they ever heard these messages? What do they do about these messages, if they are heard? Many colleagues retain the status quo by choosing to ignore these messages, or at least never comment to one another about what these messages seem to be saying about the relationship.

An examination of this rich, analogical information is quite risky. An engagement coaching process often is needed to precipitate this type of discussion. The coach will identify his own impressions of the emotional state of his client and indicate what steps he observed that led him to making inferences regarding their attitudes or emotions. The coach then invites verification and inquiry from his clients regarding their own feelings and nonverbal expressions. While in a counseling session, a counselor may indicate something about the way she is feeling about her clients, or about how she is interpreting their nonverbal behavior, she usually does not expose the reasoning that lies behind these observations and interpretations. Coaching, however, is a much more open process, conducted among potential peers. Both the engagement coach and client explore and discuss their inferences, the logic behind them and their conclusions openly.

Axiom 5: Symmetry, Complementary Relationships or Mutuality Inform Communication

The final axiom of communication concerns the nature of the relationship between colleagues. In *symmetrical* interactions, colleagues tend to mirror one another. As one person becomes more assertive or inspiring, the other person also becomes more assertive or inspiring. Emphasis is placed on minimizing the inherent differences between people. Everyone begins to look like everyone else (the organization man and organization woman). Conversely, in *complementary* interactions, colleagues attempt to achieve a maximization of differences, with one colleague assuming the superior (one-up) position, while the other adopts the inferior, secondary or one-down position. The relationship between Kathy and Dave is clearly complementary in nature, with Dave serving in a one-down position to Kathy. Ironically, both of these people seem to create complementary relationships in many of their other working relationships, with both Kathy and Dave serving in one-down positions.

Both parties typically help to build the symmetrical or complementary relationship. "It takes two to tango" and it takes two to form either kind of relationship. For Kathy to assume a one-up position, Dave must also agree (at least implicitly) to assume a one-down position. Furthermore, he must find some indirect gratification in playing this role if it is to become a stable pattern in his relationship with Kathy. Otherwise, they would both be competing for dominance and a symmetrical relationship would be formed. Alternatively, neither might wish to be dominant and a relationship of *mutuality* and partnership might emerge. We have found in our engagement coaching experiences that some colleagues seem to relate easily to one another in either consistently complementary or symmetrical relationships; other colleagues have found ways to be together that are more flexible, dynamic or built on mutuality.

These then are the key ingredients in the brew called engagement coaching. We begin with a dash of good communication skills that lead to open and trusting interactions, and then mix in thoughtful reflection on the axioms inherent in effective interpersonal relationships. In the Resource Section of this book we have provided additional tools that can be used in engagement coaching. These tools can be deployed specifically when a coaching client is facing a particularly difficult engagement with a subordinate. The coach can assist by helping her client prepare a script for this engagement, by helping her client assess the type of defensive detours often used by this subordinate (or assessing the detours to which her client is himself most vulnerable) and by helping her client identify (and perhaps practice using) several interactive strategies that enable her client to retain control of this potentially volatile engagement.

Empowerment Coaching

Two of the most respected experts on empowerment, Cynthia Scott and Dennis Jaffe (1991), have noted that empowerment concerns new ways of people working together. This new mind-set requires, as Goodwin Watson (Watson and Johnson, 1972) noted many years ago, a fundamental shift in personal attitude. Scott and Jaffe describe the shift in this way: "employees feel responsible not just for doing the job, but also for making the whole organization work better." (Scott & Jaffe, 1991, p. 4) Watson would suggest that empowerment also requires a shift in team process. Scott and Jaffe (1991, p. 4) speak similarly of how "teams work together to improve their performance continually, achieving higher levels of productivity." Finally, Watson would encourage a shift in organizational structure if empowerment is to occur. For Scott and Jaffe (1991, p. 4) this would mean that "organizations are structured in such a way that people feel that they are able to achieve the results they want, that they can do what needs to be done, not just what is required of them, and be rewarded for doing so." Any effective empowerment, then, must ultimately involve a wide range of strategies and tools that impact on the structures, processes and attitudes of individual employees, work teams and the overall organization. A masterful empowerment coach, by extension, is in the business of helping his client identify the *structures, processes* and *attitudes* in her own organization that can most effectively contribute to these new, empowering ways in which members of her own team can work together.

The Keys to Empowerment

We believe that the key to "empowerment" lies not only in the ways in which people work together, but also in the manner by which individuals and teams specifically work in the domain of ideas. Empowerment proves itself first in the realm of ideas: the structures, processes and attitudes of an empowered and appreciative organization should be conducive to the generation, testing and implementation of ideas. Empowerment and appreciation concern the creation of settings and the development of individual and team capacities to work with ideas. Empowerment exists when ideas are being freely generated, when ideas are being discussed and tested, and in particular when differences in opinion regarding ideas are not only tolerated but actually welcomed as the basis for further dialogue and further development of a solution or new program. Only when the currency of ideas flows freely in an organization, so that employees are "bought in" and engaged in debates, does empowerment begin to also translate into the freedom to act, implement, innovate and carry full responsibility.

> Only when the currency of ideas flows freely in an organization, so that employees are "bought in" and engaged in debates, does empowerment begin to also translate into the freedom to act, implement, innovate and carry full responsibility.

We can't begin to review all of the many ways in which empowerment can be engendered in an organization and ways in which an empowered coach can assist her client. We have decided to start by focusing on the stages of team development that underlie the creation of an empowered team, since empowerment is not possible in a solitary context. In today's flatter and matrixed organizations and in a networked economy, managers need coaching about how to create or enable fairly autonomous and highly interactive teams. We then turn to several general suggestions concerning team leadership, roles and evaluation. We focus at the end of this chapter on four building blocks of team empowerment and relate these four building blocks to the concepts of appreciative team empowerment.

The Nature of Effective Team Meetings

Coaches frequently deal with issues involving the inadequate use of meetings: their clients complain about how these waste their time, or about how hard it is to get everything done in the meetings they chair, or about the conflicts that arise when differences surface. "You and I have simply got to stop meeting this way" is the name of a once popular and now classic book on how to improve meetings. This title contains some depressing truth for most of us as well as a touch of whimsy. Although we spend a better part of our lives in them, we are not very skillful in either planning for or conducting meetings; hence, usually do not look forward to being assigned a leadership role in a team. Typically, we do not relish the role of team member either, preferring instead to spend our time doing tasks that are more enjoyable and/or immediately rewarding.

When we do attend meetings, the yield is often not something of which we can be proud. This seems to be particularly the case in our contemporary world where the tasks often seem to be complex and elusive, and the processes of review and approval are sometimes quite complicated. One distraught manager at an East Coast organization in the United States reports that:

> "…according to my "logical" calculations, we are now ready to have a team reaction to the individual reactions to the interim reports so that the original committees can prepare final reports based on the team reactions to the individual reactions to the interim reports to give to the new committees so that they can make new interim reports based on the old final reports by the original committees based on the team reactions to the individual reactions to the interim reports."

While sympathy and empathy for this distraught manager may be warranted, it is not particularly helpful. Some general suggestions are offered in this particular chapter along with some particular insights about how teams change over time. These latter reflections are necessary correctives to any one set of general guidelines about effective meetings, for the tools and procedures that may be effective at one stage in the life of a team will be ineffective at another stage.

An experienced corporate training director we knew recently suggested that six steps be taken by a leader in order to improve meetings. His wisdom holds true:

1. Prepare carefully for the meeting. Capitalize on the natural, inherent influence of your position of leader.

2. Act so as to encourage expression of ideas and protect and preserve the ideas and feelings of each individual member.

3. Assure from the outset that there are clearly conceived and announced objectives.

4. Check from time to time for understanding.

5. Conclude the meeting with a restatement of the major points brought out during the session and state clearly any actions to be taken.

6. Thank the team for its participation and urge the members to put their new learning skills to use.

A similar set of common-sense suggestions was proposed a few years ago by an unknown author who called them "The Ten Commandments for Successful Meetings."

1. Call meetings only when necessary

2. Use meetings only when involvement of other people is essential

3. Include only the appropriate people

4. Prepare the meeting place

5. Always start on time

6. Set a time limit

7. Always provide an agenda in advance

8. State the purpose at the beginning

9. Practice good team dynamics; and

10. Use stand-up meetings whenever necessary

Both sets of common-sense guidelines talk about the need for careful pre-meeting planning, clarity about the purpose of the meeting, and the use of effective team process skills. The Ten Commandments for Successful Meetings speak in addition to the basic consideration of whether a meeting is actually needed; and, if it is needed, how to keep it short. The stand-up meeting (often called a "huddle") is being used with increasing frequency to reduce the time needed to set up a room and to provide an inducement (the fatigue of standing up) for the team members to keep their comments short and the meeting brief. The Ten Commandments for Successful Meetings list also speaks to the basic consideration of team size. A smaller size team is usually a more efficient and effective team, provided the team is large enough to encompass all or most of the required areas of information and expertise. The Ten Commandments for Successful Meetings suggest that consideration be given to whether each specific person should be invited to the meeting.

These basic considerations being offered in the Ten Commandments for Successful Meetings are particularly important in many American organizations, where the norms of democracy and accessibility dominate. It is hard in this day-and-age to declare that a meeting is not needed, for this usually implies that one person will be taking a unilateral course of action on a particular matter. It is also difficult to not invite someone to the meeting for this usually implies that this person's opinions are not worth consideration by the team. Thus, while these basic considerations are important, they do not yield easily to solution in contemporary organizational environments.

> If a conscious effort is made to help team members answer the appropriate questions at each stage of the team's development, the transition to the performance of stage four can be made more quickly and directly.

The guidelines that have just been enumerated from several different sources provide an entry into the more detailed descriptions of empowerment that we offer in this chapter. We turn now to a consideration of the team development stages that necessarily modify the general guidelines that have just been offered and that define the ways in which the members of a team can come to fully appreciate the complex dynamics of their team and can effectively share leadership in directing this team toward successful completion of its assigned task. A masterful empowerment coach can be particularly helpful to her client when assisting him in identifying the particular developmental stage of his own team and, in turn, helping him identify the most appropriate meeting design and actions to be taken at this developmental stage.

Stages of Team Development and the Meetings that Serve Them

As anyone who has worked within teams knows, these dynamic systems change over time. The behavior of a team and of the individuals who compose the team changes at different stages of the team's existence. We behave differently in teams that have just been formed than we do in teams that have been in existence for several weeks or months; teams function differently when they are just getting started than they do when and if they settle into a smooth routine.

The most widely used model for the developmental sequence of small teams, was identified by Bruce Tuckman (1965), and it concerns two distinct areas of behavior. First, almost all teams come together to get something done. Teams have agendas to cover, problems to solve, decisions to make. Behavior related to getting the job done will be called *task behavior*. Second, teams are made up of people. Whether they wish to or not, members of a team will establish interpersonal relations with each other over the course of the team's development. Behavior related to the interpersonal dimension of the team's life will be called *interpersonal behavior*. Tuckman proposes that teams follow a predictable pattern of development over time in the areas of both task behavior and relationship behavior.

Stage I: Forming. When a team is first established, it will inevitably go through a period of organization and orientation. In the area of task behavior, this is a period of orientation to the task. In this stage the team will be concerned with identifying the task at hand and in deciding what information and experience will be relevant to that task. In essence, the forming stage will be devoted to establishing the ground rules under which the work of the team will be conducted.

In the area of interpersonal behavior, the forming stage will be concerned with testing and dependence. "Testing" refers to attempts by team members to discover what kind of interpersonal behavior will be acceptable to other team members and to the formal leader of the team. "Dependence" refers to the tendency of team members in this early stage to rely on the formal or informal leaders of the team to provide structures and guidelines for interpersonal behavior. In the realm of task behavior, team members in the forming stage attempt to answer the question "What is the task of this team, and how will I be able to contribute to that task?" In the realm of interpersonal behavior, team members in the forming stage attempt to answer the question "What kind of behavior is acceptable in this team, and how am I to behave in this team?"

Stage II: Storming. The second stage of team development is characterized by some degree of emotional response. In the area of task behavior, the storming stage will be characterized by an emotional response to the demands of the task. To at least some extent, team members will experience some resistance to the demands the task will apparently be placing on them. If the task is relatively easy and if the experience and expertise of the team members seem adequate to the task, this resistance will be relatively minor and may even go unnoticed. If, however, the task appears extremely difficult, or if the members of the team are uncertain of their abilities to accomplish the task successfully, this resistance may be quite intense.

In the area of interpersonal behavior, the second stage of team development will be characterized by interpersonal conflict. Hostility may be directed by team members toward one another or toward the formal leader of the team, perhaps as a way of expressing individual differences or of resisting the continued imposition of structure on individual behavior. A sense of unity will not be present, and conflict may polarize around certain key issues. Essentially, the team will be experiencing a conflict between wishing to remain in the relative security of stage one or move into the unknown of perhaps closer interpersonal relations that may be established in the future. In the realm of task behavior, team members in the storming stage attempt to answer the question, "Am I emotionally ready to deal with this task?" In the realm of interpersonal behavior, team members in the storming stage attempt to answer the question, "Do I really want to work with these people!"

Stage III: Norming. The third stage of team development is characterized in both areas by increased openness and communication, as the team realizes that its prior conflicts point out the areas in which they need to establish some ground rules, agreements or "norms". In the area of task behavior, the third stage will be characterized by the open exchange of relevant interpretations. Information, ideas, and opinions relevant to the task will begin to be negotiated by team members as they settle down in earnest to getting the task done.

In the area of interpersonal behavior, the third stage of development is characterized by the development of team cohesion. In this stage, team members accept the team and one another; and, as a consequence, develop an important sense of team unity. Team harmony becomes important in this stage, and interpersonal conflict may be avoided to help ensure that harmony. In the realm of task behavior, team members in the norming stage attempt to answer the question, "What relevant ideas and opinions do I have that will help us accomplish this task?" In the realm of interpersonal behavior, team members attempt to answer the question, "How can I help contribute to continued team unity and harmony?"

Stage IV: Performing. In the fourth stage, emphasis is placed on constructive action directed at the successful completion of the task. In some sense, the distinction between task and interpersonal behavior fades here, for the energy that was previously invested in interpersonal issues now will be devoted to the task. In the area of task behavior, the final stage of team development may be identified as the emergence of solutions. It is at this stage that genuine attempts are made toward the successful completion of the task. In the area of interpersonal behavior, the fourth stage can be described as functional. Because the subjective issues of interpersonal relationships have been dealt with in the first three stages, team members can now function objectively as instruments of effective problem solving. In the realm of task behavior, team members in the performing stage attempt to answer the question, "How can we successfully complete this task?" In the realm of interpersonal behavior, team members attempt to answer the question, "What can each of us contribute to the successful completion of this task?"

A distinctive appreciative approach to team empowerment would require that each of these roles be understood and honored by all team members.

If teams develop through predictable stages over time, as Tuckman's model suggests, three consequences for team leaders and members become apparent. First, a developmental sequence in teams is in some sense inevitable. The inevitability of the phases also applies to long-term work teams when staff changes occur, when organizational or market changes seriously affect a team's circumstances, or there is, simply, a change in leadership. Team members would be well advised to provide time for (renewed) team development. A high level of task performance cannot be expected from teams at early stages in their development, or if they miss the attention required to completing each phase thoughtfully.

Second, leaders can help teams move smoothly from stage to stage. If a conscious effort is made to help team members answer the appropriate questions at each stage of the team's development, the transition to the performance of stage four can be made more quickly and directly.

Third, this four-stage model of team development can help team leaders and members diagnose current problems the team may be having as a function of a particular stage of the team's development, thus de-personalizing what may appear as conflictive or disruptive occurrences.

Forming, storming, norming, performing: the four predictable stages of team development can provide a powerful insight for an empowerment coaching client and, in turn, for team members into what is happening to them and what they can do about it. They can appreciate and thereby better cope with the stress and apprehension that accompany any shift in the functioning of the team or leadership roles over time. As mentioned above, this stage theory can also help an empowerment client and members of her team determine which guidelines are most appropriate at particular times in the life of the team. Guidelines concerned with team membership, acquaintance, and the availability of information are obviously more important at the forming stage of a team, whereas guidelines concerned with agendas, team decision-making operations and clarity about actions taken are more important for teams at the performing stage. Nevertheless, some of these latter guidelines might be appropriate at early stages of team development, not to enhance team productivity but rather to provide some structure that helps to reduce anxiety and accelerate movement toward the performing stage of the team.

Lately, practitioners often add a fifth stage, called *"adjourning"*, to signify the formal ending of a team, or at least of a specific project or mission. It can also be used, as can the former four phases, by long-term working teams who see the benefit of punctuating their work with celebrations and who sometimes have to deal with the dismissals of team members. From a task standpoint, loose ends have to be completed, legacy materials passed on. The question becomes: "What have we really accomplished?" At a personal level, there can be some grieving mixed in with the celebrating, and the question becomes: "How do I want to remember this journey and with whom will I remain in touch?"

The Nature and Function of Meetings

Not all meetings are being conducted for the same purpose. A masterful empowerment coach will often help his client identify the primary purpose(s) associated with a specific or regularly-scheduled meeting of her team. The specific purpose for which a meeting is being conducted will often determine the most appropriate procedures for conducting the meeting, appropriate leadership and follower-ship roles, and so forth. We must learn how to appreciate and then respond in an appropriate way to the diverse purposes being served by any team. In other words, *form should follow function* in an effectively run team meeting. It is essential, therefore, to examine the different types of meetings one might encounter before discussing alternative ways of conducting these meetings.

Types of Meetings. Several different taxonomies have been offered in the identification of meeting types. They share many common properties. A taxonomy of meetings as defined by their primary goal might consists of:

- Meetings that inform

- Meetings that instruct

- Meetings that define or plan

- Meetings that clarify

- Meetings that create

- Meetings that resolve or decide.

We propose a similar list that focuses on five meeting types that encompass somewhat broader purposes:

1. Information flow

2. Decision-making

3. Two-way communication

4. Introduction of change

5. Team spirit

When a coach prepares her client for a series of challenging meetings, or is helping a leader develop his own meeting protocols for very specific purposes, such taxonomies can be extremely useful.

> *Information Flow*: As organizations become more complex, specialization increases; and the dissemination of information becomes more difficult. Meetings are most often designed to facilitate the flow of information and bring various units of the organization into alignment around shared information. In many of the organizations we work with such meetings are under attack, because people rightly perceive that information could be disseminated in writing by digital means – face and phone time being at such a premium. But human attention is selective, so physical presence may often still be the only way to ensure that people actually received *critical* information.

> *Decision-Making*: Meetings are often called for the purpose of making joint decisions. People are more inclined to be enthusiastic about carrying out directives and implementing decisions if they have been involved in the planning and/or decision-making process. Increasingly, more specialized people have to pool their information in order to create a more complete data set. As with many statements in this book, this may be assumed to be a basic tenet of all managers. As coaches, however, we marvel often at driven senior leaders, who are caught in their routine of shouldering most major decisions themselves in heroic ways, who discover through coaching, with often child-like delight, how much more productive (and fun) joint decision-making can be.

> *Two-Way Communication*: Distinct from the one-directional, slow and clumsy email or voice mail exchanges we all live with, meetings still provide people with the best opportunity to ask questions and seek clarification with regard to direction

from higher levels of management. They also provide team members as well as the leader with an opportunity to present, test and debate their own ideas and suggestions regarding matters under consideration. The coach has to attract their client's attention to the proportion of talking time between them as leaders and their team members; help them observe if they give their opinions first or last, and how well they listen to and engage with others' ideas. Such behavioral choices will determine if team engagement in decision-making debates will be genuine and active, or passive (and silently resistant).

Introduction of Change: Meetings provide an excellent forum for introducing changes. Meetings can bring the principal actors affected by the change together to insure that all the implications are considered and analyzed. Necessary revisions and modifications can be discussed and finalized before the changes are implemented. Follow-up meetings can serve as effective evaluation instruments to make certain desired results are being achieved. The pace of today's economy has accelerated the rate of change in every work unit in the world. The coach will point out to the client that most meetings might nowadays contain an element of change management, requiring attention to changes in expectations, plans, roles, degrees of authority, etc. All such changes are accompanied by human visceral reactions that the meeting leader has to allow to surface and resolve, so they don't stray underground — or into the hallways.

Team Spirit: Meetings can be a valuable tool in developing a spirit of teamwork. No organization can be successful and expect to show a profit if its employees are not pulling together. One of the primary challenges of globalization is the dispersed nature of today's teams and the difficulty of infusing virtual meetings with the same spirit that face-to-face encounters can generate. That is why virtual or dispersed teams increasingly use social media, using social sites both for personal and professional purposes. Ultimately, it has always been informal relationships that have kept teams going, and leaders who encourage and model that behavior demonstrate that they are in synch with the times.

When these lists are pulled together (along with other comparable lists of which these two are representative), four primary, overarching purposes stand out with reference to team functioning. These are

1. Soliciting and/or disseminating information

2. Conflict management

3. Problem solving

4. Decision-making

They relate directly to the four stages of team development. While all communications can appear in every meeting, the forming stage is best expedited by effective data-communication, just as a team most successfully addresses the storming stage by means of effective conflict management. The norming stage uses the processes of effective problem solving with great frequency, while the fourth stage, performing, is heavily reliant on the processes of successful team decision-making.

Information Dissemination Meetings. The first of these four types of meetings is least extensively discussed in the literature—but is probably the most frequently used. Many staff meetings, general organizational meetings, advisory team meetings, and administrative cabinet meetings serve this function. It is essential that the team members are made aware that the meeting will be of this type before building an expectation that decisions will be made or problems solved at the meeting. This first type of meeting often is more expendable than are the other two types, since other means of data dissemination are available. Before calling such a meeting, one might want to consider the following line of reasoning to determine if it is necessary.

Information-handling meetings provide. (1) a forum for exchanging ideas, (2) an opportunity for stimulating our minds, and (3) a means of presenting information to many people at once. But our empowerment clients can accomplish most of these purposes without meeting in person. Before an empowerment client calls her next meeting, she should figure out what she would like to happen there, and then see if an alternative procedure might be a better, more cost-effective way to get the same job done.

> When the situation is either very good or very bad, people will look to a person in a position of power for leadership in moving toward the achievement of goals.

Routing schedules are the simplest form of information transfer. Instead of meeting to pass around information, send it around to relevant people for them to read at their convenience. Reply comments can come back to you the same way. This method is excellent for exchanging ideas, providing and receiving stimulation, presenting information, and the like. If, instead, a meeting is really chosen for informational purposes, it should be used to instruct as well as inform, to define, plan, or clarify. Such meetings must simultaneously provide a forum for two-way, immediate communication, thereby building team spirit and team acceptance of changes that have been made in the organization. An effective informational meeting should include avenues for not only dissemination of information (which, in isolation, can be done by other means) but also team members' feedback on this information and an exchange of pertinent information among all members of the team. More will be said about this type of meeting later in this chapter.

Conflict Management Meetings. Even with effective communication, members of a team will create or become involved in conflicts that disrupt team functioning. In fact, it is precisely because communication has begun to flow in a team that members of the team begin to recognize their differences of opinion and differing styles and values.

As the leader of a team, an empowered and empowering client can take several courses of action to mediate a team conflict. First, the leader can help each party to the conflict get out their version of the conflict in a systematic manner, and then call on the team to assist in managing or even resolving the conflict.

Second, she can call on a third person in the team to mediate between the two parties - assuming that this person is neutral, respected by both parties, and open to this difficult role. Alternatively, under conflict conditions, the leader can bring in an outsider to consult on the issue or identify the person in the team with the lowest stake in the outcome of the issue and ask this person's opinion.

Third, a client can simply give each party sufficient airtime to present their grievance or perception of the problem. Frequently, conflicts erupt primarily because one or more members of the team have not found space in which to talk and react to other ideas that have been presented.

Fourth, an empowerment coach can employ the tools of paraphrasing or polarity management (Johnson, 1992) to resolve conflict. Frequently each party to the conflict has not heard the other side of the argument clearly. A paraphrase by a neutral party or leader will often be heard long before comparable words are truly heard from the "adversary." Finally, perhaps the best way to manage conflict is by trying to avoid it. This can be done, in part, by surfacing and defusing the dominance of "personal agendas" during meetings.

In our work with leaders, making them aware of their own conflict management styles is critical if their meetings are to fulfill this purpose. Coaches will help their clients to notice where their preferences lie in terms of "turning into the storm" or looking the other way.

Are they avoiders or confronters? And when they do address conflict, do they approach it factually, emotionally, calmly or aggressively? A team's conflict resolution abilities are improved or hindered greatly by their leader's role modeling. Coaches will sue instruments or reflection to build a manager's essential self-knowledge and self-regulation in this regard.

Problem Solving Meetings. The third type of team meeting is often the most difficult to manage, yet also the most important. Team members use the meeting to identify and solve problems. While this is the most effective use of team resources, the problem-solving meeting is rarely employed, perhaps because of the difficulty inherent in its management. Knowledge about effective problem solving processes in teams abounds but is insufficiently employed in actual team meetings.

As an alternative to (or in advance of) the problem-solving meeting, a multi-round questionnaire procedure can be used to clarify the problem and/or solicit alternative solutions to the problem. Known as the *Delphi technique*, this procedure is particularly effective when used with people who are busy or have incompatible work schedules – a particularly apt tool for dispersed, often global teams.

 It is difficult for any team member to be both actively engaged in the work of the team and detached enough to observe its processes in detail.

A circulating notebook has also been suggested as an alternative to the problem-solving meeting: Instead of meetings to brainstorm or solve a problem, an empowerment client can send around a statement of what she wants to accomplish and simultaneously set up a Notebook to which everyone can contribute. The Notebook, freely accessible, becomes the repository for thoughts, ideas, and idle speculations—the same comments a client might hear at the meeting she might have called. An empowerment coach can then direct people to look back through the Notebook to see what others have contributed and to respond directly or contribute a new idea or approach. Each week the client (or another member of her team) copies the new contents of the Notebook and routes it to everyone in on the project; she presents a new, sharper focus to keep the team moving forward. These Notebooks are great for problem solving, brainstorming, exchanging ideas, and gaining consensus or agreement. Blogs and other internet-based dialogue tools have precisely facilitated this sort of remote problem-solving. It will appeal more to analytical, technical, sometimes introverted types who think while writing than to people and teams whose personality heavily favors live interaction—but the new economy leaves few people a choice to opt out.

Decision Making Meetings. The fourth type of meeting involves decision-making regarding specific courses of action. Typically, the formal governance bodies of an organization and/ or the administrative teams in an organization use meetings for this purpose. However, meetings often are wasteful because a decision has already been made prior to the start of the meeting – or the leader's mind appears made up, closed to other input. If the meeting becomes nothing more than "window dressing," it tends to produce alienation and resentment rather than any feeling of ownership for a decision that has already been made. A coach can support a leader who prepares for a decision making meeting by making sure her mind is open, that she has designed a good decision-making process and is willing to utilize advocacy as well as inquiry. Empowered and empowering leaders and their coaches know how to use consensus-building processes, or – if those fail – voting methods in order to bring matters to a conclusion. In a flat, dispersed world, where close supervision can't be counted on to "enforce" decisions, the degree of buy-in generated in these meetings is the gold standard by which their success can be measured.

Team Leadership

Each of these four types of meetings requires somewhat different roles and procedures. It is essential, therefore, that a team leader who is engaged in empowerment coaching be clear about the nature and purpose of the meeting being called, and that team members be informed of its nature and purpose before arriving at the meeting. This is the key to empowerment and to an appreciation of complex team processes.

Members of teams play a wide variety of roles. Following is a description of various team roles that are played in each of these three types of meetings. A distinctive appreciative approach to team empowerment would require that each of these roles be understood and honored by all team members. Some roles relate to team leadership, others to team follower-ship. An appreciative team will enable and encourage all members to identify for themselves and enact a useful and meaningful role in the team. This role should contribute directly to the productivity of the team and provide the member with a sense of accomplishment and contribution. A wide range of roles in teams must be performed in virtually all teams; hence, there is plenty of work to go around. Unfortunately, one or two members of a team often assume most of the essential roles in the team. This procedure overburdens leadership and under-utilizes and bores follower-ship.

The nature and function of leadership in teams have been debated and studied from many different perspectives for many years, and several theories have emerged. Understanding some of the theories of team leadership may help empowerment clients not only to exhibit leadership themselves but also to encourage it in others.

The trait theory, situational theory, and interactive theory of leadership. The three team leadership theories that seem most appropriate to the daily practices of contemporary organizations are *trait theory, situational theory*, and *interactive theory* of leadership. Before the middle of the 20th Century, the debate focused on whether team leadership was the result of characteristics possessed by a person (trait theory) or the result of a specific and unique convergence of events, needs, roles, and skills operating in the team (situational theory). According to trait theory, a team leader is inevitably a leader; situational theory would have it that team leadership is a result of forces that lie outside the leader's control.

Most researchers and theorists during the second half of the 20th Century concentrated on identifying characteristics (traits) that are common to team leaders. These correlational studies may reveal several dominant traits of leadership, but they do not account for the variation in team leadership behavior. The latter can often be better explained by the situation in which leadership is exhibited. Situational leadership theory suggests that different types of leadership are needed for different times and in different settings. (Blanchard, Zigarmi, and Zigarmi, 1985; Blanchard, Woodring, and Laurie Hawkins, 1998) Situational theory is based on the assumption that leadership is dependent upon the willingness of others to follow. People will follow those who they believe will give them what they want, and people want different things in different situations. Therefore, changing situations call for different types of leadership.

In more recent years another theory, the interactive theory, has emerged. It emphasizes the *interaction between the characteristics of the leader and the team-based situation* in which leadership is being exerted. Tannenbaum and Schmidt have identified seven different behaviors that they postulate will occur as a result of a certain balance in a team between the amount of power and influence held by the leader and that held by the followers. When a team leader has considerable power and influence in the implementation as well as formulation of decisions, then *unilateral decision-making* on the part of the leader will frequently be observed. Conversely, if the leader has limited power and influence—as is often the case in contemporary organizations—then *collaborative decision-making* is essential. In this situation, leadership is most likely to occur if the leader clearly and consistently relates institutional goals to the goals and needs of those working within the institution.

Autocratic behavior under conditions where power and influence are diffused inevitably leads to weak and ineffective leadership.

Rensis Likert(1961) proposed a related interactional model of team leadership. He identifies four types of team leaders.

1. The *exploitive-authoritative* leader has little confidence in other people and rarely involves them in decisions. This style of team leadership seems to work best in a hierarchical and production-oriented environment.

2. The *benevolent-autocratic* leader has a condescending attitude toward others. Decision-making at lower levels is done within prescribed limits. This style often seems to be dominant in human service, educational and public institutions, where there is a long tradition of paternalism between administrators and staff, and between staff and those being served by the institution.

3. The third style, *consultative-democratic*, is that of the team leader who has substantial confidence in members of his team. Communication flows up and down the organization. There is a high level of trust, and many decisions are made at lower levels. This style of leadership is most effective when the staff is highly trained and professional and when the goals of the institution are clearly defined- unfortunately an infrequent juxtaposition of favorable conditions.

4. The fourth style, *participative* leadership, is found among leaders who are people oriented, who frequently consult with members, and do all they can to help others perform their duties. Communication takes place in a friendly atmosphere and is often directed toward relationships rather than task issues. This style is best suited to organizations of human service rather than production. Participative leadership may be appropriate in a complex project involving highly skilled, intelligent, and self-directed people. Under the best of conditions, participative leadership reflects the collegiality for which many contemporary organizations strive. Usually neither participative nor consultative leadership is appropriate under crisis conditions or when only a few people in the organization possess the expertise necessary to solve complex technical problems.

The final and probably most sophisticated interactional theory is called the *contingency* theory of team leadership. First proposed by Fred Fiedler (1967), this theory holds that the relationship between a leader and members of a team is the most important factor in determining the leader's influence over the team. Next in importance is the structure of the task; and third, position power. Under most circumstances, if the leader is well liked by a team that has a definite task to perform, and if his position of power is widely accepted by the team, it will be fairly easy for him to be a successful leader. Furthermore, a task-oriented leader performs best under conditions when she has either a great deal of influence over team members or none at all. Leaders who are oriented toward relationships in the team rather than the team's task tend to perform best when they have moderate influence over the team.

Fiedler's theory of contingency leadership predicts that when the situation is either very good or very bad, people will look to a person in a position of power for leadership in moving toward the achievement of goals. When things are going well, members of the institution follow the leader because he is associated with success. When things are going badly, members of the organization look for strong rather than permissive leadership, which might contribute to even greater disintegration. Under moderately stressful conditions, followers prefer moderate leadership so that everyone has the opportunity to express their ideas and contribute to the improvement of the situation.

In summary, traits and situations are both important. An effective leader must be both eclectic and sensitive in his or her application of different leadership styles. No one type of leadership is always appropriate but participative modes may best serve the leader who lives in the usually turbulent (though not desperate) conditions of today's organizations.

Leadership and Emotional Intelligence. Coaches will also find a useful model in the six leadership styles identified by Goleman, Boyatzis and McKee in *Primal Leadership* (2004). Their two key contentions are very important for the empowerment coach.

1. First, certain leadership styles are most effective at certain points in a company's or team's evolution and for certain organizational tasks. For example, a *pacesetting* style is suited to engendering urgent and flawless execution when the unit's survival depends on it). Nevertheless long-term morale responds better to some styles (*coaching, affiliative, democratic*) than others (*commanding, pace-setting*).

2. Secondly, leaders must have a comfortable range and repertoire of styles, since no one or two preferred approaches will suit all challenges and all corporate life-cycle phases. While the *visionary style* most often builds a high degree of resonance and moves people towards shared aspirations, for example, it will need to be complemented by one of the other styles when it's time not just to set direction but to engender planful implementation or organizational learning.

Adopting and perfecting a new leadership style requires enormous self-awareness, commitment and consistency. We admire a mid-career executive client, who recently performed quite such a feat. She had risen to the head of a very sophisticated marketing research firm, based on her exceptional intelligence—brilliant analytics and a natural empathy that helped her insightfully understand audiences. She was an affiliative and coaching leader, under whom staff learned a lot. Since organizations inevitably move outstanding performers to ever higher levels of management responsibilities, Lisa was tapped, in her early forties, to become the head of all research functions, over a vast number of employees. Coaxing and teaching, she realized in the coaching sessions, were going to be insufficient tools for the dramatic re-direction she intended to implement in her new realm of responsibility. But assertiveness was never her strong point. Slender, petite and blond, she wasn't even sure that people would ever take her as seriously as necessary.

Lisa also harbored a fear of going overboard in her authoritative response to the urgent situation of explosive growth in which the company found itself; in their industry, you can't staff up fast – learning is highly specialized, on the job and takes one or two years. Reflection led Lisa to understand that what she needed above all was courage. We suggested that, in parallel to the coaching, she enroll in a martial arts class. By her own account, the fact that she "can now throw a 300 pound guy" has given her access to a calm but firm, thoughtful but much bolder leadership style and an energizing vigor which her team shares.

Evaluating Team Meetings

In evaluating the effectiveness of an appreciative team meeting with regard to empowerment and the generation of ideas, it is important for an empowerment client, with the help of her coach, to look at the success of the team in meeting its general purpose: sharing information, managing conflicts, solving problems or making decisions. It is also essential for the team members to evaluate the longer-term outcomes of the ideas that have been generated and, in particular, the actions that have been taken based on these ideas. Has there been clear accountability assigned? Has there been follow-through?

The evaluation should also focus on the processes whereby the team works on the task. Typically, the real problem resides not in the technical capacity of the team members to meet its objectives, but rather in the processes being used by the team. Alternatively, a team might call in an outside consultant or assign one of its own members to the role of process consultant. This person is usually not the empowerment coach—though executive coach Mary Beth O'Neill (2007) very successfully blends these roles. The process consultant is to help a team identify and hopefully solve its own problems. The process consultant does this by encouraging team members to become more aware of and to openly discuss the processes of the team, as well as the outcomes of these processes, and ways in which these processes can be improved.

Typically, a process consultant will observe the team in operation for a limited period of time, usually for one or two sessions. The consultant will then make comments on the process of the team: leadership functions, communication patterns, decision-making processes, conflict resolution strategies, and so forth. The process consultant will often make use of questionnaires. Just as no one leader can provide all of the functions needed in a team, so it is difficult for any team member to be both actively engaged in the work of the team and detached enough to observe its processes in detail.

Usually, one member of the team or an "outsider" (consultant or team coach) must be assigned to this detached *observer* role. If the person does come from inside the team, her new services will not be wasted. A process observer can contribute as much to a team's success as does the most active and resourceful member of the working team. Unlike recording secretaries, the role of process observer should be passed around the team, though team members should receive some training in this role or at least do some reading about process observation before assuming this role.

Obviously, we have only touched on a few of the dimensions of empowerment coaching. If interpersonal engagements are complex, then group and team dynamics are even more complex—exponentially more complex!! Empowerment coaching is particularly valuable for this very reason: organizational clients can always "use a hand" or benefit from a "second set of eyes" or "a second mind" working on the challenges inherent in team leadership and team participation. We have provided additional resources in the second half of this book that empowerment coaches find of great value when assisting their clients. These resources range from a description of multiple leadership roles in a meeting to a three-tiered model of the work actually being done in groups.

Opportunity Coaching

Special opportunities arise in many different ways when working in an organization. One can be applying for a new job, making a major presentation at a conference or board meeting, or simply preparing for an important review of one's own performance over the past quarter. Some of the most valued coaching is done when a client wishes to seize and make the most of an opportunity, whether it is for career advancement, for making a real difference in the operation of their department, or for convincing a group of respected colleagues that a new idea or innovative product is going to work.

Typically, an opportunity comes with added stress, as well as the potential gratification and anticipation associated with successful engagement of the opportunity. An effective organizational coach will assist her client with the stress, while also helping him prepare for the event. At a different level, the effective organizational coach can assist a leader with the broader strategies associated with helping other members of the organization to maximize their opportunities—particularly by providing stimulation and challenge as well as appreciation and support.

> From an appreciative perspective, the micro-lab is particularly aimed at identifying those skills that are already being effectively used by someone who is faced with a challenging opportunity, so that these skills might be used more often and in more appropriate settings.

A substantial amount of preparation for specific opportunities can occur in one-on-one coaching sessions, and the coach can balance challenge and support for her client, and provide role-play and other "rehearsal" formats. To complement that kind of work, we would like to offer a description of two strategies that we have found to be particularly helpful in balancing challenge with support by including additional participants beyond the coach and the leader being coached . They both involve additional players (in many ways serving as "auxiliary coaches)" and produce a powerful form of "rehearsal". These two related strategies are variations on something that is often called the Leadership Lab. Both labs provide a venue in which one can safely prepare for an opportunity or reflect on the dynamics occurring in the midst of the opportunity. We turn first to the more general principles involved in both forms of the Leadership Lab

Coaching Focused on a Protagonist's Opportunity: The Leadership Lab

A formal leadership lab requires a group setting, but many of its principles are applicable to one-on-one coaching as well. In fact, the reason we are including this methodology here, in the playbook of a masterful coach, is that it is the individual client (called the "protagonist") who is at the center of the leadership lab process, just as he is during one-on-one coaching. Even though a coach will inevitably need group facilitation skills in running a Lab, it is this focus on the individual client (the protagonist) that distinguishes the lab from other forms of working with groups: interventions like team coaching, where the "client" is the whole team, or the facilitation of group processes, where the facilitator is commissioned to guide the whole group, collectively, towards their chosen outcome. In the Lab, all coaching benefits and centers on an individual.

The individual protagonist role might be taken by a senior executive who is preparing to present a tough issue to his board, by a new manager who is preparing to launch her vision vis-à-vis a new team, or by a supervisor preparing to "sell" a change idea to his management team.

The name "leadership lab" has been assigned to signal that this coaching resource is intended not only for men and women in senior roles, but also for anyone in the organization who might serve in a temporary leadership position (such as chair of a committee) or might become a formal leader in the near future. It should be noted that some organizations find it very hard to frame the issue of leadership in nonhierarchical terms. For these organizations, leadership refers to someone in a position of formal authority. The term "learning lab" often replaces the term "leadership lab" in these organizations. This is perfectly acceptable, given that learning certainly resides at the heart of this dynamic organizational coaching process.

Whether taking place in what is called leadership laboratories or learning laboratories, this model of opportunity coaching provides a safe setting in which current or future leaders can test out alternative ways in which to deploy their distinctive strengths, especially when facing major opportunities (and attendant critical challenges) they have identified in the lab. Leader lab participants contract for feedback from their coach and other lab participants and receive this feedback after testing out strategies in a simulated work environment. Typically, lab participants test out several different strength-based strategies, building on feedback they have already received in the lab as well as insights they have gained from observing and providing feedback to other lab participants.

The Client-Centered Lab provides other lab participants with the chance to see their colleagues at work and to realize that most leadership skills and problems hold little regard for functional boundaries.

The leadership laboratory as a powerful coaching model can be traced back many years—to the social-action sessions that were held by Jacob Moreno (Moreno and Fox, 1987) as he prepared men and women to make an impact in their community. While this process eventually wound up as a much more therapeutically oriented tool called "psychodrama," it was initially very much a process that concerned the provision of a safe setting (sanctuary) for people to sort out and engage their leadership skills when faced with a challenging opportunity. Several approaches have been developed over the past twenty years in the design of leadership laboratories. We will focus in this book on two of these approaches: the Leadership Micro-Lab and the Client-Centered Lab.

I. Preparing for an Opportunity: The Leadership Micro-Laboratory

A basic sequence of performance, feedback and repeat performance, and a focus on specific skills, lie at the heart of the Leadership Micro-laboratory process. Dwight Allen and his colleagues at Stanford made five basic assumptions about this type of micro-lab learning.

1. Micro-lab performance is real. Although the work environment is simulated, the performance reflects reality.

2. Leadership Micro-labs lessen the complexities of normal work environments. The size, scope and duration of specific leadership tasks are all reduced.

3. Micro-labs focus on training for the accomplishment of specific tasks. These tasks all relate to the opportunities that are opening for the lab participants. These tasks might concern team building strategies, presentation skills, management techniques, or conflict-management.

4. Leadership Micro-laboratories allow for increased control of practice. In the practice setting of micro-labs, all of the key parameters (time, number of participants, methods of feedback, and so forth) can be manipulated. As a result, a high degree of control can be built into this opportunity coaching program.

5. Micro-labs greatly expand the normal feedback dimension in a coaching process. Immediately after addressing a specific challenge, the client receives feedback and a critique that can be immediately translated into practice when the client repeats her performance shortly thereafter.

A typical micro-lab session begins with one of the participants volunteering to be the focus of attention in this session. This person (as in all Leadership Lab models) is called the protagonist. It is critical that no participant is ever required or subtly coerced into being a protagonist. Some lab participants learn by doing, while others learn just as much from observing and reflecting on the laboratory experience. (Kolb, 1983) The protagonist plays a specific role in a particular opportunity context—such as making a presentation before a board of directors or providing negative feedback to a subordinate. This role-play typically only represents a small fragment of the total performance. This brief role-play usually lasts no more than ten minutes. It is recorded on video and observed by the coach as well as the other lab participants.

At the completion of this role-play the other lab participants provide feedback to the protagonist on the session. The protagonist and coach review the feedback, view parts of the video recording and, in general, discuss the performance. Using an appreciative approach, attention focuses on areas of distinctive strength and ways in which the protagonist's strengths can be more consistently and effectively deployed. Once the analysis is completed, the protagonist is given a brief period of time to rethink her strategy, incorporating into it the information received from the other lab participants, the coach, and the video recording. The protagonist may then perform the role play once again and the feedback process is repeated.

Central to the idea of micro-lab learning is the belief that effective performance consists of a number of discrete, identifiable activities that can be isolated and taught. Although the specific skills will vary according to the needs of the particular program, several skills—often called *micro-skills*—are characteristic of most complex interpersonal situations and may be particularly salient for people who are faced with challenging opportunities:

> *Set induction*: The ability to prepare other people for what one wants them to hear or learn. This is often done through a story, an analogy, a demonstration, or a leading question.
>
> *Stimulus variation*: The ability to vary the pattern of interaction with other people, which includes such elements as physical movement, gestures, voice level, and ability to draw attention to important points.
>
> *Silence and nonverbal cues*: The ability to use nonverbal messages to move a discussion.
>
> *Reinforcement*: The ability to use both verbal and nonverbal messages to encourage and influence the performance of other people.

Questioning: The ability to ask clear, stimulating and encouraging questions.

Use of examples: The ability to use both verbal and visual examples at appropriate times in a discussion.

Closure: A complement to set induction, the ability to bring an interaction to a close in a way that not only summarizes the essential points and conclusions of the interaction but also optimally moves the relationship (after a particularly important interaction) to a new level of understanding and effectiveness.

These skills or others that may be identified as desirable often become the focus of attention in a micro-lab. It must be pointed out, however, that such a set of skills does not imply an ideal or prescribed model of effectiveness; instead, micro-lab coaching aims at refining and increasing the range of skills available to individual clients as the demands of the situation require. From an appreciative perspective, the micro-lab is particularly aimed at identifying those skills that are already being effectively used by someone who is faced with a challenging opportunity, so that these skills might be used more often and in more appropriate settings.

A micro-lab program can be conducted for a maximum of four to six participants over a four-day period (usually in one intensive period of time, though, in many instances, sessions are offered weekly over two to three months. Participants focus on certain leadership functions and the achievement of certain leadership competencies. Reflective and instrumented coaching processes are often employed to encourage deeper and broader analysis of current strengths and styles.

> Coaching clients and members of a team must be appreciated for all of the talents they "bring to the party," not just those that are most visible and commonly honored in our society.

By the second or third session, a performance cycle begins. In each cycle, a participant is given the opportunity to engage in one five-minute performance. The other participants observe this mini-performance and are often asked by the coach to take notes on the protagonist's use of specific competencies or distinctive strengths that have been the focus of earlier sessions. Additional didactic sessions are often offered in these extended workshops regarding other competencies or additional reflective or instrumented coaching sessions are held to help participants identify distinctive competencies and particularly challenging situations in their work life. A second cycle is initiated. Often the protagonist will take on the same challenge as in the first cycle, but now making better (or at least different or more extensive) use of his distinctive competencies, new insights regarding this challenge, or specific strategies and tools being described in the workshop. Additional didactic sessions are interspersed and a third cycle typically is offered before the workshop is brought to a close with a discussion of ways in which to transfer these newly acquired insights and skills to the real world of organizational life.

Micro-labs have a number of obvious strengths. The micro-lab is a highly focused activity that allows participants to work on one skill at a time. It provides a safe environment in which to experiment and practice. It provides both rapid feedback and a chance to put that feedback to immediate use through a second performance. Furthermore, by breaking down a complex act into clearly identifiable skills, micro-labs make leadership behavior more accessible: a set of skills that can be learned and a process of interaction that is neither mystical nor necessarily private. Leadership becomes a deliberate, public enterprise that can be observed, analyzed, and learned. Finally, as we shall see when we turn to possible modifications of micro-labs for use in opportunity coaching, one of the greatest strengths of the micro-lab is its flexibility. Although micro-labs may become rather elaborate, the basic sequence—perform, analyze, and perform again—is one that can be used in many different settings.

Like any approach to opportunity coaching, the Leadership Micro-lab has its limitations. First, the micro-lab may be too elementary for some clients. In spite of the obvious logic of the component skills approach, many experienced coaching clients resist micro-labs as unnecessary and even disruptive dissections of an activity that is organic, whole, and unified—even though many of these same clients will defend such rational analysis in their own area of technical expertise. Objections may be raised to the short time limit of a micro-lab session. Many clients may feel, perhaps with some justification, that such a limit does not allow them sufficient time for the natural development of an idea or practice of a skill. There are also obvious logistic problems involved in bringing together very busy people, equipment (that may or may not work) and a coach. Even a modest micro-lab requires careful planning and organization.

Finally, it should be noted that micro-labs are focused exclusively on immediate performance; they do not deal with the values, attitudes, and structures which surround the work environment and which profoundly influence the performance of the leader in this setting. Micro-labs can doubtless help employees be more effective in their leadership functions—and that is an obvious benefit. These labs, however, are not likely to cause a participant to rethink or reframe the assumptions and implications that lie behind the way she performs. Both reflective and instrumented coaching can be of great value in bringing those who face executive challenges to this second level of analysis and insight.

II. In the Midst of Opportunity: The Client-Centered Laboratory

Like the micro-lab, a Client-Centered Laboratory (CCL) provides a safe, controlled environment in which men and women who face challenging opportunities may identify distinctive competencies, refine already existing strengths, or develop skills. It differs from the micro-lab in that the protagonist herself determines the strengths or skills that she wishes to refine or further develop. As in the case of the micro-lab, the CCL is usually staffed by a coach and is conducted for three to six participants. When not serving as protagonist, lab participants play roles as leaders, followers, subordinates, bosses or participants—whatever is needed to help the protagonist in meeting their opportunity challenge.

The coach is responsible for directing and controlling the process, which begins with the establishment of a contract between himself and the protagonist. This contract consists of a specific list of issues or aspects of performance about which the protagonist wants feedback. Someone about to make a presentation before a board of directors, for instance, may want to know how the directors are likely to respond to the structure and flow of her presentation. What about her use of examples or her pacing? Another participant who is about to facilitate a planning group may request responses to the interest level of the experience or the kind of questions she is asking. The protagonist and coach work out the details of this contract prior to a laboratory session or at the start of the session.

The second step in a Client-Centered Laboratory process, as in a micro-lab, is the performance of a five to ten minute role-play by the contracting protagonist. This session may be self-contained or one segment in a longer sequence of activities. Several of the participants can be used as role players for a particular session. The participant who is to be the focus of the session may request them to role-play certain kinds of employees or supervisors (hostile, apathetic, young, and so forth) or she may simply ask them to be themselves. The role-play is followed by the feedback session, during which the protagonist receives information from both the coach and other laboratory participants on those aspects of her performance contracted for earlier.

Finally, as in the micro-lab, the protagonist is encouraged to repeat this process, incorporating into her second session information gained during the replay and feedback periods. Given that the CCL is not as focused on specific skills as the micro-lab, there is much more for participants to ponder at the conclusion of their first session. In recognition of this difference, the Client-Centered Lab varies from the micro-lab in that the second performance usually does not take place immediately after the first. Rather lab participants are encouraged to think about their feedback and benefit from the feedback being given to other participants after their own performances.

While CCLs are very flexible, they typically take on one of ten forms.

1. The first type of lab focuses on interpersonal relationships and no roles are assumed by anyone in the lab. Rather, the lab provides an opportunity for the protagonist to try out a specific approach that is not directed to any specific person. For instance, the protagonist might want to be more assertive in expressing his dissatisfaction with other employees' performance and will use the lab to test out several hypothetical situations.

2. The second type of lab also focuses on interpersonal relationships. However, one or more specific roles are assigned to other lab participants. They assume the role of a specific person or specific type of person with whom the protagonist wishes to work in a more effective or sensitive manner.

3. A third type of CCL involves the assuming of roles in an interpersonal relationship. However, in this instance the roles are reversed. The protagonist takes on the role of another specific person or type of person—with another laboratory participant assuming the protagonist's role. In this way, the protagonist can gain greater empathy or at least a greater appreciation for the perspective being assumed by this other person.

4. The fourth type of lab focuses on group leadership. No one in the lab assumes an artificial role. Rather, the protagonist tests out various leadership strategies with other participants being as natural as possible. Simulations of specific tasks or types of group functioning are often used in this fourth type of leader-centered laboratory.

5. The fifth type also involves group leadership issues, though with this type other lab participants assume specific group roles—seeking to replicate the actions or reactions of a specific person or type of group member. The protagonist can focus in this fifth type of lab on their strategy for working with a particularly difficult group.

6. The sixth type of lab once again involves role reversal. A protagonist might wish not to play the leader, but instead get the feel for membership in a specific type of group. Someone else takes the leadership role so that the protagonist (who usually occupies the leadership role) can gain a better appreciation for the group as experienced from a different perspective.

7. The seventh and eight lab types both involve preparation for a major presentation. The protagonist might be preparing to make a major speech or applying for a new job. She might instead be rehearsing for a press conference or an upcoming presentation to a Board of Trustees. The seventh type of lab requires no role-playing. Lab participants simply respond naturally to the presentation and offer candid (and hopefully appreciative) feedback to the protagonist. The protagonist is given the chance to try out a specific approach that is not directed to any specific group of people.

8. Conversely, the eighth type of lab is directed toward a particular audience. Lab participants assume the roles of specific people or specific types of people operating in a group context and provide feedback to the protagonist from the perspective of this specific role.

9. There are two other types of client-center labs that can be particularly useful for a protagonist who faces an opportunity challenge. A difficult decision must be made and the protagonist uses the laboratory (like he would use a reflective coaching session) to sort out and clarify aspects and dimensions of this decision. The ninth type of leadership lab involves no role-playing. The protagonist is at a "fork-in-the road." He presents several alternatives to a panel or jury (composed of other participants in this lab). These panel or jury members assume no particular perspective, but render their judgment regarding the alternative decision-points that the protagonist is considering.

10. The tenth type of leadership lab is perhaps the most demanding—and potentially enlightening—of the ten alternatives. The protagonist must make a decision and in tracing out the alternatives, the protagonist identifies various aspects of herself that are involved in this decision: the protagonist presents several alternatives to the panel or jury (other participants in lab). Members assume specific and differing aspects of self or represent interests or perspectives of specific and differing constituencies. They render their individual judgments regarding alternatives based on this aspect, interest or perspective.

A CCL coach can make use of many different tools and techniques. Her creativity will increase as she takes on a variety of lab issues and as she looks to other lab participants for ideas regarding how to address a specific issue that one of the participants has identified. She can make use of a monologue during which the protagonist reflects out loud, usually while walking around the lab space. This "walk-about" often generates new perspectives and provides other lab participants with rich material on which to comment when reflecting back to the protagonist.

The CCL coach might even wish to use a process called *Rashamon* (named after the famous Japanese movie in which several different versions of a single story are being portrayed). When used as a lab technique, Rashamon requires that several lab participants listen to or observe the actions of the protagonist, then leave the room. They come back into the room, one at a time, to report on what they have seen, heard or concluded regarding the protagonist's work. In this way, the protagonist receives several independent versions of what he said or did. A temporary role-reversal can also be engaged. The coach (or a lab participant) assumes the role of the protagonist and the protagonist assumes another role for a short period of time (usually no more than one or two minutes). This technique can be used with any of the ten lab types (as well as in individual coaching) not just the types based on role-reversals. Many other techniques also can be introduced, though the lab need not be highly complex, nor does the coach have to entertain the lab participants. The lab can be run in a very straight forward manner with the coach primarily serving in the role of clarifier, orchestrator and rule-keeper (appreciative, constructive, and focusing on the interests and stated needs of the protagonist).

 Effective coaches are always leaning into the future with their clients. Coaching means business!

The Client-Centered Laboratory shares many of the strengths and weaknesses of the micro-lab. It is focused, controlled, and relatively safe. It can heighten awareness of leadership processes. It can open up dialogue between colleagues. It has the additional strength of providing participants with control over the process, for the skills to be observed are defined by the protagonist and not by the coach or program. On the other hand, a CCL (like micro-labs) can have logistics problems, and may meet initial resistance.

Aside from its primary intention of providing the individual protagonist with controlled information about her performance, the Client-Centered Lab provides other lab participants with the chance to see their colleagues at work and to realize that most leadership skills and problems hold little regard for functional boundaries. In addition, a CCL conducted with participants who serve as role-players will often generate a general and useful discussion that may itself be a new experience for many of these participants. Finally, the opportunity to give constructive feedback may be a valuable learning experience for all laboratory participants who must give feedback to other employees in their on-the-job setting.

On the one hand, we have found that both engagement and empowerment coaching are "easier sells" than opportunity coaching—particularly when this third form of Behavioral coaching is being conducted through the use of Leadership Labs. On the other hand, we have also found that coaching clients are often most motivated and most open to new learning when faced with a challenging opportunity and a safe peer-based environment in which to think and experiment . And we have found that the Leadership Lab provides an excellent opportunity for clients to gain new skills and new insights with the help of not only their coach but also their fellow participants in the Lab. It is worth fighting through the logistical challenges of establishing a Leadership Lab, given the potential "big bang" payoffs resulting from this model of Behavioral coaching.

Conclusions

The multi-dimensional approach to Behavioral coaching that we have described in this chapter is founded in the principle of appreciation (as are all of the coaching strategies and models presented in this book). Our approach to Behavioral coaching is appreciative in at least five ways.

First, this multi-dimensional approach to engagement, empowerment and opportunity coaching brings out the *latent strengths and resources* of all coaching clients. One begins with the assumption that a client has skills, knowledge and aptitudes that can be of great benefit to their colleagues, their team and their organization—provided that one's client and other members of her organization fully appreciate these talents and the environment of the interpersonal engagement, team empowerment, or opportunity-focused Leadership lab is conducive to the display and nurturing of these talents.

As a cautionary noted, Scott and Jaffe (1991, p. 42) offer the following insightful observation about non-appreciative perspectives:

> Many managers [in contemporary organizations] spend much of their time
> disqualifying people, making up reasons why their people won't do what the

organization wants them to. . . . They expect the worst from people. . . . . Not surprisingly, the manager usually finds that these negative beliefs turn out to be correct. He or she is right, but for the wrong reasons. The manager doesn't see that he or she has created a self-fulfilling prophecy. By acting in such a way that the team did not achieve the desired results, the manager proved his or her negative assumptions to be correct.

Just as negative assumptions can be self-fulfilling, so can positive assumptions about people's strengths and competencies be self-fulfilling.

Second, the approach being presented in this chapter recognizes the *multiple leadership roles* that a coaching client can embrace. Everyone can be a leader in performing certain tasks or engaging in certain areas of team functioning, at a certain time and in a certain place. Andy Warhol once suggested that each of us can be famous for fifteen minutes. While this may be a bit of an overstatement mixed with profound cynicism, it is possible, from an appreciative perspective, for each coaching client and each member of a team to find herself in a leadership role at some point in the life of an organization. The client has only to acknowledge this leadership role, be alert to the moment that calls for this role, and allow it to emerge and be honored by other members of the organization. As Cynthia Scott and Dennis Jaffe (1991, p. 32) propose specifically with regard to team empowerment:

> In the empowered work team, everyone has the responsibility that was tradition-ally given the leader. If anyone sees a problem or has an idea, they are responsible for bringing it to the group. The idea must be respected, and everyone should be engaged in looking for ways to grow and develop. It's not enough for just the [the people in formal leadership roles] to do this.

Third, an appreciative approach to Behavioral coaching recognizes not just the multiple lead-ership roles played by a client in challenging interpersonal situations or as a team member but also the many other contributions to be made by the client or other team members. In recent years, we have come to recognize that people possess "*multiple intelligences*" and that these many different competencies are often unacknowledged in our society. One of these forms of intelligence, often called emotional intelligence, has been acknowledged as particularly important in all organizational settings. (Goleman, 2006) Coaching clients and members of a team must be appreciated for all of the talents they "bring to the party," not just those that are most visible and commonly honored in our society, such as technical and analytic skills, decisiveness, planning and perseverance.

Employees who are appreciated by their organization are expected to influence their own individual and the collective future of their organization. As a result, appreciation tends to add pressure to a client and team members rather than reduce pressure. As Blanchard and his associates (Blanchard, Carlos and Randolph, 1999, p. 6) have noted: "Leaders who empower people are placing additional *responsibilities for results* on the team members. That is right: empowerment is not soft management. But even though it places high expectations on people, team members embrace empowerment because it leads to the joys of involvement, ownership and growth."

The information we have presented is appreciative in that it enables a client to better understand and appreciate the subtle and often complex dynamics of the interpersonal relationships, the teams and the opportunities they face within their organization. Contemporary organizational dynamics researchers and experienced organizational coaches have provided us with many valuable insights and suggestions regarding *effective interpersonal and team processes*. As clients of masterful Behavioral coaches, men and women in organizations gain a fuller appreciation of these complex processes; as a result, they can better tolerate and even enjoy the complex drama of organizational life, while also learning how better to influence the outcomes of their relationships with other people and the teams of which they are members.

Finally, it is important to note that an appreciative approach to Behavioral coaching is embedded in the emphasis being placed throughout this chapter on not just generating ideas but also enabling the client to confidently translate these ideas into personal action. Behavioral coaches and their clients are seeking ways to translate items of discussion and dialogue into steps, toward realization of clearly articulated intentions, based on shared and consensually validated information.

The appreciative core of Behavioral coaching is manifest when the masterful coach disposes of a rich choice of practices and approaches in preparing the client for new, sustainable, and possibly transformative behavior. While the models we offer are very powerful and proven, coaches continuously develop novel approaches to Behavioral coaching. Effective coaches are always leaning into the future with their clients. Whether it is through assisting a client to effectively engage another person, to empower a group, or to meet the challenge inherent in a major opportunity—Behavioral coaching means business!

Chapter Five

Decisional Coaching

Historically most organizational coaching has been deficit-based. The classic definition goes something like this: "Coaching is a relationship in which the coach helps the client to meet developmental goals and/or performance outcomes to serve the sponsoring organization and their own growth." This is a deficit model because the client is considered deficient in the skills or capabilities needed to meet company expectations. This perspective is mirrored in the primary importance of the objective organizational standards the client wants to attain. The Decisional coach may therefore be more tempted to act as an expert consultant advising the client what to do.

The balance of power (as represented on the side of the coach by expertise and organizational sponsorship) shifts when organizational coaching is engaged from an appreciative perspective. The power equity is important because the client can respond to his/her interests instead of the influence of the authority figure, the coach. Based on the needs of his client, the coach may instruct, model, pose questions, give feedback, and have an open ear. The client and coach metaphorically walk side by side. Appreciative coaching is based on a fulfillment mode. The coach's work is assisting the client to grow into the best professional person they can be. The contracting discussion with the sponsoring organization clarifies that the objective of the coaching is to help the leader "play at the top of her game." The organization then has the chance of deploying the evolved leader in the best possible way if/where the leader profile fits their needs. That is how enlightened organizations use coaching interventions, and why they strive to build coaching cultures: in order to maximize the collective potential of their most important assets.

Before turning to each of the three models of Decisional coaching (reflective, instrumented and observational) we identify a key principle that underlies all three of the Decisional coaching models and that, more generally, distinguishes an appreciative approach to organizational coaching from other approaches. This principle is called *first and second order learning and change*. We then turn to a key strategy that evolved from the principle of first and second order learning and change—the strategy called *reframing*.

First and Second Order Learning and Change

The concept of first and second order learning and change is central to the processes of Decisional coaching. We begin this discussion with a brief hypothetical conversation that illustrates the first and second order. This conversation takes place between a supervisor, Fred, and his subordinate, Alan:

> Fred: Why don't you just try harder?
>
> Alan: Would you get off my back! I'm already working as hard as I can! It just won't work.
>
> Fred: O.K., maybe we should add one or two more people to your crew.
>
> Alan: No! That would only make things worse. I would have to devote all of my time to training these new guys.
>
> Fred: Well, I give up. What do you think could be done?
>
> Alan: I don't know, but I'm feeling desperate—I guess like you must feel. Maybe we need to be a little less ambitious. Are we trying to do too much? Or maybe we've taken on the wrong assignment. Maybe our division is simply unable to meet this goal. Or maybe we've approached this problem in an entirely wrong way.

This discussion between Fred and Alan is typical of those that occur in many organizations from time to time. The issue they are addressing resists solution—in large part because it is a complex problem rather than being a one-dimensional puzzle. More (or less) of the same thing—*first order change*—is tried with no results. People try harder or they ease off a bit. No difference. More resources (money, people) are thrown in or pulled out of the project. There is still no appreciable effect.

Someone like Alan comes along to suggest the unthinkable. Maybe the problem statement itself should be reviewed and even redefined. Maybe a goal was set too high or too low, or a person or department is conceived as a barrier when actually a resource (or vice versa). This re-conceptualization of a problem requires a *second order change* instead of the first order change that is usually initiated when a problem is encountered. One of the primary roles of the Decisional coach is to encourage her client to think the unthinkable and to ponder alternative ways of conceptualizing a problem. Decisional coaching is also appreciative at a personal level: A coach encourages her colleague to re-conceptualize his own strengths and opportunities.

> The power equity is important because the client can respond to his/her interests instead of the influence of the authority figure, the coach.

The notion of first and second order change finds its origins in two unlikely fields of study: linguistics and experimental psychology. We will briefly detour to these two fields to better explain the nature and use of the powerful techniques associated with second-order change.

Meta-Language

One of the dilemmas faced in recent years by linguists and philosophers who study languages and their use is that one must use language in order to discuss language. In discussing the inability of most languages to describe ongoing, organic processes, one must make use of a specific language which is itself limited, static and unyielding. This paradoxical condition concerning the use of language to talk about language was addressed by the British philosopher Bertrand Russell. He observed that any system, words, or taxonomies that are being used to describe a particular collection of objects or experiences can't itself be a part of this collection. (Whitehead and Russell, 1910-1913) In other words, we must somehow move outside of a system when we are trying to describe it.

In a similar manner, Gregory Bateson (1972, p. 180) has reminded us that a map of a territory is not itself the territory. A map of Seattle, Washington, for instance, is not Seattle but only a map. Similarly, the word "cat" can't scratch you. The word "chair" is not actually a chair but only a representation of a type of furniture. These examples are obvious and even trivial. We often find ourselves, however, in the difficult and puzzling situation of not being sure whether we are addressing the real problem or only a representation of the problem.

We encounter people (often ourselves) who confuse the concept (for example, "super-ego") with the reality that this concept is supposed to represent. Thus, we search for the location of the superego in the cerebral cortex, rather than accepting the concept as a useful metaphor to describe a complex set of human activities and experiences. We must somehow be able to distinguish between the map and territory, between words and things, between first-order language that describes things and second order language that describes how we use language to think about things.

Learning How to Learn

Experimental psychology represents an entirely different field of study. Yet a similar problem was confronted in the 1940s and 1950s. Animals that were being run through a maze learned how to execute a particular maze more rapidly and with fewer errors over time. This is not big news. Behaviorists have known this for many years. However, there was something much more intriguing that occurred. The animals were able to run through a new maze more rapidly and with fewer errors than animals that had never been exposed to a maze. Apparently these animals learned not only how to run a specific maze but also how to run mazes in general. This same phenomenon has been observed in the learning of many other types of tasks and puzzles—as performed by human as well non-human subjects. This phenomenon has been labeled the establishment of a learning set or, more simply, *learning-how-to-learn*.

We not only learn how to do something (such as running through a corporate maze of contradictory policies and procedures and subtle norms and rituals) but also learn how to learn (i.e. interpret reality and adapt) even more rapidly and thoroughly in the future. We learn the corporate maze very slowly in our first job, usually through trial-and-error and with a fair amount of embarrassment. Later, in a second or third job, we learn how to run the corporate maze much more rapidly and with fewer mistakes or painful memories.

First and Second Order Change

In the case of both meta-language and learning how to learn, two levels of activity seem to be taking place simultaneously. On one level, people are using language and are learning how to perform certain tasks. On the second level, they are using language to talk about language and learning how they learn to perform certain tasks. Similarly, there are two levels at which change seems to be taking place.

At one level, change can be conceived as the acceleration (facilitation) of a desired transition or deceleration (blocking) of an undesirable transition. A first-order change effort, for example, might involve increasing the efficiency of an existing accounting system or extending the length of a training workshop. This type of change represents a transition in organizational structures, processes or attitudes. It requires only that a person or organization perform more or perform less of something than now is the case. Such a change can usually be measured in quantitative terms. It is rather easily observed and understood. It is usually associated with resolution of an organizational puzzle. First-order change occurs frequently in the lives of individuals and organizations; it is how most routine tasks are absolved. Often it is hardly even noticed if the quantity of change is minimal.

A second level of change occurs when there is a transformation in some structure, process or attitude in an individual, team or function. Organizational transformations involve qualitative shifts. Something is altered in form in such a way that the old ways of measuring it no longer hold. An organization, for instance, installs a new and radically different accounting system rather than seeking to improve the current system. Rather than being lengthened or shortened, a training program is abandoned in favor of some other kind of intervention.

Second-order change is always abrupt and noticeable and may often be confusing to those involved. It may occur dramatically and suddenly or it may arise from a series of smaller, first-order changes that eventually require a second-order change: the straw that broke the camel's back. To stay with the straw metaphor, one piece of straw on the ground becomes two pieces of straw when a second piece is set down beside it. At some point, when a certain number of pieces of straw are laid on top of one another, we no longer have separate pieces of straw but rather a haystack. The haystack is a single, coherent whole that can be identified by a single word. A qualitative, second-order change has taken place, based on several, incremental first-order changes. Similarly, a child at some point becomes an adult. A team of people becomes an organization. A set of minor irritations or unresolved organizational puzzles become a problem.

First-order change involves gradual evolutionary alteration in some system, whereas second-order change involves abrupt revolutionary alteration. The end of a first order change may represent a qualitative difference from the beginning. However, each change that is made will be minimal and may represent no qualitative difference from the immediately preceding change. The change can be considered transitional rather than transformational. It is usually defined as normal change.

We must somehow be able to distinguish between the map and territory, between words and things, between first-order language that describes things and second order language that describes how we use language to think about things.

This evolutionary strategy holds one major advantage. This type of change is likely to be more acceptable and less stressful for a greater number of people than would be the case if the change were large and abrupt. First order change is burdened, however, by one major disadvantage. In the slow, progressive movement toward some goal, the sense of direction and motivation to be found at the beginning of the change initiative may be lost. As a result, the change effort simply can fade away before the goal is attained, or the change effort becomes misguided and ends at a quite different point than first intended.

Second-order, revolutionary change represents a profound transformation in the person or institution. It represents a paradigm shift. (Kuhn 1962) Because the second order change appears abrupt, the motivation to begin and a sense of the direction in which to continue usually remain intact during the course of the change. Levels of stress and resistance to this transformational change, however, will be great. Typically, power (and sometimes even manipulation) is required to bring about this type of change.

Contemporary leaders often feel at a loss when faced with the choice between first and second order change. Neither option seems very attractive. Change is slow and ineffective or it is rapid, intense and potentially destructive. While a leader may be in a position to exert power to push for a change, such an approach often backfires or at least reduces the leader's credibility. A leader can also manipulate other people; most leaders have the interpersonal skills to be persuasive communicators and excellent salesmen and women. Leaders who are seen as hustlers, however, also lose credibility. Decisional coaching enables a leader to consider other approaches to change—particularly through use of a process called reframing.

Reframing

Reframing encourages a shift from first to second order conceptualizations of a problem, yielding valuable insights (second-order learning), creative solutions or even recognition that a problem does not in fact exist. A leader reframes an issue with the assistance of a Decisional coach by taking one of three approaches:

- Defining the goals associated with a specific problem in a new way.
- Describing the current context within which the problem exists in a new way.
- Identifying a new set of strategies for solving the problem.

The Reframing of Goals

In one magazine article, organizational coaching is described as a process that helps "managers, entrepreneurs and just plain folks . . . define and achieve their goals—career, personal or, most often, both." (Hamilton, 1996) While we would suggest that most coaches do much more than this, this statement does identify an important coaching model, namely reflection on and then planning for implementation of goals. In many instances, individuals and organizations tend to work hard to accomplish a specific, elusive goal (first order), rather than reconsidering whether or not this goal, in its present form, is actually important or worth-while. This is where reframing can add new perspectives. Problems inevitably involve a discrepancy between the current and desired states of a system. Many problems can be at least partially solved by reconsidering the importance, relevance or the very nature of the desired state.

We turn, by way of example, to a personnel problem facing Susan, manager in a medium-sized high tech firm. She is not satisfied with the work of her subordinate, Ralph. Susan firmly believes that Ralph needs to change his behavior, yet she also knows that she is sometimes perceived as a hard-driving manager who sets goals that are too high for her managers. Is she being accused of pushing too hard because she is a female? Perhaps her hard-driving reputation is nothing more than her commitment to the company. Or is she really setting goals too high? If she is being unrealistic in setting goals, then her problem with Ralph (and perhaps with other managers) might best be solved not by finding new ways of motivating her managers or by introducing new technologies (first-order change), but by helping her managers to re-examine their priorities and potentially re-adjust their production goals according to valid strategic imperatives (second-order change).

The conversation between Susan and her coach, Alicia, might go something like this:

> Susan: I can't seem to find an effective way of getting Ralph to meet the goals I have set for him. He keeps offering excuses rather than solutions and frequently pushes his problems up to me or down to his own subordinates. Yet I know Ralph is trying hard and that he has hired great people who work hard. He is particularly effective in motivating new employees. I wonder what I can do to make these goals a reality.
>
> Alicia: It sounds like you have tried several different strategies. [Susan had already identified three different approaches she has taken in working with Ralph,

ranging from incentive plans to suggesting a reorganization of his department.] Why is it important that you achieve these production goals?

Susan: Because we established these goals in our five-year plan for Ralph's department.

Alicia: Why is it important for you to accomplish the goals set in your five-year plan?

Susan: If I don't accomplish these goals, it will look bad for my division and—frankly—for me and my own future in this organization.

Alicia: How do you know that other people in this organization expect you and your division to meet these goals?

Susan: Well, the five-year plan says that we should . . . but actually I don't really know how important these goals are for our CEO or the other division directors. We rarely seem to talk about our five-year plan during our Executive Council meetings. It's often frustrating for me. I seem to be the only one who is interested in that crazy plan!

Alicia: So why are you so interested in that "crazy plan"?

Susan: You know, that's a good question. Sometimes I worry that I might be using the five-year plan as an excuse. Maybe I rely on these goals because I'm ambitious and look for any argument to get my managers motivated.

Alicia: So, you're a very ambitious person and this leads to increased productivity on the part of other members of your division—including Ralph. They want to help you achieve your ambitious goals. I wouldn't even be surprised to learn that they want to achieve these goals because of their loyalty to you, rather than because they are interested in the five-year plan. Is this possible?

Susan: Interesting. You know, I'm not sure.

Alicia: Maybe this is something you could find out.

Susan: Yeah. Let's talk a bit about how I could find this out.

Alicia: And you might also want to reflect on what your goals would really be if you didn't have to rely on the five-year plan. Or perhaps you might verify how relevant the 5-year plan really is to the CEO and the company's future. If it's critical, you might want to reflect on ways in which you could influence the other managers and your CEO to either take the five-year plan more seriously... or maybe replace or adjust it.

Susan: I would like to discuss this five-year plan issue at some time in the future. But right now . . . I would like to re-examine my own goals for this division in this new light and, in particular, the goals that have been identified for Ralph's department.

Susan and Alicia move on to explore other aspects of Susan's problem with Ralph. However, at this point Alicia has already been valuable to Susan in helping her reflect on one aspect of her problem with Ralph. Specifically, Alicia has helped Susan reframe a set of goals. What specifically are the approaches available to Alicia as a Decisional coach?

Goal Replacement. One goal can be replaced by a second goal that is more closely affiliated with an individual's or an organization's true interests. A coach like Alicia might ask her client questions like:

- What do you really want to see happen?
- What do you/your department really need?
- What is even more important than this goal?
- What would happen if you really took this goal seriously?
- What would you like the outcomes of this project to be?
- What would you like to celebrate three years from now if you were very successful in this unit of the organization?

When forced to clarify goals, a manager like Susan often can be more successful simply by directing her efforts more consistently toward the truly important goals of her division or organization. Other coaching strategies (particularly Aspirational coaching) that emphasize the clarification of one's purpose or broader goals also provide leaders with an opportunity to establish and monitor their goals; however, the Decisional coaching process additionally encourages leaders to reflect on her actions and question their choices from a higher level of awareness (second order change).

Espoused and Enacted Goals. A leader can also be encouraged by her coach to examine her current behavior and the behavior of other people in her department, division or organization against their respective goals. She engages in this Decisional process in order to consider whether or not the current, enacted behavior exemplifies the espoused goal or actually another, as yet unidentified, goal. A coach might ask his coaching colleague:

- If you are not moving very effectively toward your espoused goal then perhaps this is not truly the goal toward which you are working. What might this goal be?

- If you were someone from Mars who came to your unit and observed what is being done and what people are talking about, what would you assume to be the goals and purposes of this part of the organization?

- How do you think members of your unit benefit from the way(s) in which your unit now operates?

- What are some of the unspoken truths about this goal around here?

Seemingly irrational or counterproductive actions often yield *secondary gains* for an individual or organization. (Bandler and Grinder, 1979) A work team that never meets its production quota may be meeting its real goal: controlling the operations of the company. All of the other production units of the company must adjust their work schedule around this slower unit. Similarly, the director of a social service agency may actually want to retain control over all aspects of the agency's operations. He attempts to keep the organization in a state of crisis to justify his active involvement in all parts of the organization.

If a client can identify these secondary gains/benefits and the goals that lie behind these goals, then she can identify other behaviors that more successfully meet these goals or that meet these goals without hindering the work of other people in the organization. This is an appreciative approach to addressing a seemingly intractable process. One first appreciates the secondary gains—then looks to other strategies for achieving these gains. Given the work team's interest in influencing the overall operations of the company, for instance, one can set up new structures in the organization that enable workers to influence production decisions without having to resort to surreptitious production slowdowns. Similarly, the social service agency director can be encouraged to employ alternative methods of being involved in all aspects of agency operations without having to resort to crisis management.

We learn the corporate maze very slowly in our first job, usually through trial-and-error and with a fair amount of embarrassment.

Sequencing and Timing of Goals. Alicia can use a third Decisional approach to coaching. This approach involves the re-sequencing of existing goals: one goal no longer is considered to be in conflict with another but rather is conceived as enabling the other goal to be achieved. Two members of a management team, for instance, argue about whether the company should spend its money on a new marketing venture or on a major new research and development initiative. The argument is best reframed by asking whether or not the achievement of either of these goals is likely to increase or decrease the achievement of the other goal.

Rather than argue about the isolated importance of either of these goals, one can reflect on sequence and timing. A coach might ask:

- Would the new marketing venture, if successful, increase the probability that a research and development initiative will be mounted and funded?

- Would a successful R&D project enhance the prospects of a new marketing push?

By reframing a conflict in terms of synergistic sequence rather than isolated importance, one can break up many log-jams concerning program priorities.

Appealing to a Higher Level Goal. One can also re-conceptualize a coaching issue by appealing to a higher level goal. This can move an individual or organization from a first order to second order conceptualization of a coaching issue—in particular a problem or dilemma. A coach might ask:

- You have identified X as a goal, while Ralph has identified Y. In what ways are these goals compatible? Is there an overarching goal about which you can both agree?

- What goal(s) can all members of your executive team agree on?

A masterful Decisional coach can often assist her client by focusing on meta-level outcomes, so that the client can negotiate differences with other members of her organization at a point of common agreement and need. (Bandler and Grinder, 1979, pp. 160-162) Two production teams, for instance, might disagree about quality control. A Decisional coach can help one or both leaders of these teams reframe their argument by first seeing if they can agree on a definition of quality standards. Then, given that definition, they can design a series of pilot tests to assess the effectiveness of each quality control procedure.

Managers may also experience internal conflict regarding priorities. Perhaps part of Ralph's problem concerns the number and diversity of goals that have been assigned to his department. He is confronted with what we described earlier as a rugged landscape. There are many peaks rather than there being one dominant peak. At another level, we might wonder if part of the problem resides not in the landscape but rather in Ralph's predisposition to dreaming. Is Ralph a bit of a dreamer because he is trying to escape from a set of conflicting priorities? Are his dreams nothing more than a mirror of the disparate or mis-aligned goals that have been placed on his department by other dreamers in his organization? He might become more effective as a manager if he is given a clearer and more strategically congruous set of goals. At the very least, Ralph and the people who report to him will become more fully accountable for accomplishing departmental goals if these goals are thoughtful and explicitly aligned with one another.

The Reframing of Contexts

As in the case of goal reframing, there are several ways in which a masterful Decisional coach can help her client reframe the context within which he is operating. First, the Decisional coach can encourage her client to re-interpret the so-called facts associated with the context in a different way. Second, she can encourage her client to shift his attention from one aspect of the context to another. Third, a masterful coach can help her client re-punctuate the events that occur in a particular context, so that the cause and effects associated with each of these events are redefined. We will briefly describe each of these approaches.

Re-interpreting Facts. Any context can readily be interpreted and described in a variety of ways. A second order change in the prevalent interpretation may have a profound impact on an individual or organization. One can reframe an interpretation of a context by choosing to focus on the strengths and resources inherent in the situation rather than focusing on its weaknesses and deficits. This appreciative perspective can be very effectively employed as a means to effect change. As Watzlawick, Weakland and Fisch (1974) noted in their thoughtful analysis of the reframing process:

> To reframe . . . means to change the conceptual and/or emotional setting or viewpoint in relation to which a situation is experienced and to place it in another frame which fits the "facts" of the same concrete situation equally well or even better, and thereby changes its entire meaning . . . . What turns out to be changed as a result of reframing is the meaning attributed to the situation, and therefore its consequences, but not its concrete facts—or, as the philosopher Epictetus expressed it as early as the first century A. D.: "It

is not the things themselves which trouble us, but the opinions that we have about these things."

A quite poignant example of the reframing of facts and its potential power is found in a story about Anti-Semitism. The eighteenth century philosopher Moses Mendelssohn, who looked very "Jewish," was walking down a busy street in Berlin. He accidentally collided with a stout Prussian officer. "Swine!" bellows the officer. "Mendelssohn," replies the philosopher with a courteous bow. (Novak and Waldoks, 1981, p. 82) In this case, the potential recipient of an insult chose to reframe the context by first shifting the referent of the other person's insult back onto the person delivering the insult and then cushioning this shift with courtesy.

> If a client can identify these secondary gains/benefits and the goals that lie behind these goals, then she can identify other behaviors that more successfully meet these goals or that meet these goals without hindering the work of other people in the organization.

By reframing the context, Mendelssohn places the responsibility back on the insulter. The Prussian officer may choose to accept the reframe and consider the whole matter to be a misunderstanding that resulted in a sign of courtesy from the person being insulted (a variant on turning the other cheek). Alternatively, the Prussian officer can view the whole thing as a very unsuccessful attempt at delivering an insult that ended up with the other person winning the battle. The latter choice would probably be unacceptable to the proud Prussian, hence leaving him with no option other than the appreciative reframe. A remarkable interaction!

The self-fulfilling prophecy that Robert Rosenthal (1966) made famous (often called the "Pygmalion effect") further exemplifies this model. If one person judges another person as stupid or unmotivated, and interacts with them from that attitude (e.g. talks down at them, withholds information and encouragement) then the labeled person is likely to end up acting unmotivated and less competent, whether or not he initially was so inclined. People inadvertently comply with our expectations of them, because we treat them differently, depending on how we view them. Thus, if we choose to enter into an interpersonal relationship with a positive mind-set, we will interact with the other from an appreciative perspective, and then this person is likely to relate in a positive manner toward us and be as productive as they can – thus having the greatest chance of fulfilling our positive expectations, and validating our original frame of mind.

In order to help a manager notice what expectations he might hold (and no doubt act out) towards a colleague he perceives as under-performing, a Decisional coach might ask her client:

- Be honest with yourself: are you sharing information generously with this person, or sometimes withholding it?

- Are you available or unavailable to this colleague when they need your guidance?

- Do you appreciate their work product and encourage their good accomplishments, or are you primed to look for errors and disappointments?

- Do you give them feedback and coaching, or are you withholding your input, leaving them in the dark?

- Is your body language and tone of voice with them open and receptive, or curt, impatient or even punitive?

The work of Erich Fromm (1947) and Elias Porter (Porter, 1976: Phillips, 1991) uses a similar kind of reframing in defining a person's interpersonal weaknesses as his strengths used inappropriately or in excess. One must first acknowledge that a weakness is also a strength that, under most conditions, produces positive results for us. One must also acknowledge the secondary gains obtained from existing behavior patterns—much as in the case of reframing goals. Thus, *rather than attempting to "eliminate a weakness," we need only modify the extent to which it is being used or the setting in which it is being used.* This is a central feature in masterful coaching: focusing on a client's abilities and helping a client recognize and perhaps create the settings in which these strengths are fully and appropriately deployed.

The CEO of a non-profit, for instance, who is an excellent speaker and socializer, is ineffective in working with troubled members of her local community on a one-on-one basis. Her verbal skills help her in the first situation but not in the second. She is rewarded for being verbally active when working with many people, but not when she is expected to be a quiet and sympathetic listener in attending to complaints of members of her community. She could try to improve her ability to work one-on-one. This would be a first-order change. A second-order reframing by this administrator could involve a shift in her job assignment. She could assign the responsibility for meeting with individual members of her community to other members of her staff, reserving more of her work with these constituencies to large team gatherings. Rather than focusing on her weaknesses, this administrator is encouraged by her Decisional coach to focus on her considerable skills in working with large teams and groups. In recognizing that these skills are distinctive and appropriate in most settings, she may become less nervous about being quiet enough in the one-on-one setting, and with the reduction in anxiety and in the frequency with which she works with other people she might eventually feel less need to be highly verbal. It is at the moment when a person does not have to feel threatened that she is most inclined to open up to alternative behaviors.

People inadvertently comply with our expectations of them, because we treat them differently, depending on how we view them.

Alicia takes a similar approach in working with Susan. Susan can be encouraged to reframe the problem she is experiencing with her direct report, Ralph. Susan can be encouraged to focus on Ralph's strengths and on ways in which Ralph can more frequently be placed in settings where these strengths are effectively employed. Perhaps, he could be more actively involved in strategic planning, so that his tendency to dream becomes appropriate and helpful to the organization. Ralph might also be asked to assist with new employee orientation in the company, making use of his capacity to inspire and motivate. He might be assigned to more start-up operations or given the opportunity to work autonomously on more projects. In order for any of these options to be explored, Susan must first be willing to reframe her perceptions of Ralph, focusing on his strengths, achievements and potential, rather than his weaknesses or failures. This is the essence of an appreciative approach to Decisional coaching.

Shifting Attention. This second way in which to reframe context requires a shift in attention—to another aspect of the context. Often attention is shifted to an area that has been denied, ignored or forgotten. (Bandler and Grinder, 1982, p. 166) A seemingly naive outsider asks: why isn't George at the meeting at 7:00 a.m.? Everyone knows that George has a drinking problem. The outsider brings up this issue. A Decisional coach often serves this same role. She asks the un-askable question about the forbidden topic. In this case, the un-askable question is: why isn't George at the meeting and what is this organization going to do about his chronically unreliable scheduling? The Decisional coach couples the challenge of this difficult question with a supportive attitude. Her coaching client soon realizes that he can discuss this issue in a reasonable manner, while keeping George's welfare in mind. He begins to address the problem of George's alcoholism, as well as attendant problems, for the first time.

At other times, a topic is broached by a Decisional coach that previously was simply ignored or not recognized as distinctive and influential in the life of a person or organization. The culture of an organization, for instance, strongly influences the behavior of employees, yet is rarely given much direct attention. Dress codes reinforce status differences. The jargon used by various units in the organization not only defines status differences but also sensitive boundaries and barriers between certain teams. Attention to the dress and language of an individual or organizational unit, and open discussion about the impact of this dress or language, often leads to new cultural insights and changed behavior patterns. In the case of Ralph's performance as a manager, perhaps the culture of his department (or of the entire organization) encourages a split between the real and the espoused, and places people in conflicted roles with regard to living with short-term pressures without long-term clarity of purpose..

Re-punctuating Events. By shifting time perspectives and definitions of beginnings and endings, we can often gain a new perspective and a new set of solutions to complex, ongoing problems. This third approach to contextual reframing concerns the "punctuation" of specific events that occur within a specific context (Watzlawick, Weakland and Fisch (1974, pp. 54ff). We already introduced this concept in our chapter on Behavioral coaching when describing how coaching can be used to address interpersonal issues (*engagement coaching*). Any series of interactions between two people, two units in an organization or two organizations can be punctuated in a variety of ways, depending on the perspective of the person or persons doing the punctuating. One party to a conflict, for instance, might identify the absence of the other party at a critical meeting as the point when the conflict started (hence the responsibility of the other party). The second party might punctuate this same series of events quite differently: He did not attend the meeting because of the first party's abusive behavior at a previous meeting. When did the conflict begin? Who is responsible? This all depends on how the continuous, interrelated stream of events is interpreted. Is Ralph a dreamer because other members of his department can't get off the ground and refuse to identify ambitious goals? Or are other members of his department highly realistic because Ralph is always out there dreaming of some unattainable goal? Both are probably the case. It all depends on how the sequence of events is punctuated.

Any problem or conflict can be reframed by asking a client to consider alternative punctuation. As a Decisional coach, Alicia might ask Susan:

- What if you were to consider point B rather than point A to be the time when Ralph's performance difficulties began? Would the problem look any different from this vantage point?

- What if we were to go back two months and look at some of the earlier events that might have influenced your perceptions of Ralph's working relationships and managerial style? What might Ralph's problem look like if we were to focus just on the events of this past week?

- What would be Ralph's interpretation of the causes for the problems being experienced in his department right now?

A significant perceptual change can often occur through reframing long before overt change in behavior becomes readily apparent. In many instances, individuals and organizations move through periods of apparent stagnation or dormancy. They may actually be gradually re-examining and reframing their perceptions of the context within which they live and work. A major developmental spurt may follow this period of conceptual reorganization, leading an outsider to conclude that there are sequential stages of stabilization and change.

The Reframing of Solutions

The field of creative problem-solving is filled with examples of reframed solutions. People generate new and quite different solutions to complex problems through the use of such longstanding think tank techniques as *brainstorming,* (Clark, 1958) *synectics* (Prince, 1970) and *conceptual block-busting.* (Adams, 1974) With regard to ways in which to change human behavior or organizational life, two stand out as being particularly effective.

One of these is paradoxical in nature and is usually labeled '*prescribing the symptoms.*' (Watzlawick, Beavin and Jackson, 1967) The other is in many ways equally paradoxical, for it concerns the use of existing features of the system to create a new system. Both of these approaches begin, as do goal and contextual reframing, by acknowledging the power of existing conditions and the need to work in an appreciative manner with and through these conditions rather than fighting against them.

Any series of interactions between two people, two units in an organization or two organizations can be punctuated in a variety of ways, depending on the perspective of the person or persons doing the punctuating.

It should also be noted that both of these approaches are controversial, for they often seem to require that a trick be played on the person or organization that is being changed. While goals and contexts are usually reframed with the full awareness of all participants, solution reframing often seems to take place without that awareness. On the other hand, solution reframing is particularly effective in helping people and organizations move out of situations in which they are "stuck"—for which there appears to be no adequate first-order solutions.

Prescribing the Symptom. We offer a classic example of this approach. It concerns a restless child who is unable to fall asleep. The more the child is encouraged to fall asleep, the harder she will try to relax. Paradoxically, she is less likely to relax given her concerted effort to fall asleep. Instead of encouraging the child to relax and fall asleep, an astute parent might instead encourage the child to stay awake: "See if you can stay awake for fifteen minutes!" When the child tries to stay awake and attempts to keep her eyes open, then she is likely to fall asleep. As adults we often follow the same path. We tend to fall asleep in front of the television or at the theater. Later, we lie wide-awake in bed.

In an organizational setting, the always-late manager chooses to employ this same paradoxical model with the encouragement of his coach. Rather than showing up at a meeting fifteen minutes late (his usual practice), the manager is asked to work on showing up twenty minutes late. He has to wait five minutes before walking into the meeting and in doing so realizes that he controls his own time. Next week he shows up ten minutes late, then fifteen minutes late, then five minutes late, then ten minutes and then five minutes early. Finally, he shows up on time. He discovers that he can, in fact, arrive on time.

Masterful Decisional coaches often help their clients with these types of difficult situations. Clients who hold negative (and potentially distorted) images of other individuals or units of the organization are encouraged by their coach to actually distort their images of the other person or unit even more. Their coach might also ask their colleague to distort their perceptions of the image that they think the other person or unit has of them. The client then reflects on the secondary gains he receives from these distorted images, as well as the evidence he holds regarding the validity of these images. Organizational issues often only become clear when considered in their extreme form. With the support of his coach, a harried manager can often confront embarrassing distortions with a sense of humor and greater appreciation for the power of stereotypes and untested assumptions. Alicia might suggest this approach when coaching Susan regarding Ralph's tendency to dream while his department is confronted with serious problems. Rather than trying to get Ralph to become more realistic, Susan might actually ask Ralph to become even more visionary and might place him in roles that are highly visionary (such as chairing a task force on new ideas for the organization).

Susan (and Ralph) may discover that he soon grows weary of this one-dimensional role. After all, he does like to be realistic on occasion, particularly when completing a specific project about which he cares. Some people thrive under conditions of opposition and lose all motivation when they get exactly what they want. Alternatively, Alicia could suggest that Susan herself become more of a dreamer and less of a realist when working with Ralph. A colleague reports that she often copes with her visionary boss by out-dreaming him. When she becomes a dreamer, then her boss suddenly becomes realistic, asking "do we have the money to complete this?" or "are you sure this will work?" Susan might similarly out-dream Ralph and thereby (paradoxically) move him into a more realistic role. Other members of Ralph's staff could use Susan as a role model and similarly take on more of a visionary role in their relationships with Ralph.

Using the Existing System. This second solutions-reframing approach is actually a hybrid of the other forms of reframing. (Bandler and Grinder, 1982, p. 171) The existing resources and dynamics of the system (individual or organization) that is being changed are framed in positive terms. Forces that are resistant to change, for instance, come to be seen as the bases for stability in the newly changed system. Many years ago, Seymour Sarason (1973) observed that revolutionary leaders must bring in managers from the old regime to help bring stability to the new government. His observation seems to still hold true. Kurt Lewin and his colleagues similarly noted that any planned change effort must be followed by *refreezing*—a process that brings stability back to the system. (Lippit, Watson and Westley, 1958)

People who resist a change can themselves become invaluable resources in promoting and planning for the change. Many resistors, for example, point to past history when declaring that a planned change will never be successful: "We tried that ten years ago and it didn't work." Rather than arguing with or ignoring this person, one asks him to help plan for the new change effort so that some of the mistakes that occurred ten years ago can be avoided. The skeptic can also be made the historian of the new project or can assist in the design of its evaluation. Alternatively, those who are usually the innovators and proponents of new ideas—men and women like Ralph—can be placed in the role of program auditor or member of a panel that reviews new program proposals. This helps to shake up old roles and provides everyone with new perspectives on one another and the organization.

coachbook *A Guide to Organizational Coaching Strategies and Practices*

...isional coaches can help their clients reframe sources of resistance as assets in yet another way. Typically, policies and procedures are set up to thwart new enterprises. Yet these same policies and procedures that often make it difficult to start something new also make it difficult for anyone to stop the new venture once started. A large organization is often the perfect place to try a new idea. After all, it takes one to two months to find out that something new is being tried. It then takes another month or two to gain the attention of those in the bureaucracy who have the authority to do anything about this new venture—and another two to three months to work through the channels to block it. By this time, the new venture may have proven its worth and can make it on its own. As the popular adage from the 1960s goes: "it is easier to beg for *forgiveness* [after an action step has been taken] than to ask for *permission* [before the action step is taken]."

Reframing: Potent and Problematic

These various reframing tools are not without their own problems and certainly should be used by Decisional coaches and their clients with discretion and ethical awareness. They significantly expand the repertoire of a Decisional coach and make significant change possible in difficult and resistant circumstances. The very forces that bind people and organizations to one way of doing things can be used as levers for change. With such powerful tools we must be certain that these individuals and organizations actually desire the proposed change and trust the intentions and competencies of those aiding in the reframing process.

One coaching client will find a solutions-oriented reframing most helpful, while another may find it more beneficial to focus on the framing of a current or desired state. In working with Susan, for instance, Alicia may think that the most important role she can play is to be reflective with Susan about her relationship with Ralph. Susan might decide that they should focus on Ralph's problem. They might both decide instead (with Ralph's concurrence) that Alicia should coach both Susan and Ralph—focusing on the relationship between them rather than on either Susan's perceptions of Ralph's problem or the solutions Susan will initiate to solve Ralph's problem.

In many cases, reframing is most beneficial when directed toward a client's blind spot—the spot where this leader is absolutely certain there is no room for change in perspective. The purpose of Decisional coaching is not to show anyone "the right way" in which to relate to one another, solve problems or make decisions. It is rather to provide both challenge and support and to help a client reflect on her own thought processes, identify her own distinctive strengths and competencies, and take actions that are appropriate to her own value system and aspirations.

Keeping this powerful reframing strategy in mind, we will now turn to a description of three Decisional coaching models (reflective, instrumented and observational) and begin with reflective coaching.

Reflective Coaching

Whether or not one makes use of either *instrumented* or *observational* coaching methods when engaged in Decisional coaching, one will inevitably spend some time as an organizational coach using the methods of *reflective* coaching. Typically, reflective coaching is most intensely engaged when starting work with a Decisional coaching client and when bringing this work to a close. As the reflective coaching process meanders, new directions emerge on the path.

A masterful reflective coach needs to keep and maintain the integrity of the coach's role. When the energy of conversation shifts, the coach needs to clarify the shift. The shift may move from Behavioral coaching to reflective coaching. For example, "You seem to be talking more about your reasons for confronting Harold. Our agreement was to focus on how best to confront Harold's resistance to the issues around employee relations. Do we want to re-negotiate our goal agreement?" Similarly, after reviewing an instrument, it's a natural flow from instrumented coaching, in which results from an assessment instrument are reviewed by the coach and client, to reflective coaching when results from this assessment instrument suggest a change in one's functioning as leader of a specific department.

> A colleague reports that she often copes with her visionary boss by out-dreaming him. When she becomes a dreamer, then her boss suddenly becomes realistic, asking "do we have the money to complete this?" or "are you sure this will work?"

Reflective coaching involves a process of "walking with" one's colleague through complex problems related directly to their job and indirectly to their entire life. Reflective coaches challenge their clients' basic frames of reference and assumptions, while simultaneously supporting them in facing their demanding roles as leaders. An appreciative perspective supports reflective coaching. In taking an appreciative perspective, a coach deeply values his client by willingly engaging in a dialogue from an assumption of mutual respect and a search for discovery of distinctive competencies and strengths. Cooperation is recognized as a value. Within this context, the client feels safe to explore capacities and issues to develop and unfold her deeper self.

Reflective coaching also begins and ends with the inherent assumption that the ultimate insight about a client resides within him rather than in other people. Initially, this would seem to be a rather solipsistic and isolating assumption—and it certainly can lead to isolation if a client chooses to rely exclusively on his own perceptions and resources in making a decision or acting upon this decision. The primary purpose of reflective coaching is precisely to ensure a break out of this isolation. The reflective coach serves first as a *witness* to the reflections of his client and serves second as a *sounding board* (or perhaps more accurately a *mirror*) that enables his client to observe from a point of detachment his own internal processes.

The Process of Reflective Coaching

Specifically, the reflective coach provides witness and support in three related domains. The reflective coach helps her client:

- Identify and clarify central *intentions* in his life, role and organization.

- Collect and analyze valid and useful *information* regarding his life, role and organization, especially as related to central intentions.

- Generate and test out a maximum number of viable alternative *ideas* with regard to central intentions and taking into account relevant information.

Having dwelled in each of these three domains, the reflective coach engages her client in a process of reflection that creates client ownership for the intentions, information and ideas that have been articulated through this reflective process.

The reflective coach who operates from an appreciative perspective does not criticize or even extensively comment on the deliberations of the person she is coaching. This is unnecessary, for the most powerful tool for change and correction is always one's own self-awareness and recognition of one's own internal (in-)consistencies. Over the past twenty years, social scientists have learned that this is the case even when one is considering changes in the political and racial attitudes of those who were carefully taught to be afraid of those who are different from themselves. People must come to their own personal (and very private) realization that their biases cause a mismatch between their own espoused values and the actions they take in the world. People who make decisions in organizations must similarly find a way to confront their own "gremlins" and their own inconsistencies. That is the only way in which genuine and enduring change takes place.

During the reflective coaching process, a client relies primarily on information derived from his own internal ruminations. For this internal process of critical reflection to be successful, the coach must not only provide a complementary amount of interpersonal support, she must also provide the type of questions that yield new perspectives and insights—the second-order process we described above (also known as "transformative" learning). (Mezirow and Associates, 2000)

The Role of the Reflective Coach

The reflective coach must always be flexible and responsive to the unique style(s) and needs of the person she is coaching. Thus, there are no "hard and fast" rules for the reflective coach. Nevertheless, there are certain roles that a reflective coach is likely to assume when working with a client. Furthermore, there are certain levels that are likely to be reached at various points during the coaching session, as the reflective coach and her client reflect critically on the client's own decision-making (internal decisional) processes.

The reflective coach will inevitably assume two roles: as questioner and as witness. As a person who *asks "good" questions,* the coach should seek to accomplish the following:

- Provoke dialogue between the client and coach (usually by both establishing trust and posing "difficult" questions).

- Encourage a shifting (even if only temporary) of perspective on the part of the client (reframing of existing perspectives or exploration of new perspectives).

- Encourage exploration of thethree coaching domains of information, intentions, and ideas.

As a *witness* to the client's reflection, the coach provides three invaluable services that are often not explicitly acknowledged by either the client or coach:

- Space for a public verbalization by client: the client "hears herself think."

- Empathetic and appreciative listening by coach: the client learns that what she has said is neither   "off the wall" nor "totally unique" – yet what she has said is also appreciated by the coach as part of the client's own unique life journey and narrative.

- Accountability on the part of the client to the coach: the client knows that "someone who cares about my success has heard what I said and what I committed to doing."

The Levels of Reflective Inquiry

While reflective coaching is often an unpredictable process—similar to improvisational jazz and theater in many respects—there are, still, a few reflective coaching moves that have been found to be particularly effective when engaged in a Decisional coaching process. Specially, we propose that an effective reflective coaching process often involves moving back and forth through seven specific levels of analysis. Each level offers a different perspective and a different reflective lens.

1. The reflective coaching process often begins at Level One with the client reporting on their *Observation* of a specific event. The reflective coach will begin with a request: "Tell me what happened." or "Tell me what you are seeing in this email."

2. Given this initial observation (and the narrative or brief story accompanying this observation), a coach and client can begin moving toward Level Two: an examination of the *Data* that has been obtained. The coach asks: "What did you see that is relevant to your immediate concerns and interests?"

3. From here a coach and client can move to a Third Level, which is concerned with the *Meanings* that a client assigns to the Data that has been gathered. A relevant question is: "What does this mean for you?" or "How does this data relate to an important issue in your (work) life?"

4. Level Four involves the identification of and analysis of *Assumptions* that underlie the Meaning the person has assigned to the Data. The coach asks: "How do you know that your observation is accurate?""How do you know that the meaning you assigned to this data is appropriate?" This will either help validate the assumptions the client made, or clarify any misperceptions he had formed or even lead to a total shift in perspective, if needed,

5. At Level Five, the coach is helping her client access some *Conclusions*. Several questions are often asked at this level: "What do you want to do about this situation?" "What can be done to address your concerns about what you have observed?"

6. These questions inevitably move the client and coach to Level Six, which is concerned with *Beliefs*. The coach asks: "Why do you think this decision is appropriate?" "What

makes you think that taking this action in this situation will lead to success?" "How confident are you that this will be effective?"

7. Finally, at Level Seven, *Action* takes place, based on the Conclusions reached and the Beliefs that support these conclusions. In post-Actions reviews, the coach will be encouraging her client to reflect on the actions taken, by asking: "What did you actually do?" "What occurred when you took this action?"

In subsequent sessions of reflective coaching, a coach and client can now *reverse* the levels of analysis. As reflective coaches we begin with Level Seven and the post-*action* review questions already associated with this level: "What did you do?" and "What occurred when you took this action [what were the consequences]?" "What worked, what didn't work, in your view?" We then return to Level Six and a focus on *Beliefs*. In encouraging our client to reflect at this level we now ask: "What does the way in which this action went (more or less well) tell you about the world and about you in this world?" The Fifth Level is now concerned with how our client reached *Conclusions* with regard to the world they engage. A coach accesses this level when asking: "What have you learned from this action?"

The reflective coach serves first as a *witness* to the reflections of his client and serves second as a *sounding board* (or perhaps more accurately a mirror) that enables his client to observe from a point of detachment his own internal processes.

At the Fourth Level, a coach now encourages her client to reexamine the *Assumptions* being made (based on the Conclusions reached). One of the questions that might be asked by the coach encourages a client to enter again the Domain of Information: "How do you know you are accurate in your assessment of this action and its actual or potential impact?" Another question encourages the client to move into the Domain of Intentions: "What was this action intended to accomplish?" Yet another question encourages movement into the Domain of Ideas: "Why do you think this was the appropriate action to take?" From here a coach and client can move back to the Third Level, which is concerned with the *Meanings* that a client assigns to the specific Assumption or set of Assumptions he has made that led ultimately to his Beliefs regarding outcomes and the Actions taken (and more immediately to the Conclusions reached). Relevant questions include: "How does an important issue in your life relate to the action you took?" and "What are you discovering/learning about the resolution of this important issue by virtue of the specific action path you took?"

The coach is now ready to assist her client in moving back to the first two levels. At Level Two, the client revisits the *Data* that has been collected—now with greater clarity regarding the lens through which he is gathering (and interpreting) this data. The coach will ask such questions as: "What do you now think are the most important facts to know about the situation you confronted?" "About what facts are you most confident and about what are you now less certain?" The reflective coach is not so much challenging the validity of her client's data as encouraging her client to revisit his data analysis—and realize that there are other interpretations that might be entertained and other perspectives that might be taken when viewing the current situation. These alternative interpretations and perspective may, in turn, have led, eventually, to different decisions and a different course of action.

Finally, at Level One, the coach encourages her client to reconsider the *Observation* he initially made. The coach now asks: "Tell me what you now think happened?" The reflective coach encourages her client to construct a new narrative, based on his journey up and down the levels of analysis. The labels for each level and the key question(s) to be asked at each level can serve as a format for documenting the levels of reflection that are being engaged. The coach and client may either move from Level One to Level Seven, or from Level Seven to Level One—or (as we have proposed) from One to Seven and back again to One. The word "level" in no way is intended to imply that one form of inquiry is more "important" or more "advanced" that another form. It is the process of moving up and down the levels that is critical to the reflective coaching process.

We offer additional recommendations regarding reflective coaching in the Resource section of this book. Several coaching processes are recommended that build on provocative questioning strategies. Each of these processes promotes and enhances reflective inquiry.

Instrumented Coaching

Kurt Lewin wrote many years ago about the three stages of planned change that change (and learning) occurs only after an "unfreezing" process. For many people who are facing leadership challenges, the processes of self-reflection or of being observed by another person are simply too threatening: They do not "unfreeze" through these processes, but rather tend to become even more "frozen" in their current images of self and their behavior patterns. Many of these reticent clients will find instrumented coaching to be effective, as will those leaders who are thirsting for more "information" about themselves and about their impact on those around them. They will find a certain amount of detachment in the review and analysis of personality classifications, competency ratings - or in the numerical information or verbatim quotes presented, for example, in a multi-rater feedback report. In the latter case, they will appreciate not only the privacy afforded them in their own initial review of this information but also the confidentiality afforded those who complete the feedback edition of the survey and/or the organizational culture survey. Everyone is afforded a certain amount of protection and distance, which sets the stage for a preliminary and often quite tentative exploration of one's own personal perspectives and values (reflective coaching).

> People must come to their own personal (and very private) realization that their biases cause a mismatch between their own espoused values and the actions they take in the world.

Multi-rater instrumented coaching even tends to arouse curiosity about the bases upon which other people arrive at their perceptions of the client's attitudes and behaviors: "Is it something I do or is it what other people do when they are around me or is it something about the organizational culture in which we work and relate that leads to these perceptions and assumptions about my behavior?" This in turn may lead to a growing interest on the part of reticent or inquisitive clients in a fuller and deeper understanding of their own personality as well as the culture in which they are operating. Based on this new understanding and appreciation of their own personality as it interplays with the culture of their organization, these coaching clients might even wish to receive feedback from an *observational* coach regarding their real-time performance in a variety of roles.

The Purposes of Instrumented Coaching

Instrumented coaching enables clients to learn about their *personality preferences* but also to receive feedback from other people about how their behavior is perceived. The client and her coach can then use this information to reflect on the extent to which the client's behavior patterns do seem to be dependent on the *work environment*. When an appreciative approach is taken, the client will gain valuable insights regarding the nature and scope of her strengths, as well as discover the settings and roles in which other people perceive these strengths as valuable or not, and the intentions other people may assign to the client's (over-)use of these strengths.

Instrumented coaching that measures *organizational cultures* also offers clients the opportunity to assess the environment in which they work so that they might better understand the interplay between the setting and their behavior. This information and subsequent reflection yield rich insights regarding the roots of a client's behavior.

- To what extent is the coaching client operating in accord with her environment and to what extent is she swimming upstream, behaving in ways that seem to be incompatible with the dominant culture of her work environment?

- To what extent is her natural style compatible with the natural culture of her organization?

- How much does she have to tolerate or give up?

- How much does she have to change or act in a manner that seems foreign to her?

- What is the likelihood that she will adjust to her environment?

- What is the value (for both her and her stakeholders) of her adjustment to the environment?

- On the other hand, what is the potential impact or influence she can have on her environment? At what cost?

When information about the work setting is coupled with feedback from other people with whom the client interacts, the coach and client can move into an analysis of the client's behavior and identify ways in which the client can make fuller and more consistent use of her strengths. The client may choose to:

- Move more often into settings that encourage and enhance her strengths.

- Become more patient with herself when working in a setting that is incompatible with her strengths, and apply self-care when making such efforts.

- Discover ways in which to ensure that other people see her strengths and better understand the reasons why she behaves as she does.

- Discover ways in which to more regularly receive clear and accurate feedback from other people with whom she works regarding her behavior and how it is interpreted.

- Explore how she wants to grow by expanding her behavioral and leadership repertoire, and the benefits this would provide, personally and professionally

Distinctive Features of Masterful Instrumented Coaching

Instrumented coaching can involve as little as a simple discussion by a coach and her client about the results of a specific inventory that the client has completed. Masterful coaching, however, involves the careful and focused selection of specific instruments for specific coaching *areas of focus*. To assist coaches in selecting an appropriate instrument, we have included an extensive list of appropriate and easily accessible instruments in the Resource section of this book. What makes instrumented coaching most effective and distinctive, furthermore, is the use of *three levels or tiers of assessment* and attention to *critical incidents* in the life of the client with linkages to the present. Finally, we find that masterful instrumented coaching often involves focusing on a specific and more recent *critical incident* that exemplifies the issues being addressed by the client during her instrumented coaching sessions.

1. Contracted Area of Focus

The first distinctive feature of the masterful instrumented coaching process concerns the identification of that aspect of her work life on which the client initially wishes to focus attention. We turn back to the case we presented previously of Susan and her Decisional coach, Alicia, to illustrate this first feature. Recall that Susan was having problems with one of her managers, Ralph, who was always being a visionary when he should have been more realistic and was rarely able to give straight feedback to his subordinates regarding their performance or problems.

> Multi-rater instrumented coaching tends to arouse curiosity about the bases upon which other people arrive at their perceptions of the client's attitudes and behaviors.

Because of this dissatisfaction with Ralph, Susan indicated to Alicia that she was initially drawn to the assessment of her own interpersonal style. She wondered if she simply was unable to work with Ralph because of differing ways in which they operate with one another and with other employees in the organization. Given the problem Ralph was having with other managers and given Susan's own difficulties in working with some of her other managers, Susan was also interested in the broader issue of organizational culture—particularly with regard to communication styles and how the culture of her organization fits with her own preferred interpersonal style.

II. Three-Tiered Assessment: Self-assessment, Multi-rater and Cultural

Alicia's work exemplified a second distinctive feature of the masterful instrumented coaching process. After she involved Susan in the selection of an assessment questionnaire that was related to the aspects on which Susan wished to focus, Alicia went a step further. She introduced three different kinds of questionnaires. One elicits Susan's own *self-perceptions* (in this case regarding her interpersonal style). A second elicits *responses from other people* with whom Susan works regarding Susan's interpersonal style. A third questionnaire asks a random sample of employees to indicate the dominant styles and *norms of their organization* with regard to interpersonal styles. This three-tiered approach of the instrumented coaching process provides Susan and Alicia with a much broader foundation for their work together.

By making use of three different kinds of questionnaires, instrumented coaching directly addresses several of the most telling criticisms directed at self-assessment questionnaires alone – that they provide too narrow a perspective. The three-tiered instrumented coaching process solicits feedback not just from the client but also from other people who work with the coaching client. In this way, a second level of analysis is engaged: Susan learns not only about her preferred interpersonal style and dominant attitudes and values regarding interpersonal relationships, but also about how other people see her and the extent to which there are discrepancies between her own self-perceptions and the perceptions of others.

Frequently, self-assessment questionnaires are administered to leaders in a workshop setting followed by a brief theory session. They are then provided with an interpretation of the results, sometimes based on normative data from a broad sample of previous respondents. The typical assessment process usually concludes at this point. Even when a multi-rater assessment is included, the manager rarely has an opportunity to compare his data to what his cultural environment or his own job actually require, let alone build on the information through reflection with a coach.

III. Critical Incident Analysis

There is yet another distinctive method used in the instrumented coaching process. This process engages the client and coach in the examination of specific, critical incidents in the recent life of the client. These incidents reflect and are, in turn, illuminated by the insights already gained by the client from the instrumented coaching process. Furthermore, specific critical incidents are selected precisely because they directly relate to the perceptions of self and others and to the characteristics of the work environment with regard to personal styles, attitudes and values.

Alicia, for instance, may have directed Susan's attention to a specific (and important) interaction she has had recently with Ralph that exemplifies some of the issues she has identified through the instrumented coaching sessions in which she has already engaged with Alicia. By focusing on this critical incident, Susan not only may learn something about how to relate to Ralph when addressing this important issue (or a similar issue) in the future, but will have been able to test her own personal insights against the reality of a challenging situation. The critical instance analysis becomes the anvil on which a coaching client can forge a revised sense of self and a revised repertoire of behaviors that are aligned with the distinctive environment in which these behaviors will take place. More guidance about the utility of the critical incident analysis appears in the Resource section of this book.

Descriptive vs. Normative Assessments

In addition to the three distinctive characteristics just mentioned, a masterful coach will keep in mind the critical differences that exist between instruments that are *descriptive* in nature and those that are *normative*. What exactly are the differences between these two types of instruments and why are these differences so important? First, we will turn to the nature of the differences. A descriptive instrument is one which has no right or wrong answers; no one rating is better than any other rating. For instance, a question on a Descriptive instrument might be about whether a person prefers to be highly analytic when attempting to solve a problem or prefers to be more intuitive. Neither an analytic nor an intuitive approach to problem-solving is necessarily better or worse (other than in the minds of people with a strong preference for analysis or intuition). In most instances, a Descriptive instrument concerns the styles, preferences or perspectives embraced (consciously or unconsciously) by the person being assessed. The Myers-Briggs Type Indicator (MBTI) is a classic example of a Descriptive instrument. It is not better or worse to be Extraverted or Introverted, Sensing or Intuitive, Thinking or Feeling, Perceiving or Judging.

By contrast, a *normative* instrument is one in which there are evaluative differences between the ratings at one end of a scale and those at the other end. For example, a Normative instrument might include an item that asked the rater to determine the extent to which the person being rated (himself or some other person) is an effective communicator. This is not about style. No one we know prefers to be a poor communicator. These instruments are called normative because there are implicit (or explicit) norms built into the instrument. Effective communication is good and ineffective communication is bad. Effective supervision and delegation is good and ineffective supervision and delegation is bad. This is not a matter of style or preferences or perspectives, it is a matter of competence.

> There is a tendency for each of us to hold two different theories about human behavior. One of these theories concerns our own personal behavior. The second theory concerns the behavior of everyone else.

This distinction between Descriptive and Normative instruments is not just academic. It is not just a point of discussion among psychometricians (the men and women who build these instruments). It is a critical distinction for organizational coaches to draw when they are deciding with their client about what type of instrument to use. Descriptive instruments are less likely to generate resistance than a normative instrument. Most clients can hear that they have certain preferences or a certain style. It is much harder for them to hear (or read) that they are not very competent in certain areas. Not only are they likely to be threatened but also often surprised by the challenge to their competency, especially if their Normative ratings are low in several areas. Substantial research supports the conclusion that managers (and other employees) who score low on Normative instruments also tend to overestimate how other people view their performance. They might be ineffective in their work in part because they don't realize that other people view their work in a negative manner. Thus, it is a double personal shock in many instances, when a client receives poor Normative instrument ratings: "I am not performing well in this area; my colleagues don't appreciate me… and I wasn't even fully aware of this!" This is particularly the case when the Tier Two data is coming for multiple sources (as we shall discuss in a later section of this chapter). Thus, as we note in this later section, the Normative instrument data must be treated in a very careful manner and the release of this data should always be accompanied by supportive coaching services.

Normative instruments are also best used and discussed *in conjunction* with Descriptive ones. ("I now understand how my personality preference causes part of the perception others have of my performance and my behavior".) Adding the cultural Third Tier component further contextualizes how and why the performance of the person is viewed as fitting or not fitting the organization.

Descriptive instruments offer their own unique challenges. First, we should be aware as coaches that multi-rater descriptive data might not be as threatening as normative data; it is precisely for this reason that descriptive data is also much easier to ignore or dismiss as "interesting" but not very informative. Recipients might indicate that this is "nothing new – I have known this for a long time…ask my wife." They might also dismiss the data from other people as being quite biased and "inaccurate." Conversely, other descriptive data recipients often take the information they have received too seriously: "Am I really this person that they describe? Have I really been this wrong about myself all these years?" As in the case of normative date, the recipient of descriptive data should always be assisted in the interpretation of the data by a masterful coach. The coach can help provide sufficient support ("This is only one snapshot of you, it is not your inescapable destiny") and sufficient challenge ("This portrait of you is real in the sense that some people see you this way and they are likely to respond to you and anticipate that you will respond to them through these lenses"). Furthermore, the coach will often benefit from knowing something about the conceptual structure that underlies the descriptive instrument being used. In this way, the coach becomes a teacher and a guide to new dimensions and perspectives in the self-awareness, the self-image and ultimately the life of her client. This role of teacher and guide is particularly appropriate if the descriptive instrument is theory-based rather than empirically-based (a distinction we are about to draw in the next section of this chapter).

Thus, when preparing to use a normative instrument, a coach should prepare for potential resistance and - in the case of a multi-rater process - should assist her client in sorting through the sometimes conflicting and sometimes harsh appraisals made by other people to find the nugget of truth and the grain of insight that can be used for improved performance and decision-making. When preparing to use a descriptive instrument, a coach should build a strategy that encourages a serious but not uncritical review of the data being presented and that should be used to teach the coaching client more about the match or mismatch between their own internal perceptions (Tier One self-assessment) and the perceptions of the client that are held by other people with whom they interact (Tier Two assessment by other people).

Descriptive Instruments

As we begin our discussion regarding the use of Descriptive instruments in organizational coaching, it is important to focus briefly on the distinction we just drew between empirically-based and theory-based instruments.

> The moment when a leader receives a massive amount of normative feedback from his co-workers is never stress-free, and some people describe it as game-changing or life-altering.

Some descriptive instruments (such as *16 PF* and many career planning instruments) are *empirically-based*. An extensive amount of data is collected and these data are usually analyzed through use of complex statistical tools (such as factor analysis). In the *design* of these instruments, people who are already known to be oriented in a specific way (style, preferences, perspectives) are given a large number of questions to which they are to respond. Those questions that are answered in a specific manner by a majority of respondents with a specific style are considered representative ("typical") and placed in the formal questionnaire for public use. For instance, items with which all or most successful musicians agree are selected for a questionnaire that measures preferences for musical expression or appreciation.

By contrast, a *theory-based instrument* (such as the Myers-Briggs Type Indicator) begins with the theory (in this instance, the personality theory of Carl Jung) and constructs questionnaire items that correspond to or are directly associated with this theory. Thus, a theory that differentiates analytic from intuitive thinking would contain items on the questionnaire that ask about the extent to which the respondent works on complex issues by doing careful analysis or responds quickly in an intuitive manner.

Typically, the theory-based Descriptive instruments are much better as a tool of organizational coaching than are empirically-based Descriptive instruments. The empirically-based instruments serve an important function as predictors of later success in specific careers (Normative instruments are also very good predictors in many instances). When it comes to generating rich dialogue for coaching conversations, however, it is usually better to have a solid theory that underlies the results of the Descriptive instrument. A client and coach can readily talk about the implications of being highly analytic or highly intuitive. It is much harder to trace the implications of having a musical aptitude or of knowing that one's style or perspective is commonly (or not commonly) found among managers in a certain kind of organization. The Myers-Briggs Type Indicator has been widely used by professional coaches precisely because it can readily evoke insightful and extended dialogue between coach and client. We will now turn to a more detailed exploration of the ways in which each type of instrument can be used in a masterful way.

Internal and External Sources of Information about Self

Leaders may wish to first concentrate primarily on their own internal sources of wisdom and insight when seeking to improve their performance or manage complex problems. These clients usually prefer to just participate in reflective coaching sessions, especially if their coach adopts an appreciative perspective. However, given the sponsoring organization's expectations and needs, other leaders have to consider not only their own perceptions but also the perceptions of other people about them. They want to compare their own internal perspectives and insights with those of the men and women with whom they work. Such coaching engagements often include instrumented coaching—and, in particular, descriptive instruments. These clients ask their coach for assistance in gathering and helping to make sense of data gathered from many sources. Ideally, instrumented Decisional coaching provides both the data from other people and the vehicle for interpreting these data.

Typically, the coach administers one or more descriptive self-assessment questionnaires to his client. These questionnaires help the client identify preferences and potentially choose to expand her repertoire of behaviors. The instrumented coaching process, however, moves beyond simple self-assessment. The coach administers a comparable descriptive questionnaire to others with whom the client works. For instance, this two-tiered descriptive coaching procedure is often used when a coach and client make use of the Strength Deployment Inventory (SDI). This widely—used inventory includes both a self-assessment form (Tier One) and a form requesting feedback from other people with whom the person completing the SDI works. The Tier Two feedback form yields data in the same categories as the Tier One SDI.

The two tier descriptive assessment can sometimes become even more expansive. The organization may require that a normative instrument be used to calibrate the leader's performance or profile against a certain internal or national benchmark. Some instruments actually combine normative and descriptive items. The Decisional coach may also wish to administer an organizational environment, climate or culture inventory that is aligned with the Tier One (self-assessment) and Tier Two (assessment by others) questionnaire. Through use of this Tier Three questionnaire, the coach helps his client assess the interplay ("fit") between her personal style preferences, values, attitudes and practices and the environment or organizational culture in which she works. With this information in hand, the coach reflects with the client on ways in which her styles, values and attitudes are manifest in the dilemmas and challenges she faces daily.

Following are some of the questions that a Decisional coach, using a set of descriptive instruments, might ask her client after administering Tier One, Two (and Three) instruments:

- What's new, surprising, perplexing, frustrating in the data?
  [the identification of "coachable" issues and engaging the process of unfreezing]

- What does this suggest to you about potential strengths and opportunities?
  [an appreciative perspective and engaging the process of learning]

- What are the settings in which this strength is most apparent and/or in which this strength flourishes?
  [a contextual perspective/situational effectiveness]

- What does this suggest to you about ways in which your strengths get you into trouble?
  [an appreciative perspective and further engaging the process of learning]

- What are the settings in which you are "deskilled" (have no access to your strengths) and/or in which you make inappropriate use of your strengths?
  [a contextual perspective/situational ineffectiveness]

- So What? What patterns, insights and conclusions about yourself and your work can you see now?
  [an invitation to interpret and synthesizing the data from a new perspective]

- Now what? What does this suggest about actions you might take in the near future?
  [an appreciative perspective (leaning into the future) and engaging the process of refreezing]

Together, the coach and client discover or invent ways in which to further enhance use of the client's strengths to notice, replace or de-fuse the habits she no longer finds productive and optimize the presence of conditions in the workplace that complement her abilities.

Two Theories Regarding Self and Others: Trait and State

We are all inevitably curious about the ways in which we are perceived by other people and the extent to which we fit into the environment and organizational culture in which we work; furthermore, psychologists have found that there is a tendency for each of us to hold two different theories about human behavior. One of these theories concerns our own personal behavior. The second theory concerns the behavior of everyone else.

 An observational approach to coaching requires and even encourages an opening up of boundaries within an organization.

Our personal theory suggests that we act the way we do because of the setting in which we find ourselves. "I am very talkative because I have been asked to teach this seminar, because everyone else in the room is being quiet, or because I am quite knowledgeable about this topic. In other settings I am likely to be very quiet, particularly when other people have been given the role of teacher or have more knowledge about the topic under discussion than I have." This same reasoning applies when each of us identifies the reasons why we are assertive, passive, jovial or depressed. We exhibit a specific pattern of behavior primarily "because" of the situations in which we find ourselves. We are not only contextual leaders. We are also contextual followers, listeners, observers, speakers and participants. Psychologists use the term *state* to identify this theory. We act in a specific way because of the state or context in which we find ourselves.

We hold a quite different theory about other people. This second theory suggests that other people act the way they do not because of the setting or state in which they find themselves but rather because of some enduring and overriding personality *trait*. Their leadership style is built-in or acquired early in life, as is their style of communication, conflict-management and problem- solving. "You can't teach old dogs new tricks." And people don't change just because you place them in a new job. They may seem to be different, but this change is temporary or artificial. Thus, the person running the meeting is naturally talkative. He loves to run meetings and will seek out any opportunity to speak. He isn't being talkative because of the setting. He is always talkative. It's a personality trait—rather than being determined by the state or context within which the person is operating.

In his best-selling book, *The Tipping Point*, Malcolm Gladwell (2000, p. 160, 163) identifies this second theory as the Fundamental Attribution Error (FTE):

> . . . human beings invariably make the mistake of overestimating the importance of fundamental character traits and underestimating the importance of the situation and context. We will always reach for a "dispositional" explanation for events, as opposed to a contextual explanation. . . . Character [however] isn't what we think it is or, rather, what we want it to be. It isn't a stable, easily identifiable set of closely related traits, and it only seems that way because of a glitch in the way our brains are organized. Character is more like a bundle of habits and tendencies and interests, loosely bound together and dependent, at certain times, on circumstance and context. The reason that most of us seem to have consistent character is that most of us are really good at controlling our environment.

Ironically, Gladwell's analysis of the FTE is itself an example of the attribution error. Gladwell is assuming that somehow "human beings inevitably make the mistake . . . ." This would suggest that FTE is a fundamental character trait rather than situation-based. Perhaps, there is something in contemporary social systems that provoke this error. Perhaps there is some pay-off for assuming that people tend to act in a consistent manner—and perhaps Decisional coaches (with the help of a set of descriptive instruments) can help their colleagues sort out the times *when* the assumption of consistency is appropriate and when it is inappropriate.

Obviously, both of the theories are partly right and partly wrong. We are products of our environment. However, we also have certain enduring traits that lead us to certain settings and that move us to behave in certain ways regardless of the setting. As we noted in our previous discussion of reflective coaching, our assumptions and theories about our own behavior and the behavior of other people can be distorted and self-fulfilling. Reflective coaching is particularly effective in a client's review of assumptions and theories about the behavior of other people. Instrumented coaching, on the other hand, is particularly effective in reviewing the assumptions and theories that clients hold about their own personal behavior—particularly when a descriptive instrument is being used during the coaching engagement.

Normative Instruments

During the first decade of the 21st Century, the so-called 360-Degree feedback process has become the most commonly used form of Normative assessment in organizational settings. Coaches and organizations use many different 360-Degree feedback formats. Their selection depends upon the needs of the person being coached, the policies, practices and preferences of the organization with regard to feedback instruments, and sometimes the budget that has been allocated for this data gathering process.

The Multi-Rater Assessment Process: A multi-rater feedback questionnaire will best be administered after the coach has a clear understanding of the presenting issues and the context and purpose of the coaching engagement, so she can select the appropriate instrument or – if an *interview 360* is performed – the right interview questions to use. This will determine how oriented the questionnaire will be towards work performance (is the client a good manager?) or toward personality, behavior and values issues (how ready is the client for a larger leadership position?) Questionnaires that are sent to subordinates and peers must be consolidated anonymously – best filled in online on a protected site to which only the coach and the instrument administrator have access. Since return rates are often low, we encourage leaders to enroll a sufficient number of observers that the results can still be meaningful to them—even if only two-thirds responded. We have found that the leader's choice of his raters (with input from other human resources or organizational stakeholders) and his own communication with them explaining that the leader himself has initiated this inquiry go a long way towards maintaining the client's self-respect, sense of control and thus openness to the returning data.

Even though the Decisional coaching process is oriented toward development rather than evaluation, the information obtained from superiors through Normative instrumented coaching can, as we noted earlier, be highly impactful and sometimes even disruptive. Regarding feedback confidentiality, bosses are in a category by themselves. Most employees have only one boss and, even if several matrix bosses are involved, the superior(s)'s responses can't and should not be kept anonymous – after all, every employee deserves to know where they stand in their boss' estimation at any time. One might be concerned under these circumstances about how candid certain superiors' responses will be, especially if a superior has avoided giving such input in the past. Interestingly, we find again and again that bosses who have difficulty holding people accountable face to face or who find it hard to address behavioral issues in-person "write their hearts out" in such 360 instruments. At least then, a new conversation can begin, facilitated by the coaching process.

Normative Instruments and the Coaching Process: In the contracting phase of an engagement, coaches will want to ensure that the superior is an integral part of the coaching process, understands the developmental nature of the Normative instrumented coaching process, and agrees to provide honest feedback to her subordinate through the questionnaire. Many masterful coaches rightly refuse to start an assignment until the supervisor has updated her feedback with their employee. A coaching conversation with the superior is often needed as a reminder that it is the boss' responsibility (not the coach's) to provide direct and candid performance expectations and feedback to the leader. Once the superior and person being coached both understand and support the developmental nature of this process, the superior's Normative feedback can be handled openly, as it will provide more texture and detail but no unexpected fundamental surprises to the client. This instrumented feedback subsequently helps the boss to engage as a mentor and supporter with the client in his progress. As part of the multi-rater feedback process, the person being coached will also complete a self-evaluation form which indicates his level of self-awareness and also *de facto* predicts his expectations of how the subordinates, peers and superior might respond to the questionnaire.

The Data Debrief Meeting: The data from all this input will then need to be analyzed, summarized and debriefed by a coach. In practice, that is not always the case. Brutus and Derayeh (2002) looked at the 360° feedback processes of 100 organizations and found that those interventions which had failed to meet expectations did not include an appropriate debriefing process for the participants, leaving them to decipher their feedback data virtually unsupported. The lack of supervisor involvement or even HR support in helping an employee make the most of the gathered input at best nullifies potential value and at worst leaves managers confused, discouraged or angry.

The moment when a leader receives a massive amount of normative feedback from his co-workers is never stress-free, and some people describe it as game-changing or life-altering. So it has become a best practice not to hand over raw (or even summary) data to a client without the presence of a coach, who can guide and support the client during his first (often emotional) reactions. When a computerized instrument is used, the coach shares the anonymous, numerical data report with the client, including any verbatim comments. However, when the coach has designed and applied a verbal, personal interview 360, fewer and fewer coaches believe that those raw rater responses (even unattributed and grouped) should be given to the client verbatim. A thematic summary with some quotes and illustrations work best in helping the client accept and digest the information.

During the debrief process of a Normative instrument, the Decisional coach might find that her client may immediately (or upon reflection prior to the next session) identify very different themes than the ones the coach has prepared to talk about. The coach's interpretation of the data remains a working hypothesis until the client confirms or invalidates or contextualizes the data. Considerable sensitivity and tact is needed. The effective coach must even be willing to abandon her conclusions entirely. Although no specific guidelines can be established for the conduct of this meeting, clearly the primary objective of the session is to help the person being coached explore with the coach his strengths and, in the most supportive manner (and environment) possible, any developmental agenda he may have.. While the coach knows that the ultimate expert in his work-life issues is the leader himself, she will be testing possible blind spots or defense (or deflection) mechanisms of the leader all through the conversation.

After the data review meeting(s), when some agreement has been reached concerning the client's strengths, an action plan is typically developed based on all the input and driven by the priorities the client wishes to achieve. (As we will describe below when discussing Performance-Based Feedback, there are other sources of data that should inform a full-fledged development plan and long-term coaching engagement agenda.) In many organizations, the client, with the support of the coach, shares his key learnings with his key stakeholders - at a minimum with his boss, whom he thus engages as an informed mentor and supporter. The coach also guides the client to consider how to express appreciation and maybe even share insights with his other observers and raters. (How do colleagues feel when they spend time giving thoughtful feedback to a leader but never hear back?)

When team issues are involved, a team meeting in which the leader shares a few learning highlights and insights he has gained can be an excellent opportunity to clarify any ambiguous messages the data might have contained. Demonstrating the posture of a *learning leader* often strengthens respect and trust by the team (at least in western egalitarian cultures, where leaders are not expected to "know it all"). What about closing the loop with peers or other external stakeholders who have given input? Sharing some learning highlights with such raters individually and asking "what else are you hearing about me that I'd find useful?" creates alliances and engages colleagues in each other's development. Those leaders who wish to model true continuous learning, also establish a habit of asking their stakeholders (regularly) for ongoing feedback in the areas in which they want to grow.

Are multi-rater Normative instruments fit to track developmental progress? The Center for Creative Leadership (1998) reported its findings after years of research:

- 360 instruments are mostly designed to represent a snapshot in time, and very rarely to track change.

- When re-administering the instrument, the numerical changes in the ratings are rarely significant because:
  - Observers may have changed;
  - Raters may have mentally "raised the bar" since they gave input, *expecting* progress;
  - The context and challenges of the job may have changed.

- Re-administration does yield useful information when it includes:
  - A limited, appropriately selected number of raters, and very few, specific questionnaire items, limited to the client's areas of focus;
  - Space for verbatim, qualitative comments, which always provide the most telling input.

When these methods are put in play, positive progress trends can certainly be documented.

Cultural Context

As we noted earlier, the instrumented coaching process does not necessarily stop after Tier One (self-assessments) or Tier Two (assessment by other people). It can move beyond the perceptions of self and others to an analysis of the work environment itself (Tier Three) and the relative match or mismatch between this environment and the client's strengths, preferred style, attitudes, values and work practices. This level of analysis counters a common criticism that self-assessment questionnaires fail to take into account variations in a person's style, attitudes and values as a function of the situation in which they find themselves. To what extent, for instance, is Susan's difficulty with Ralph caused (or at least exacerbated) by the organizational culture in which they are both immersed? Perhaps the culture favors confrontation and rational analysis. Ralph's softer and more visionary style might not be supported by this culture. But is his style such a bad thing? As long as he produced the practical outcomes/results his department needs to achieve, his particular, distinctive approach would perhaps help to balance off the linear and cold style that is so dominant in this organization, thus acting as a retention factor for his team members.

On the other hand, the cultural analysis may reveal that there are two dominant subcultures in the organization—one that emphasizes direct, clear and rational communication, the other emphasizing intuition, flexibility and warmth. Susan might discover that she and Ralph are respective champions of these two subcultures and that their conflict is in some ways a struggle between these two differing approaches. This would make the successful resolution or at least management of their conflict that much more important, for it could serve as a model for other members of the organization who are caught up in similar tensions between two potentially useful complementary polarities.

Such benefits have encouraged us to create and include several cultural assessment tools in our Resource section, for use by external and internal coaches. Coaches who work in the same organization over an extended period of time and have performed extensive interviews with its stakeholders about "how a leader succeeds in this company" also gain - informally - a significant cultural insight for the benefit of their clients. Just a caveat: Such inquiries need to be refreshed. Business conditions and cultural norms are shifting faster in the 21st Century organization than ever before.

The message is clear. Instrumented coaching processes are powerful and they must be handled, like any other powerful weapon, with great care. Whether the instrument is Descriptive or Normative in nature, irreparable damage can be done if the client, for example, is left alone with the data, unsupported. Much good can come from the use of two and three tier assessments, yet these appraisals must be done in a thoughtful and appreciative manner, with substantial follow-up and a direct link with other organizational coaching processes—and particularly the observational coaching processes to which we now turn.

Observational Coaching

This third model of Decisional coaching is likely to have the longest-term and most tangible impact on the clients being served by a masterful organizational coach. This form of coaching moves beyond self-reflection and the perceptions of other people to the impact of real behavior on real people in real time in real situations. It is the model of Decisional coaching that most often overlaps with the processes of Behavioral coaching.

Observational coaching options include the opportunity for a coach to go into actual workplace settings with the client (called "on-site" observational coaching or "shadow" coaching). Live shadow coaching has the enormous advantage of providing "just-in-time" feedback that is easiest for the leader to hear and understand, given the immediacy of the experience. Very senior managers, who can no longer be sure that they ever hear unvarnished feedback from their colleagues, find that a coach who observes them in action and holds up a mirror to their behavior is a most trustworthy and valid source of information.

As part of a new leader on-boarding assignment, a coach recently listened to a new CFO's call with Wall Street analysts (at his request). It was striking how self-assured and competent the CFO sounded when answering certain questions, and how evasive on others. His CEO jumped in twice and "rescued" the situation by filling in the data with which the CFO had not been forthcoming. As the coach described what he had seen to both the CEO and the CFO, he was able to help them gain a new agreement for the future: The CFO explained that his vagueness was intentional when he didn't yet want to share something with the analysts; the CEO therefore committed to watching such cues and not second-guessing his CFO or undermining such instances of strategic reticence. Without this early observed tension and the ensuing feedback, the CEO could have easily concluded that he had hired an insecure or unpredictable communicator as CFO, while the CFO would have chafed under a seemingly distrustful boss.

Facilitating an Observation-Based Feedback Process

Observational coaching provides the greatest opportunity for clients to learn and build on their strength when given immediate feedback on live situations and/or when given the opportunity to review video-recordings of their performance. The coach can observe meetings, observe the client on the phone, responding to emails, reviewing (and attending) presentations or participating in conference calls.

The basic steps of this model of observational coaching include:

1. Contracting: creating a clear, mutual understanding of what is to be observed and evaluated by what criteria and for what purpose

2. Setting the stage: logistics, knowing the work, learning the nature of the problem

3. Enactment: the actual work process

4. Feedback: based on the contract, providing information and insight

5. Re-contract: clarify understanding, criteria and parameters for the next round

6. Re-enactment: a chance to observe the skill in practice again and provide feedback.

On-site observational coaching can be extremely rich in data and provide a significant foundation and complementary information for either reflective or instrumented coaching. To qualify as coaching (versus performance evaluation), however, the client needs to retain control of this process. The coach's primary role is to expand the base of information available to her client. Furthermore, like both reflective and instrumented coaching, on-site observational coaching is based on appreciation of a client's distinctive strengths and how they play out in his work-context, rather than focusing on either the client's personal problems (the domain of counseling) or the problems of the organization (the domain of consulting).

Contracting – The Initial Meeting: Observational coaching can start off a coaching assignment or be used as a tool during an ongoing coaching relationship. A conversation dedicated to clarifying this particular approach is required in either case. The purpose of this meeting is primarily for the client to be clear about the purpose and general sequence of activities that will take place, and feel that she is at the helm of a process that will serve her. If the client has reservations or misgivings about any of the activities, these should be explored in detail.

The coach should take this opportunity to (re-)emphasize the confidential nature of the relationship, identify specific aspects of the client's job, behavior or relationships on which to work through observation and, in general, decide at the outset whether the client's needs and interests can be met by this observational coaching process.

Team coaches can produce major insights for team members:
the video speaks for itself, and it speaks volumes.

The critical part of these early conversations is to agree on what some of the questions are that the client wants answered through the observational feedback, what she commissions the coach to look out for and what criteria or parameters will guide the feedback she receives. Such considerations will then determine what work-events the coach should attend and observe. For example, if the client wishes to learn about the effectiveness of her executive presence in senior meetings, or about her ability to keep a remote team engaged during a three-continent conference call, specific occasions need to be set up to showcase the client in action. Beyond such specific goals, the client will invite broader observational feedback by the coach, thus further shaping her future coaching agenda.

Observing the Client at Work: This is often the most sensitive part of the observation-based feedback process and what differentiates observational coaching process from either reflective or instrumental coaching. The person being coached must be willing to expose himself to open observation and other members of the organization must sometimes also tolerate being observed by the coach.

In many cases, a peer (informal or internal coach) serving as an observational coach will be perceived as less intrusive than will an observational coach coming from outside the organization. The outside coach will sometimes be viewed with suspicion, especially if the person being coached is being encouraged to participate in the observational coaching process by someone above her in the organization. Clear guidelines regarding confidentiality must be made explicit to the whole group, reiterating that the coach provides no information about her client's or anyone else's performance to anyone in the organization or about members of the group to each other. Keeping that covenant under all conditionsis a fundamental (and often challenging) competence exhibited by a masterful coach. Embracing an appreciative perspective in all interactions will also help reduce fears and build support for this inevitably intrusive process.

Clear guidelines should also be established regarding a client's use of information from the observational coaching process in any review of his own performance. This is often a rather complex issue. On the one hand, the client owns the information collected about his performance by his coach. On the other hand, if the person who is being coached wants to use this information to demonstrate his competence or achievements, such data can only represent a part of an overall evaluation.

As an insider, a peer coach is less likely to be caught in the dilemmas associated with the label of external expert. However, there are still many occasions for conflict of interest. If guidelines aren't clear, a peer coach can easily be drawn into the performance review of a colleague she has observed. Furthermore the internal coach may be viewed with even greater suspicion than the external coach if potentially political factors are involved. An employee who is being observed by a peer may be concerned about the long-term confidentiality of observations, conversations and reports, since today's peer coach still remains tomorrow's co-worker.

Even with clear guidelines, observational coaching might stir up fears and resistance because it rattles boundaries. An observational approach to coaching requires and even encourages an opening up of boundaries within an organization. The struggle regarding acceptance of observational coaching in an organization is worthwhile, however, for this process usually leads not just to successful coaching but also to a climate of ongoing learning: the person being coached and observed role models and promotes the stance of a life-long learner interested in personal development. When the observational coaching process is infused with an appreciative perspective, it can bring down the barriers of defensiveness in the whole participating system.

The person being coached should be observed in a variety of different settings. Typically, he will be observed in one-on-one meetings with subordinates, in group and committee meetings, in on-going supervision and delegation activities, in meetings with members of the organization from other departments, in meetings with outside stakeholders, customers or board members, and in informal conversations. An initial unstructured visit by the coach in several of these settings is usually helpful to get a feeling for her client's job. The coach is introduced to others, then invited to observe interactions in an unobtrusive manner.

Depending on the scope of themes established for observation in the early contracting conversations, a single observation of a representative meeting or of a half-day in the daily life of her client may be sufficient, or additional visits may be appropriate. Certainly, if her client works in several different settings and plays several different roles in the organization, the coach should observe the person she is coaching on multiple occasions, including some high-pressure and high-stake situations.

> Masterful coaches think of it as the reality-check, the grounding, the environmental scan needed to keep the coaching from becoming irrelevant or stale by remaining limited to the dialogue between the same two people.

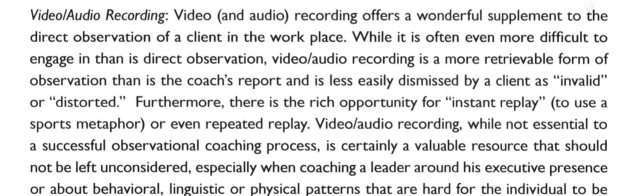

Video/Audio Recording: Video (and audio) recording offers a wonderful supplement to the direct observation of a client in the work place. While it is often even more difficult to engage in than is direct observation, video/audio recording is a more retrievable form of observation than is the coach's report and is less easily dismissed by a client as "invalid" or "distorted." Furthermore, there is the rich opportunity for "instant replay" (to use a sports metaphor) or even repeated replay. Video/audio recording, while not essential to a successful observational coaching process, is certainly a valuable resource that should not be left unconsidered, especially when coaching a leader around his executive presence or about behavioral, linguistic or physical patterns that are hard for the individual to be aware of in the moment.

The less intrusive audio recording requires the permission of the organization, of course. Like one or more observations by the coach, the meeting or event to be recorded should be as representative as possible of the client's performance on the job or a particular problem area about which the person being coached is concerned. Video recording usually is more obtrusive than the observing coach in the room. Individual clients accept and seek video recording most frequently in order to record their presentations for subsequent improvement in their public speaking skills. A video, even narrowly purposed in this way, can yield rich additional material on which the client and the coach can reflect.

As to groups, video is most accepted by teams who want to improve their communication skills. When involving a group dynamic, studies show that the video recording procedure is likely to feel intrusive and distracting for fifteen to twenty minutes if used to record small group interactions and for about five or ten minutes in larger groups... after which the group's energy tends to prove stronger than everyone's self-consciousness. Team coaches can produce major insights for their groups and the team members in this way: the video speaks for itself, and it speaks volumes.

Integrating Instrumented and Observational Coaching into Performance-Based Feedback

It is the role of the Decisional coach to ensure that the client has as much good data for his choices as possible – so that he can make informed choices about his own behavior, his growth, his career, his fit within the organization. The Decisional coach multiplies his client's options and expands his perspective. Good data, fed back in a thoughtful way opens the Window of Strengths (Chapter One) and multiplies the leader's paths to growth. Performance-based feedback (PBF) is a tool that allows for the systematic, confidential and structured exchange of ideas, perceptions and suggestions between coach and client, designed to identify and improve existing leadership strengths. We address it here, because Instrumented and Observational coaching are both integral to this feedback process.

While PBF is most valuable and most commonly utilized at the beginning of an organizational coaching relationship, it more often actually becomes a recurring loop, applied in larger or simpler forms at several critical times during an engagement. Some brief coaching assignments (especially when attached to larger group programs) end when the Development Plan is in place; but others continue for three months, six months or longer, building on the original data findings. Additionally, in complex leadership environments, there may be a change in the culture (caused by a change in the ownership or senior leadership of the firm), in the stakeholders, in the scope of the job, or in the career direction of the client... all requiring a refreshed and adjusted PBF process. Masterful coaches think of it as the reality-check, the grounding, the environmental scan needed to keep the coaching from becoming irrelevant or stale by remaining limited to the dialogue between the same two people.

The findings of the PBF are the best basis for extensive coaching assignments. Executives (not their coaches, of course!) often share some of the discoveries they gleaned from the process with their superiors, peers and team, at the appropriate time, in the spirit of uncovering their hidden strengths and developmental insights.

Six Phases of Performance-Based Feedback

While the process will always include all six phases, the emphasis on each phase and the nature of the data will change depending on the timing of the PBF within the overall coaching engagement. The first PBF process in a coaching relationship will be the most thorough, but later ones can be equally powerful, revelatory and direction-changing. The Performance-Based Feedback process involves these stages:

1. *Data collection:* In the first stage, information of various kinds is collected about the client's work and positioning in the organization.

2. *Data analysis:* In the second stage, that information is analyzed in a detailed and systematic manner by the coach. The third stage builds on this analysis.

3. *Debrief:* The data is then communicated and validated in dialogue with the client, and mined for the most relevant insights.

4. *Action planning:* Various strategies for sustaining, expanding or improving current functions are developed (often summarized in a "development plan").

5. *Implementation:* These new strategies and tactics are test-driven and implemented by the client (with and/or without the assistance of a coach, depending on the contract).

6. *Evaluation:* The final stage of the PBF process consists of the evaluation of results from the process.

Data collection: The coach will first interview the client about the context and purpose of this PBF process. What does the leader wish to achieve and/or work on? A number of insights will emerge from this interview. In addition to the self-reported perspective, depending on the culture of the organization, the coach will have secured information about the working context of the client from other sources: the sponsoring supervisor, HR, past performance reviews, etc.

The coach will be attempting to answer the following types of key questions for herself and for the client: How does the client feel about getting feedback on his performance?

What are the primary functions served by this person in this organization? What are his long-term goals and short-term objectives? What methods are used to reach these goals and objectives? How are meetings conducted? How do his subordinates show that they have completed their assigned work? How does the person being coached gain support for his program and ideas from superiors? What are relationships like with this client's peers? Does the client have any particular concerns or problems on which he would like to work? Are these concerns unique to this particular client or are they shared by other employees in this organization? Does this job fit the person?

> If there are significant discrepancies between the client's, the peers' and the subordinate's and/or superior's perception, the coach and client will wish to explore such gaps further.

Depending on the nature of the leader's job and the concerns voiced by him (as identified in the initial interview), additional information may need to be collected with the client's permission and assistance. Work product will be examined by the coach at times (are his PowerPoint presentations strategic enough?). Past performance appraisals (is there an upward or downward trend line?) or testimonials from customers or other external data will round out the picture. A Two-Tiered (Self-Assessment and Assessment by Others) or Three-Tiered (Self, Other and Culture) Instrumented coaching process is often used at this early stage, and then again (in a reduced form) at defined intervals. In addition, special questionnaires may have to be designed to assess such specific work skills as strategic abilities, project management, budget building and monitoring, relationships with the general public or customers etc.

Even at the early data-gathering stage, observational coaching may be included. This is particularly important if no Tier Three assessment can be made. Through observational coaching, the coach can at least gain an informal sense of the organizational culture in which her client is working. It is not uncommon for a coach, in the very first meeting, to find out that a critical team retreat or perhaps a global conference call is imminent. Observing the client in action first hand becomes an invaluable addition to the third-party information being gathered. When the PBF process is repeated (albeit in reduced form) at the mid-point or towards the end of a coaching engagement, observational coaching data will be more amply available and will represent the richest source of insight.

Data Analysis: At this point the coach will have collected considerable information about her client's work. Some of this material may be relatively subjective, based as it is on the coach's own impressions of her client. Some of it may be relatively objective, based on the summary of responses to the questionnaire. All of this information should now be reviewed, analyzed and organized in preparation for the data review meeting with the person being coached.

Both client and coach should prepare independently for the review meeting. The client should review any of his own past assessments, feedback and performance assessments with a view to identifying as specifically as possible particular areas or issues he would like to discuss and work on. In the meantime, the coach is doing her own preparation for the meeting. Although each coach will eventually discover or invent her own way of dealing with the wealth of data facing her, we suggest an appreciative, fairly structured four-step sequence of review, analysis and organization. Once individual coaches have gained some familiarity with that sequence they will be in a better position to develop their own approach to this rather complicated and extremely important task.

In the First Step of analysis, the coach reviews each source of information separately in an initial attempt to identify her client's strengths. First, the coach reviews her records of the initial interview and observations. She also views her observational coaching notes (if these have been gathered). On the occasions when video/audio recording are available, they will prove particularly useful at this point, for the coach can do detailed analyses, replaying the video recording as many times as she needs. She then lists with supporting data from past performance reviews and past feedback *what the coach believes to be her client's particular strengths and skills*. Although this initial assessment is quite tentative and may need to be revised on the basis of later analyses, an experienced coach can provide a different perspective on her client's work than can others and thus should consider herself to be an important source of information.

Next, the coach reviews her client's self-evaluation on the (descriptive and/or normative) assessment questionnaire(s) being used, in an attempt to identify her client's perceptions of his own strengths and skills. Information from the interview might also include the client's identification of specific problems or concerns and stories of successful use of specific strategies and styles. The interview data might also lead the coach to focus on particular skills, to investigate certain areas and to ignore others.

In examining the self-assessment, the feedback coach pays particular attention to extreme ratings. Skills that the person being coached identifies as being particularly strong are usually given special attention. Her client's self-assessment, of course, may not be entirely accurate, and the extent to which his perceptions are confirmed or questioned by additional information will provide important material for further consideration. At the end of this process, a detailed list with as much specific supporting evidence as possible is made concerning her *client's perceptions of his own strengths and skills*.

Finally, the coach reviews the subordinate's, peers' and superior's responses to the questionnaire(s) in an effort to identify their perceptions of her client's performance. Since the coach is looking for relative strengths, she should examine the overall response pattern before beginning to identify significant variations from it. Whatever process a coach employs when working with questionnaire data, she should conclude this stage with a *list of relative strengths and skills as perceived by the client's boss, subordinates and peers*. This list is typically buttressed with supporting evidence from the questionnaire results.

In the Second Step of analysis the coach draws three comparisons. She *compares her client's self-assessment to the responses of his subordinates, peers and superior(s)*. The coach should look for significant discrepancies in this comparative data. How accurate is the leader's self-perception: is he underestimating or overestimating his performance? And which groups does he play to best? Does he manage better up or down?

Significant agreement between the positive responses of self and others provides further evidence that a particular skill is a *public strength* (see discussion of The Window of Strength in Chapter One). Disagreement, if assessment by others is higher than the self-assessment, suggests a *private strength*; if self-assessment is higher than assessment by others, this discrepancy points to an *obscure strength*. Discrepancies may point to areas for further examination, depending on how critical the performance item under discussion is for the client.

These comparisons should enable the coach and client to determine the accuracy of her client's perceptions of the reactions of subordinates, peers and superior to his work and behavior. These comparisons should also help the person being coached to form hypotheses about the reasons for these perceptions and to discuss the implications they have for his leadership function (reflective coaching). If, in his self-assessment questionnaire, the client accurately predicts levels of subordinate, peer and/or superior satisfaction, this information may provide him with reassurance and reinforcement. If he accurately predicts subordinate and/or superior dissatisfaction on a number of items, this may strengthen his motivation for further reflection on his own behavior and identification of settings in which to make greater use of strengths and skills. If there are significant discrepancies between the client's, the peers' and the subordinate's and/or superior's perception, the coach and client will wish to explore such gaps further, perhaps with the assistance of a few of the actual respondents to the questionnaire.

In the Third Step of analysis, the coach begins to synthesize the information before her and to prepare a tentative description of her client's current performance, as captured in this snapshot data-set. To do this, she lists all of those behaviors appearing as her client's notable strengths and skills. Under each of these items she lists the evidence which supports this conclusion, identifies any contradictory data and makes a tentative explanation of any inconsistencies in the data, to be verified with the client. At the end of this step, the coach will have developed a fairly *extensive and well-documented profile of her client and his performance.*

At the Fourth Step, the feedback coach begins thinking more directly about the coming meeting with her client. Coaches may approach this in a variety of ways. Some feel they have more information available than can possibly be covered in a single meeting. Others take into consideration the anxious expectations of the client who is keen to get the full feedback picture. Knowing the preferred learning style of the client is most helpful here: should the data be presented in analytical form, with charts and percentages? Is this a person who, instead, will primarily be interested in the big-picture themes that are transmitted orally? Should everything be summarized on one slide or page, or is a lengthy report preferred? Is a relaxed, conversational summary most appropriate first? Whatever the format of the presentation, the coach needs to have the most critical themes and data examples at her fingertips throughout the long-term coaching engagement. Whether in one meeting or parsed out over time, the coach identifies those strengths that can most productively be leveraged right away and those parts of the insights that will be most useful to examine more in depth during future sessions.

For her debriefing report, the coach now reviews her summary of the client's stronger skills and isolates those she wishes to consider based on her answers to the following four questions:

- For which skills or behaviors is there the strongest evidence that the client's performance is outstanding?

- Which of these strengths most contribute to the client's overall effectiveness?

- Which of these strengths may best be built upon to increase the client's effectiveness in other areas?

- Is there evidence of under-use or over-use of these strengths in certain settings?

- How much and what kind of support does this client need to leverage these strengths?

Secondly, the coach identifies the most significant pieces of narrative/information which most dramatically and persuasively illustrate the strengths she has identified as possible topics for discussion. Although this may seem relatively mechanical, it is of crucial importance, for unless information is edited for the meeting there is a real danger that much time will be wasted in wallowing through undigested material or looking for particular incidents or examples. While the coach will present key themes and trends that she has identified in the data, it is important she be familiar with all of the information (not just selected examples) because her client may want to focus on or question issues other than those chosen by the coach for review.

The Debrief: Once these four steps have been completed and once the coach has thought through the approach she will use in sharing this information with her client and has established a tentative agenda, it is time for the debrief meeting. Some coaches and clients spend half a day or a day over this process, others phase out the process. The key is the care taken in adapting to the client's learning style, observing their reactions in the moment and being fully present for whatever response appears. Some clients will want to spend time analyzing and reflecting aloud about the input, others will be tempted to jump straight into "now what" action planning ("what do I *do* about that?") as an anxiety relieving strategy. However, the coach has to ensure that every client takes some quality time to process the feedback (both in the coaching sessions and then alone) so that he may be prepared to have a point of view, and form an intention that will move him into action.

Action planning: On that fertile ground of reflection, based on past personal learning experiences, the client will start drafting an action plan. The coach's freeing inquiry and perspective-shifting, spacious support adds to the potential of the plan becoming an exciting, motivating and realistic map for the person. Most clients will want to socialize at least key aspects of the plan with a limited number of key stakeholders (including their boss), who then become their advocates, peer coaches, mentors and/or supporters.

The first Performance-Based Feedback process can be completed in one or two months, depending on circumstances. People who are faced with leadership challenges have different learning styles and paces, and many prefer to self-direct their performance improvement from this point on. Some Decisional coaching programs end at this point, assuming that the client, empowered by self-awareness, richly textured outside input and a thoughtful plan, can now autonomously implement his new actions, while engaging his company-internal support system. In coaching engagements designed to last for several months, the coaching work actually begins here.

As mentioned at the outset, PBF will often be used in adjusted form several times during a coaching engagement, most commonly at the mid-point and before the conclusion of the engagement. These subsequent PBFs will benefit from more observational coaching data (and possibly video/audio) than the first cycle. The reality-check, the grounding that the PBF provides synthesizes for the client each time where they stand in their evolution on the job and where they might want to grow next. A very successful top four accounting firm partner worked with her coach at varying degrees of intensity over several years, each cycle prompted by promotions or by new, increasingly complex assignments: Once the new challenge involved creating a new global function; at another time, joining the firm's board. Changing stakeholders and objectives and new leadership demands made a new PFB process useful each time.

Evaluation: The action or development plan that an executive designs with their coach will always carry some items time-marked "ongoing" (e.g. "describe vs. manifest feelings;" "tell a story to illustrate key messages of public presentations") as well as some measurable objectives that are time-bound (e.g. "acquire the two sets of experiences needed to be ready for a certain promotion;" "complete mentoring cycles with three rising stars"). Based on the totality of objectives the client decides to pursue, the coach and the client set a time-frame for evaluating their joint effort. These evaluations may coincide at times with check-ins with the client's supervisor or HR sponsor, but they need to occur regardless, intimately, between the coach and the client, as an accountability ritual that ensures that "the ladder we're climbing is leaning against the right wall".

Coaches have innumerable questions at their fingertips to assess where the client feels they are. Some examples might be:

- How appropriate were the objectives set in the intention/the plan? Which ones have proven the most critical?

- What strengths are now used more freely and consistently?

- What over-extensions of strengths are handled with greater moderation?

- How does the client know that his abilities have expanded?

- How does he know that the organization perceives that progress?

- How have his team and the company benefited from these changes?

- How has he impacted and influenced his environment?

- How are the changes impacting the climate in his closest work-unit?

- How are the changes affecting his energy (stress management)?

- How are the changes transpiring into his personal life and getting reinforcement (or resistance) there?

- What is still missing?

Coaches who personalize their clients' results (which they might label as progress, stagnation, derailment, back-sliding… or other natural phases of experiential learning) tend to avoid such evaluations, because they might feel that the evaluation pertains to *their* coaching ability. But taking stock is a critical mutual-accountability step in any organizational coaching process. Evaluating where one stands is as valuable a leadership lesson for the client to adopt as the habit of reflecting, asking for feedback or questioning his assumptions – all potentially life-long habits embedded in the coaching process.

Conclusions: Coaching as a Temporary System

Most coaching issues are framed initially in terms of first-order, very practical but tactical/transactional changes. If these don't yield the full results toward which the client strives, the Decisional coach will move with her client to second-order, transformational changes. Sometimes, however, neither of these approaches alone suffice in terms of individual or social change. A change strategy is needed which allows for *both* gradual, evolutionary change (first-order) and change that enables an individual or team of people to retain their motivation and sense of direction while shifting in more fundamental, transformational ways (second-order). A Decisional coaching process that enables alternating movement between first and second order change can be of great value to many organizational clients.

Temporary systems offer a model of change that retains the best of both the evolutionary (first-order) and revolutionary (second-order) strategies. The desired change is initiated through the small, incremental steps of a planning or design process. At a certain point, however, a temporary system is introduced in which a short-term revolution can occur through pilot-testing part or all of the program or idea. Thus, part (or all) of the plan is temporarily enacted so that people can discover what the results of implementing the plan might be, whether or not the plan is feasible and whether or not it is truly desirable. A temporary system provides people involved in change with renewed motivation to continue the change effort (provided the results of the trial enactment are found to be desirable) and, if the trial is successful, with a clearer sense of direction. All three models of Decisional coaching (*reflective, instrumented* and *observational*) either require or can best be performed within the context of a temporary system.

A Change Metaphor: The Explorer

The function served by a temporary system might best be understood by describing the state of a mythical explorer who is fighting his way through a dense jungle in order to reach the top of a nearby mountain. He can't even see the mountain and consequently does not know if he is traveling in the proper direction. He doesn't know if his work is worth the effort, for he can only speculate about the treasures that are available at the top of the mountain. Suppose this explorer is somehow transported from the middle of the jungle to the mountaintop for a short period of time, so that he can see where he is going and can judge more accurately whether or not the journey is worthwhile. Having spent a short period of time on the mountaintop, the explorer is ready to return to the jungle with a renewed sense of direction and motivation. If the mountaintop contains no treasures, then the explorer knows that the journey should be terminated before additional effort is expended.

> A temporary system provides people involved in change with renewed motivation to continue the change effort (provided the results of the trial enactment are found to be desirable) and, if the trial is successful, with a clearer sense of direction.

Similarly, a temporary system briefly transports an innovator to the end point of the innovation. This brief, utopian experience provides both direction and motivation when the innovator returns to the normal setting. If he is disappointed with the temporary system, then reconsideration of the long-term, evolutionary task is appropriate. While the dream of the explorer to be transported, temporarily, to the mountaintop is no more than a dream or wishful illusion, implementing a temporary system for innovators is not a dream but rather a practical possibility. Just as aeronautical engineers use their wind tunnels to test their work, social change practitioners have their temporary systems.

Coaching and Other Temporary Systems

The noted organizational consultant and educator Matthew Miles (1964) has observed that there are a "bewilderingly wide" range and variety of temporary systems in our society. Miles mentions conferences, games, juries and love affairs. He also lists ad hoc task forces, intensive personnel assessment programs, carnivals and utopias. What about research projects, governmental terms of office, political and social demonstrations? He mentions these, as well as military battles, psychotherapy, consulting, institutions that have complete or nearly complete control over their clients (mental hospitals, prisons, welfare homes, half-way houses) and even schools and colleges (temporary for the student). We would suggest that Decisional coaching be added to this list. This *safe haven for reflection* may be one of the few temporary systems available to the busy client. Coaching provides rare opportunities for one colleague (the coach) to be of real help to another colleague (the client).

Miles notes that temporary systems serve a variety of functions, including compensation and maintenance (games, vocation), short term accomplishment (task force, research project), induction of change (conference, psychotherapy), re-education (socio-drama, human relations training), and education (school, utopia). This wide range of activities and functions are subsumed by Miles under the category temporary systems because he wishes to identify several characteristics that are common to many, if not all, of these systems. According to Miles, the distinctive input and process characteristics of temporary systems tend to yield certain distinctive outputs. He mentions changes in persons, relationships and actions. These are also central ingredients in masterful Decisional coaching. Personal changes that are produced in Decisional coaching sessions or other temporary systems often yield relatively permanent shifts in attitudes, knowledge or behavior. Relationships also tend to be altered as a result of experiences in temporary systems. People 'can't go home again' after powerful, penetrating temporary system experiences. Their goals and perceptions have been reframed. This certainly is the case with an effective Decisional coaching experience.

At a tactical coaching level, the skill of *designing practice actions* for the client to test-drive or solidify new desirable behaviors during or between coaching sessions was illustrated in our description of the reflective coaching process and has been identified by the International Coach Federation as being a "core competency" in effective coaching. Clients can thus pilot new attitudes, new language, new behaviors, and then evaluate their effectiveness in moving them towards their desired goal. Coaching sessions abound in post-action reviews of such temporary systems, out of which next steps and more permanent systems evolve.

In addition to the positive outputs of temporary systems, Miles identified several of their central problems and dysfunctions. First, he observes that these systems often produce input overload. Too much is happening in a short period of time. The client is overwhelmed with the challenge introduced by his coach, without experiencing the support or marshalling the resources that should accompany this challenge. Participants in executive development programs must fight for privacy and have a great deal to sort out, but no time, ironically, for reflection on their reflection. As a result, learning often is incomplete.

Second, goal setting is often unrealistic. The ad hoc character of these systems often produces a feeling of infinite possibility and an unrealistic sense that the sky's the limit. Failure and disenchantment frequently are associated with a lack of realistic goal setting in any Decisional coaching process unless this process includes not only on the re-examination of context and strategy but also the regular re-examination of goals. Another frequent problem of temporary systems concerns the complex interpersonal and task related skills that are needed to run such a system. The skills needed to create new settings and provide Decisional coaching are not widely found or nurtured in our society—as Goleman (2006a, 2006b) has noted in his widely-read assessments of emotional and interpersonal intelligence.

Temporary systems and the processes of Decisional coaching are among the most complex and challenging means by which one can move between first and second order change. These systems are potentially effective in helping leaders reframe solutions. We have already suggested, for instance, that Susan might place Ralph on task forces that either push him further into his role as visionary (and thereby paradoxically make this role less appealing) or force him to play a very different role. These task forces can act as temporary systems, just as the Decisional coaching sessions do. The task forces encourage the generation of new ideas. They also can help employees like Ralph try out alternative roles, gain new perspectives from other members of the task force who come from different parts of the organization, and gain a new appreciation of their own distinctive strengths and resources. Task forces and international assignments, for example, as temporary systems have become a common and useful talent management tool, affording both the leader and her boss a chance to "test-drive" her newly acquired competencies or yet-to-be-discovered abilities.

Together with second order change and learning, and reframing, temporary systems encourage clients like Susan to experiment with new ways of thinking and acting when facing complex problems. They offer hope to the coaching client who is confronted with a seemingly intractable situation and provide a new set of tools for the Decisional coach who has already tried everything.

Chapter Six

Aspirational Coaching

Consider a hypothetical situation that was originally presented in the first issue of the *International Journal of Coaching in Organizations* (Lazar and Bergquist, 2003): Sue Gladstone serves as department head in a contemporary corporation Sue is confronted with a set of issues; each issue is seemingly nested in another set of issues. At the heart of the matter is a difficult decision that Sue must make regarding the performance of Peter, her trusted colleague of more than fifteen years at the Exemplar Corporation. Peter's level of work has always been outstanding; however, in recent months Peter's performance has dropped off in both quality and quantity. Given that Peter is a long-term employee, respected by younger members of Exemplar, the impact of his poor performance is widespread and potentially quite damaging to the company.

This coaching issue is compounded not only by Sue Gladstone's close working relationship with Peter over many years, but also by the fact that Peter has been distracted from his work by the deteriorating conditions of his wife, Gwen, who is dying of breast cancer. Sue grieves for Peter and Gwen, and very much understands why Peter leaves work early, why he often fails to return phone calls to his customers, and why his orders are often incorrectly submitted. Any wonder, given the horrible conditions he is confronting at home? Yet, Peter is in a critical position at Exemplar. He can't easily be replaced or given a leave of absence. His performance must improve immediately; otherwise, Sue and her department are in trouble.

Sue is in need of coaching and wants it. Her coach can be of great assistance in formulating a plan for addressing Peter about his performance problems. Sue wants to be supportive and understanding, yet clear and compelling.

When and where does she meet with Peter?

What, specifically, should be the agenda?

How, in the midst of these problematic times, does she find something to tell Peter that can be reassuring and truly helpful to him?

This is Decisional coaching that focuses on decision-making, on strategizing, on "thinking through" a process and its underlying assumptions and ramifications.

There is also a second type of coaching that Sue might find to be of value. This is Behavioral coaching. It concerns her preparation for the actual meeting with Peter.

What specifically should she say to Peter?

What should she do if Peter becomes highly emotional or depressed or resigned to his unfortunate fate?

How does she talk to Peter in a way that preserves their long-term relationship, while also respecting their formal reporting relationship and the company's objectives?

Most organizational coaching concerns one or both of these critical functions in the life of a manager: decision-making (Decisional coaching) and behavior (Behavioral coaching). Yet, there is also a third form of coaching in an organizational setting that Sue could find quite beneficial. What if she was able to explore even deeper issues with her coach:

> "I am in a setting that is firmly committed to human welfare, yet I am in a position where I am being expected to confront a colleague about his performance. What I really want to do is honor my organization's commitment to the welfare of its employees. I want to comfort my colleague—be truly 'with him' during these difficult times. In broaching his performance gaps, am I setting aside one set of values, regarding my organization's commitments, in favor of another set of values, regarding commitment to the performance standards in my organization (that pays my salary)? What about my organization's commitment to satisfying the needs of our customers? How do I reconcile these seemingly contradictory commitments of my organization? How do I best express my care both for my team/department and for Peter as an individual?" Am I working in a company that places higher value on production and sales or am I working in a company that places higher value on the quality of its employees' lives?"

This may prove a cultural and leadership litmus test. Susan is dealing with a dilemma, having to balance several "rights".

 Aspirational coaching can open the conversation about how one's personal values match or mismatch those of colleagues or of the organization in which we work and the personal and organizational implications of such a match or mismatch.

A third coaching strategy directly addresses these questions. Furthermore, this third strategy seems to lie underneath both Behavioral and Decisional coaching. It is a foundation for both decision-making and performance (behavior): Called *Aspirational coaching*, this third strategy addresses issues of value and meaning in multiple contexts. Perhaps Sue first needs to address these deep, fundamental questions. Then, if she does choose to sit down with Peter, she can turn to the first coaching strategy (Decisional) for assistance in decision-making and strategizing, and, finally, to the second coaching strategy (Behavioral) for assistance in preparing for the meeting with Peter.

While not omnipresent in every coaching assignment, Aspirational coaching often harbors the explanation for why leaders feel stuck. This strategy may be of great benefit to the client (and the coach), especially if the coach concludes that the services she is offering seem to be superficial, hovering on the surface of the challenge(s) being faced by the client. Aspirational coaching may be appropriate when a coaching client or the client's team seems to be arguing in circles—when nothing seems to be penetrating to the core of what is really important and what is really happening in the client's organization. Aspirational coaching can clarify one's personal values and how those contribute to our perspective on the world. It can help one discern what's important.

What should be the focal point of our efforts?

How do we distinguish between true and false riches? True and false accomplishments? True and false satisfaction?

Aspirational coaching can open the conversation about how one's personal values match or mismatch those of colleagues or of the organization in which we work and the personal and organizational implications of such a match or mismatch. It can reveal ways in which we construct our world (expressed in the way we use language and the functions being served by language), the extent to which we acknowledge our degree of authorship in this construction, and the implications and opportunities for authorship and personal choice. (Bergquist, 1993; Budd and Rothstein, 2000, Kegan and Lacey, 2001) It can help shape a department's or a division's culture; identify when conflicts among staff members are value-based vs. practical; support leaders in developing and articulating their leadership point of view; formulate and enforce ethical and value standards; examine their own and others' congruity relative to espoused vs. enacted values ("say/do"); examine the ethical and values implications of organizational policies, procedures and market-facing approaches..

Aspirational coaching can legitimize larger conversations regarding spirit and spirituality in the workplace. How is one's work an expression of a higher calling, on behalf of a greater good? This form of coaching can initiate inquiry into "who we are being" (as distinct from what we are doing) at a specific stage in our life, and how that fits into some larger plan. From such inquiries and conversations, a leader has the chance to step back, reflect, expand awareness and observe distinction, make choices, and uncover personal truths about the mysteries that each of us harbor as human beings along with the mysteries that are embedded in our purpose for being. From such conversations can come attunement, conviction, direction, velocity and joy!

In this chapter, we identify and briefly examine four models of Aspirational coaching; each elicits inquiries and conversations that bring a particular focus, set of distinctions and anticipated outcomes.

Four Types of Aspirational Coaching

Aspirational coaching has emerged in recent years from several different roots, some of which are spiritual or religious in nature and several of which have a long and venerable history. These multiple roots have, in essence, produced four models of Aspirational coaching. While they go by many names, we have chosen to label these four models using rather common and straightforward names: (1) spiritual coaching, (2) philosophical coaching, (3) ethics coaching and (4) career coaching. Following is a brief description of each model.

Spiritual Coaching

At the heart of spiritual coaching lies the process of discernment. Through this process, a coach encourages and enables her coaching client to more deeply examine and reflect on the various "voices" that speak to him in his ongoing life. The coaching client discerns which messages in his life are aligned with his best interests and the best interests of his family, community and society. With the assistance of his coach, the coaching client also discerns which messages draw him away from these best interests.

 This model of Aspirational coaching also comes from venerable roots; one might even declare that Socrates was the first philosophical coach!

Spiritual coaching is particularly valuable for the so-called "secularist" (or non-believer) who rarely, if ever, thinks in spiritual terms. The process of spiritual coaching for this coaching client may involve a process that we call "spiritual assemblage." The coach helps her client to identify moments in his every-day life that in some ways are "transcendent"—special, filled with meaning and purpose, awe-inspiring. The coach then encourages her client to assemble these moments, bringing them together so that he might seek out patterns in this assemblage of moments. These patterns constitute the client's spiritual life—his *area(s) of ultimate concern* (to borrow a phrase from Paul Tillich, 1957). This core then allows the client to evaluate the implications and the value of his life and career choices from a much boarder (and more deeply satisfying and sustainable) perspective than the purely pragmatic one.

Philosophical Coaching

This second model of Aspirational coaching also comes from venerable roots; one might even declare that Socrates was the first philosophical coach! The primary function of the philosophical coach is parallel to that of the spiritual coach, except for the focus of the philosophical coach on a secular, rather than sacred, domain of life: learning to think, understanding the history and genesis of ideas, detaching from one's ingrained paradigms of thought. The philosophical coach encourages and assists her coaching client to probe deeply into his underlying assumptions and beliefs, and to reflect on how these underlying assumptions and beliefs relate to and impact his perceptions and actions in all aspects of life. (Marinoff, 1988: Morris, 1997)

The philosophical coaching session, for instance, might focus on the coaching client's assumption about personal freedom—both his own freedom and the freedom of other people. "What will make you feel free? When is freedom an illusion in your life and when is it truly present? Is the choice between two brands of toothpaste really freedom?" Philosophical coaching might also involve probes into the emotional life of the coaching clients. However, it is not therapy and the emotional life is addressed in a quite different manner. For instance, while a therapist or counselor might ask a patient why he is anxious and might seek to uncover the roots of this anxiety, the philosophical coach remains in the present and probes her coaching client with regard to the meaning, relevance or even usefulness of the anxiety in (his) life.

A very accomplished, highly educated and extremely driven young manager complained to her coach about her burn-out and her inability to say "no" to unreasonably growing amounts of work coming her way. Upon reflection with the coach, she began seeing how much of that extra work was generated by her own inclination to "pop-corn" ideas that benefited the company. She would then try to implement these ideas, regardless of whether she obtained the adequate resources or not. Imaginative and resourceful, she could leave no "better solution" untried. Towards the end of one coaching session, she confessed to having recently been suffering from anxiety attacks. Instead of looking for relief from the anxiety attacks, the coach helped her reframe them as a useful warning signal without which she might be destroying her health altogether. This led the client to a meditation on the potential of such physical disturbances or other mishaps—seeing them as signals to stop and take stock and listen into herself versus reacting constantly to external demands.

For leaders of teams, the examination of a leader's mental construct about what motivates people is one of the most useful philosophical discussions to be engaged in Aspirational coaching. This discussion is commonly based on Douglas McGregor's (1960) distinction between *Theory X* and *Theory Y* perspectives regarding work-force motivation. An examination of Theory X assumptions ("the employee is inherently unmotivated") and Theory Y assumptions ("the employee is inherently interested in meaningful work") helps a leader question his beliefs about humanity: what constitutes work-place motivation, and (more broadly) what is the fundamental nature of human aspirations? The coach can engender reflection, for example, on why people do good work, about work and purpose, or about the link between philosophical beliefs and action.

Our theory about humanity – be it of the "X" or "Y" type – tends to be very ingrained, linked as it is to our "personal history of ideas". One of us worked with a manager recently, who had delivered consistent results as a plant director, through behaviors that revealed his "Theory X" beliefs: he displayed distrust, micro-management, perfectionism and a corrective style that clearly let his co-workers know when he was disappointed in them. The plant was in Central America; his staff accepted his style and presumed it necessary. One wouldn't think of this as the ideal setting for philosophical coaching. But Gonzalo was an avid reader of history and very keen to grow personally and professionally. The coach invited him on an exploration of the assumptions that underlie his behaviors, asking many 'why' questions.

Why do you control every decision of your direct reports?
Because they would slacken off if I didn't.
Why do you think they'd slacken?
Because they are used to being closely supervised.
Why are they used to that?
Because that's how leaders do it in our country.
Have there been any notable exceptions in your experience?

What kind of leader do you want to be?

What kind of human being do you want to be?

Gonzalo loosened his grip substantially over a few months. But, since his teams were "trained" to follow orders, he had to become a vocal, well-read and philosophically articulate proponent of his own new approach, in order to turn the culture of obedience into one of engagement.

An Aspirational coach might set up a temporary system in the form of a two-week exercise for her client, during which the leader attempts to act out of the opposite McGregor theory. (Contrary to general belief, McGregor was not a one-sided proponent of "Theory Y" under all circumstances!) The philosophical coaching can thus directly connect with shifts to new options and behaviors that a leader consciously chooses, after thoughtful, rational considerations.

Ethics Coaching

Obviously, the issue of ethics is extremely important in the scandal-ridden world of contemporary organizational life. The critical point to be made with regard to Ethics coaching is, of course, that the coach is not trying to convince, advocate or coerce his coaching client with regard to a specific set of ethics or life values. Rather, the role of the ethics coach is to help his colleague identify and clarify her own values and ethical stances, and identify ways in which she aligns with (and ways in which she betrays) these values and ethics. (Rogers, 1964; Raths, Harmin and Simon, 1966) We have provided a set of guidelines and questions in the Resource section of this book to assist an Aspirational coach who is engaged in an exploration of ethical issues with her client.

> Our theory about humanity – be it of the "X" or "Y" type – tends to be very ingrained, linked as it is to our "personal history of ideas".

There are several additional dimensions in which ethics coaching can operate. The ethics coach can help his coaching client trace out the implications of her actions in our complex, unpredictable and turbulent world, and can help her form new ethical and value-based principles that are responsive to these challenging conditions. A masterful ethics coach can move even further with his client. He can help his coaching client expand her domain of reflection regarding values and ethics, seeking alignment between her personal and professional life, between her family and community, and between her personal interests and rights and her collective responsibilities in a changing society.

Career Coaching

Career coaching differs from the other three forms of Aspirational coaching in that it often involves inventories (borrowing from instrumented coaching), specific sets of interview questions and planning exercises. (Whitworth, Kimsey-House & Sandahl, 1998) A career interest questionnaire might be offered along with a tool that encourages identification of skills that transfer from one career to another. It tends to also be more action oriented rather than just reflective. The coach often plays the role of catalyst, cheerleader or even goad, encouraging her client to take specific steps that will move him closer to specific goals and personal aspirations in his life and career. A typical coaching issue would be to inspire in the client a sense of proactive responsibility for his career development within an institution, avoiding a passive expectation of action by management. Career coaching moments also occur when examining a client's fundamental job-fit or fit within an industry, as part of a review of apparent under-performance or during times of transition.

The most powerful gift, however, that career coaches give their clients is an appreciative mirror and articulation of the client's essential and distinctive genius (and the coach helps her client relate this genius to the market place). As we noted with regard to the Window of Strength (Chapter One), most of us take some of our greatest gifts and characteristics for granted, since they've been at our disposal for a long time. One of us has worked with an Armed Forces Veteran, now a business manager in transition, who never highlighted in interviews (or in his own mind) the discipline, loyalty and commitment he had developed during his service. An attorney in a corporate position couldn't see how it was his exceptional interpersonal sensitivity rather than just his ability to build cogent arguments that was his winning essence – until a coach shone light on this distinction.

How then does the career coaching approach to Aspirational coaching differ from personal life coaching and personal career coaching? First, when career or even life issues are addressed in an Aspirational coaching session, the focus and the starting point remains embedded in the work setting. Sue Gladstone moves into Aspirational coaching because of conflicts associated with her relationship with Peter in the workplace. It is such work place situations that yield important coaching issues that are associated with personal life and career decisions. Conversely, personal coaching that focuses on life and career issues usually takes place outside the work setting and often is engaged by people who are selecting their first job, are between jobs or are contemplating a change in career or life direction. While Aspirational coaching in organizational settings is often supported financially by the company in which the person being coached works, personal life and career coaching is typically financed by the person receiving coaching or by an organization where this person previously worked (as part of a reduction-in-workforce outplacement package).

Puzzles, Problems, Dilemmas and Mysteries Revisited

Earlier in this book we introduced the distinction to be made between puzzles, problems, dilemmas and mysteries as they are being confronted by leaders in an organizational coaching session. While all four types of coaching issues can be and often are confronted in any appreciative organizational coaching session, there is a tendency for one or two of these four types of issues to be predominant. We would suggest that *puzzles* are often addressed through Behavioral coaching. By contrast, Decisional coaching is usually appropriate and prevalent when a *problem* or a *dilemma* is being identified and analyzed. Aspirational coaching is appropriate and prevalent when the issue being considered is a *mystery* or (as is often the case) a blending of problem, dilemmas and mystery. Aspirational coaching is being employed when a client addresses the balance between his life and work, and when he is struggling with profound challenges in his personal life and in an organization he is leading.

We must make commitments while living in a relativistic world.
In order to be able to do this, Perry suggests that we need courage
and the capacity for self-reflection.

Should one person provide all three coaching strategies? We believe that it is very appropriate for a single coach to employ all three strategies when assisting another person with their complex life issues. When one person is doing the coaching, there is consistency and each issue can be more fully understood within the context of the other issues being addressed in the coaching session. Most issues are nested in other issues. Puzzles are nested in problems that are nested in dilemmas that are nested in mysteries. This doesn't mean that a coach can ignore the important differences between Behavioral, Decisional and Aspirational coaching. When there is a shift from puzzle to problem, things get more complex and less clear. The Behavioral coach becomes a Decisional coach and moves back from execution of a decision to the process of decision-making itself. Success is harder to measure and the coach must be clear with her client that they are no longer in the safe harbor of clearly defined puzzles.

Similarly, when moving from a problem to a dilemma or mystery, the coach and client must be clear that they are beginning to address issues that may have no solutions and often lie outside the ken or control of the person being coached. At this point, the coaching session often moves away from action and towards reflection, away from thoughts and towards feelings, away from a focus on means and towards a focus on endpoints and ultimate purposes. This isn't religious counseling, though some of the same questions that surface in religion and spirituality are often part of the agenda. This is Aspirational coaching.

Perhaps most importantly, Aspirational coaching isn't psychotherapy, and one must be careful about not moving across this boundary. Aspirational coaching, however, can have a healing effect and can therefore be, one might say, "therapeutic" —and the world in which we now live is very much in need of this healing type of dialogue. When addressing problems, dilemmas and mysteries, one will inevitably confront highly emotional issues that tap into long-standing fears and concerns. However, for the Aspirational coach and the person being assisted these emotions, fears and concerns are approached within the context or against the backdrop of their work, rather than as the primary focus of the coaching session.

Commitment in the Midst of Relativism

We suggest that the world in which Aspirational Coaching now takes place is one that demands a relativistic perspective—especially if our Aspirational clients do not wish to shut out what we are all now learning from the new sciences and the cognitive/neurobiological revolution. What are the tools of thought that will help us as Aspirational coaches assist our coaching clients as they face the daunting prospect of taking action in a world that is fluid and in which ethics are more situational, cultural and elusive? We propose that William Perry's description of the movement from *dualism* to a *commitment-in- relativism* offers us some valuable insight with regard to this process.

Moving Beyond Dualism

Perry suggests that many mature men and women move beyond a way of thinking in which everything is either identified as black *or* white, good *or* bad, right *or* wrong, clear *or* unclear (*dualism*). They move to a way of thinking in which there are rights *and* wrongs, and goods *and* bads that exist within a specific community of belief and are not universal (*relativism*). Thus, within a specific scientific community, certain postulates are accepted as valid and are subject to rules of verification that have been formulated by that specific community. Yet, within another scientific community a different set of postulates are accepted and a different set of rules are followed in efforts to verify these postulates. Thus, in each of these communities there are "truths"—but in neither case can truth be claimed as universal or all encompassing. We see this dynamic played out in the field of psychology during most of the 20th Century. Three warring camps—behaviorism, humanism and psychoanalysis—and many sub-camps fought against one another, yet could never make much headways, since each camp made the argument for truth using methods and criteria of validity that neither of the other two camps accepted or even recognized as appropriate to a valid study of the human condition.

> We are kicked out of three different Edens, and can feel devastated and betrayed when forced to leave each of these refuges. It is at this moment that a thoughtful and supportive Aspirational coach can be of great value.

What are the appropriate responses to this condition? The typical response is a turning to or a return to the state of *multiplicity* in which we cynically conclude that since there is no one right way or moral way to do things, then any old way is acceptable as long as there is no law against it or we don't get caught. Such a cynical posture provides some shelter against the postmodern storm. Skepticism is another protective stance: Anyone who grew up – as one of us did – in a totalitarian ideological system, which had its seductive absolute truths and world-improving tenets, could spend their life in justified skepticism toward any ideology or absolute claims of truth. At least, the cynic and the skeptic feel, we will never be fooled or made to believe in something that is ultimately found to be inadequate or dead wrong.

Multiplistic (possibly cynical) thinking is certainly compatible with a postmodern world (Bergquist, 2003). It is based on the assumption of multiple truths and multiple realities, each of which is equally valid. Ironically, multiplicity is just another form of dualism: "if there is no one truth, then there must not be any truths!" As Foucault has so often observed, in this view truth and reality end up being decided by less rational forces involving governments, political pressure, social-economic power, and subtle media-based coercion. We need not worry, therefore, about who is right; rather we must worry about who is in charge and what they believe or declare to be the truth and reality. A new golden rule applies for the Multiplist: "he who has the gold makes the rules [and defines reality]!"

Perry suggests another response to the problems of a relativistic, non-dualistic world. This is the response he calls *commitment in relativism.* This response requires the willingness to take a risk and make a commitment to something, despite the fact that there are alternative truths and realities that can make viable claims on our sense of the world. At this point, Perry moves beyond the line of argument that would be found among most *constructionists* who emphasize the point that humans construct their own reality through language and forms of thought. Perry writes of the need for mature men and women to make decisions and take stances in the face of this relativism. We must make commitments while living in a relativistic world. In order to be able to do this, Perry suggests that we need courage and the capacity for self-reflection. Both dualism and relativism that is engaged without a commitment to either personal choice or action enable one to avoid anxiety. Courage alone enables us to transcend this anxiety.

Dualism, with its clear rights and wrongs, enables us to *escape from freedom*—as Erich Fromm (1941) noted many years ago. Relativism *without* commitment enables us to float above the fray, and avoid making the tough decisions or any commitments. We can be breathtaking in our clever and often cynical social analyses. We are brilliant Monday morning quarterbacks regarding politics, corporate decision-making, and our parents' child raising strategies. Because we ourselves never have to make choices, we can successfully criticize those who do have to make decisions.

The Multiplists and Relativists do not view themselves as similar to the Committed Relativist, but instead criticize the Committed Relativist for retreating into Dualism. Like the Dualist, they confuse commitment for uncritical acceptance. In the case of the cynical Multiplist, the retreat is either a falling back into Dualism or an expedient move to commitment ("who is paying you to come to that decision?"). For the Relativist, the retreat is viewed as either an ignoring of alternative perspectives or as a "selling out" to the forces that are forcing simplification in our society. The Multiplists project their own turn to expedience onto the Committed Relativist, while the Relativist yearn for (and try to remain in) a world that enables them to stay detached and "objective."

In large part this misinterpretation of the motives and perspectives of the Committed Relativist relates to the emotion of grieving, which accompanies, for example, our "loss of innocence" when moving from Dualism to Multiplicity, for we must abandon our belief in one abiding truth. We also grieve when moving from Multiplicity to Relativism, for we can no longer embrace an undisciplined and cavalier attitude toward all purported "truths" in the world. Some ideas and "truths" are better than others, and expedient use of those truths that serve our own personal agendas are no longer acceptable. In the case of the move from Relativism to Committed Relativism, we grieve the loss of freedom and broad perspective that required no final judgments or commitments. We are kicked out of three different Edens, and can feel devastated and betrayed when forced to leave each of these refuges. It is at this moment that a thoughtful and supportive Aspirational coach can be of great value.

Multiple Perspectives Regarding Puzzles, Problems, Dilemmas and Mysteries

It is conventional wisdom to think of successful members of organizations as problem-solvers—as persons who along with colleagues identify problems, analyze causes, consider alternative solutions, and act on the solution that most promise desired results. Since the hey-day of logical positivism, we have tended to use the tools and deficit language of analysis and problem solving because *we have been taught to focus on problems.* And, as Cooperrider and others have so wisely and concisely observed, we have even gone so far as to see organizations (and, sadly, by extension, the individuals who work within them) as "problems to be solved."

We have even gone so far as to see organizations (and, sadly, by extension, the individuals who work within them) as "problems to be solved."

Not only do systems thinking and chaos theory blow the field for organizational analysis wide open, but even if we were to look at problem solving as the cornerstone of our coaching work, we would need to look closer. As we have noted throughout this book, there appear to be four different kinds of issues. Some issues (*puzzles*) have answers that readily produce intended results through systematic analysis and action. Other issues (*problems* and in particular *dilemmas*) defy simple or single solutions, and often our attempts at systematic analysis and action create new, unintended consequences. Even more daunting are issues that are beyond rational comprehension, much less systematic resolution (*mysteries*).

As one might expect, Dualists don't particularly enjoy working with problems or dilemmas, and seek in all ways possible to re-conceptualize problems as puzzles. Multiplists do not like problems either, and look to expedient (if short-term) solutions. Relativists often take delight in confronting a problem or dilemma, though they prefer to remain on the sidelines, offering multiple suggestions regarding ways in which to interpret and address the problem or dilemma, without having to come to a resolution! It is only the Committed Relativist who is willing to acknowledge that a problem or dilemma—not a puzzle—is present and who is willing to live with the ambiguity and careful deliberations that attend any careful analysis of a problem or dilemma *and* is willing to live with the inevitable emotional reactions (from multiple stakeholders) that accompany the choice of one solution or course of action over another.

For both Dualists and Multiplists, mysteries are much easier to comprehend than are problems—for mysteries are outside their control. The Dualists are likely to see mysteries as a confirmation of whatever "truth" they have received from an external source: The "good" have been rewarded, or the ultimate plan has not been revealed by the "ultimate" source of truth. Multiplists will view mysteries as further evidence that there is no solid base for assessing the validity of any "truth" and that therefore one should abandon all critical analysis: "It doesn't matter what we think or believe, since what really happens in the world is a mystery beyond our control or comprehension. . . So let's do whatever we want to do."

Mysteries are much more challenging for the Relativist and Committed Relativist who try to place a rational frame around experiences in their lives. Mysteries defy reason and leave the Relativist in a mood to become even more detached from reality, and the Committed Relativist in a mood to join the Relativist in this detachment. Having come to a difficult decision, the Committed Relativist hates the thought of some external event, over which he has no control, intervening and throwing off the carefully deliberated course of action that he has taken. We finally decide on a candidate for this new job and she must decline because of a death in her family. We have chosen the new location for our shopping mall and we find that it is located in a seismically-active region and, hence, is not suitable for development. The Committed Relativist curses the perfidious predisposition of Nature and moves back to ground zero in order to make different, thoughtful, decision. As Taleb (2010) would observe, rational and systematic thinkers hate improbably, "out-of-the-blue" events (Black Swans) that play such an important role in our personal and collective lives.

Polarities and Commitments

There is yet another challenge inherent in operating from a position of commitment-in-relativism. If choosing between left and right in a definitive way is dangerous, and if defining good and bad in absolute terms is no longer philosophically defensible, how do we make choices and decisions? Barry Johnson gave us, as Aspirational coaches, an elegant and eminently practical solution in his 1992 book, *Polarity Management* for "identifying and managing [such] unsolvable problems."

Let's review: Puzzles have simple solutions and lie within our control. Many problems have multiple solutions, are infinitely complex, and require multi-directional cooperation, since they are not subject to one locus of control. Another category of challenges, *mysteries,* can never be solved completely:"What is love?" "Why am I here?" And then there are *dilemmas*, which require action and can be moved along, but can never be resolved once and for all. Think about it: Can there be *one* ultimate answer for the choice between career and family life? Can the world conclusively choose between globalization and local needs? Can a manager choose between driving for performance and attending to his people's needs? In these cases, the "solution" has to be... both! Instead of choosing between these apparent alternatives, we are learning to "manage" rather than "solve" these dilemmas.

Many years ago, Orson Welles was featured in a unique cartoon that showed two warring factions in great dispute over a minor issue that soon became major. One day, a single member of one of the warring factions made an extraordinary (and very brave) statement. This character said: "maybe *they're* right!" Everyone and everything stopped—in amazement—on both sides of the battlefield. Members of each faction began articulating reasons why the other side was, at least in some respects, correct in their assessments, in their assignment of priorities, in their priorities. This fictitious world began to change and Welles, in his magnificent voice, ends by suggesting that perhaps the people with whom we violently disagree in the "real" world might ". . . just be right!" Such is the case for the 21st Century Aspirational coaching client. With the coach's help, a leader can acknowledge, in a relativistic frame, that there is validity in the multiple perspectives, values and ideas being offered by the various stakeholders with whom this client interacts. Knowing that, the leader still make choices in real time, navigating and course-correcting between the two polarities.

Commitment within the Context of Faith and Doubt

Coaching clients make an *existential leap of faith* when they face the complex, uncertain and rapidly changing conditions of postmodern life—when they face the post-modern edge. When leaders are willing to make decisions and commitments within the context of these postmodern conditions, with insufficient and contradictory data, without absolute guidelines, then they have found what Merleau-Ponty has described as a *truth within situation*. The American poet Wallace Stevens frames the challenge of relativistic commitment in the following way: "The final belief is to believe in a fiction, which you know to be a fiction, there being nothing else. The exquisite truth is to know that it is a fiction and that you believe in it willingly."

The movement of a coaching client to commitment without the buttressing of absolute certainties—to a truth within a situation—requires courage and a willingness to encounter an unknown and unknowable world and do the best job possible with the information and perspectives that we do have. The leader of a highly innovative human service agency that builds partnerships between public institutions has offered an eloquent statement regarding this difficult movement to commitment:

> Postmodernism deals with a crisis of faith and a crisis of knowledge. Having displaced religion's appearance of truth, science is losing its own appearance of certain knowledge. Postmodernism seems to ask the basic philosophical question: who are we? . . . who are we as organized people; as organizations?

> Unclear about what we may have gained as human beings through modernism, we are like people wandering through the darkness in a storm—we thought we were on our way towards clear daylight and calm, but have begun to ask if we are going in the right direction. Perhaps there is no calm and no daylight. Rather than attempting to move towards it, perhaps we should be learning how to be effective without it. We have lost the faith in the reality we sought and are re-looking at our organizations with the possibility that this chaos may be a transition to something that is different from where we thought we were headed... or that this chaos may be the real "reality."

Once this first courageous commitment is made by a coaching client, a bit of increased self-knowledge and empathy often come along. Our clients find a new level of appreciation for their parents, their bosses and even national leaders when they come to fully appreciate how difficult it is to make good choices in a relativistic world. With an increased level of consciousness, we become somewhat more comfortable about making commitments and about adopting a style of operating that leaves options open for an appropriate period of time and that moves the decision-maker to commitment.

Even after the decision is made, the committed relativist remains open to alternative perspectives that could lead to a modification in this decision, and follows up the decision with feedback on the effects of this decision. Chris Argyris and Donald Schön propose that the most effective decision-makers are *not* those who avoid making mistakes, but rather are those who best *learn* from their mistakes and do not continue to make the same mistakes. By assuming the role of learner, the committed relativist effectively confronts the ambiguity and often immobilizing anxiety associated with the postmodern, constructionist view of reality.

Even Michel Foucault, the critic of modernist perspectives on absolute truth, and the social historian who showed the linkages between knowledge and power, speaks in his last book of the importance of seeking truth in a relativistic world. According to Foucault, "the task of speaking the truth is an infinite labor; to respect it in its complexity is an obligation which no power can pass over, except by imposing the silence of servitude." It is precisely in the typical indifference to the ongoing pursuit of truth, according to Foucault, that knowledge and power become inextricably wrapped together in a manner that is destructive to society and human dignity. The German postmodernist Jurgen Habermas similarly proposes that it is not truth itself which is intrinsically linked to power, but rather truth-claims which could not be upheld if they were not shielded from critical probing by acts of coercion and manipulations.

What then becomes the nature of certainty and commitment for a 21st Century coaching client (and coach) in this relativistic framework? The key seems to lie in an emphasis on the process of knowing and inquiring rather than on the outcome or product of the search for knowledge or inquiry. Alfred North Whitehead first spoke of such an orientation in his portrait of a theology of process—in this sense, he was one of the first post-modernists. According to Whitehead, God is changing along with everything else—much as some scientists are now hypothesizing that the basic laws of the universe may themselves be changing over time. Walter Anderson suggests that in Whitehead's universe:

> . . . there is no ultimate reality to which things happen, and consequently we don't need—in fact should be on guard against—the absolutes we make up to describe ultimate reality. Whitehead, agreeing with the American pragmatist philosophers such as William James, with whom he had made common cause, thought that the "intolerant use of abstractions is the major vice of the intellect."

For Whitehead, James and many contemporary feminist philosophers and psychologists, truth must always be viewed within its particular context and with regard to its purpose and use. Thus, a contemporary coaching client must examine not only the outcomes of his deliberations, but also the methods and purposes that defined this deliberation. The postmodern deconstructionists encourage us to look at the words and sequencing of words as well as the message and intention being conveyed by the words. Whitehead and his process-oriented colleagues similarly encourage us to look past the outcomes of thought to the thought process itself.

> Chris Argyris and Donald Schön propose that the most effective decision-makers are *not* those who avoid making mistakes, but rather are those who best *learn* from their mistakes and do not continue to make the same mistakes.

In a world of relativity and process, how do Aspirational coaches and the leaders whom they coach grapple with the issues of faith and doubt? One answer to this question is obvious, though often ignored when talking about organizational coaching. This answer is an ingredient we have often turned to in this chapter (and at other times throughout this book). This ingredient is *courage*. 21st Century coaches and clients must find and manifest courage in order to confront the issues of faith and doubt in such a way as to find their way to commitment. Courage, in turn, is to be found only when we have found some understanding of and have properly nurtured our own inner life. Courage comes when we have been successful in integrating the disparate elements of our selves. John Sanford suggests that successful people are not those who are able to achieve perfection (or think that they have achieved perfection by repressing aspects of themselves). Rather, the successful person is someone who has acknowledged and integrated all aspects of self—including those parts that are not very mature or even acceptable to our personal sense of the ideal self, while still being willing and responsible to act with courage.

Conclusions

Throughout this book, we have identified the settings in which Decisional and Behavioral coaching can occur and how they contribute to learning, expanded repertoires and perspectives, as well as desired results. Yet the deeper satisfaction and joy of the process and the most fitting immediate outcomes are often enabled by Aspirational coaching. It can expand one's capacity to positively reframe situations to create and declare the benefit or gift that is available. Because Aspirational coaching specifically attends to one's context and values, and the meaning that stems from those foundations, it connects us with our life journey, our narrative about why (we say) we're on it, and grants opportunities for valuable learning that is essential for traveling well.

Aspirational coaching furthers personal integrity, revealing where personal values are aligned and attuned (or not) with one's actions. Clients can also distinguish the fit between personal values and corporate values. The greater the congruence, the less there is stress due to the inconsistency. Operating consistently with one's values, commitments and higher purpose can be the basis for higher levels of satisfaction and appreciation, greater sustained motivation and discretionary effort, and better business performance. Coupled with Behavioral and Decisional coaching, Aspirational coaching enables a reflection and perspective that contributes to one's experience of acceptance, wholeness, integrity, connection, gratitude, and purposefulness. These are avenues for living life joyously.

Chapter Seven

Appreciation: The Essence of Masterful Organizational Coaching

We have been concerned throughout this book with the question of how best to confront the challenges and take full advantage of the opportunities associated with organizational coaching. We have also attempted to arrive at a more definitive notion about the nature and purpose of organizational coaching, especially in contrast with counseling and consulting. In response to this concern about organizational coaching and its distinctive characteristics, we have proposed throughout this book that organizational coaching—and the comprehensive institutional developmental programs of which it should be a part—is built on what we identify as an appreciative perspective. This perspective enables us to concentrate on what is working right and how the challenges the organization is facing can best be addressed. Such a focus, in turn, helps to create a positive atmosphere for change and avoids the resistance and loss of hope for a better future that are associated with traditional approaches to coaching and leadership development (Sorenson and Associates, 1996).

Through our own experiences as organizational coaches in many different settings we have found that this appreciative perspective is best retained when one focuses on three inter-related factors in the life of men and women who face 21st Century organizational challenges. We urge you, the reader, to take these focal points into account, as we bring this book to a close with a brief description of these three points.

Focus on Unique Functions

Organizational coaching concerns a specific group of people faced with those unique postmodern challenges and opportunities that pertain to building and sustaining a working community – an organization. Their functions include vision and strategy development, planning, supervision and evaluation, decision-making, problem-solving, delegating, conflict-management, motivating and inspiring others, promoting and monitoring organizational policy, strengthening values and mission, and mentoring other members of the organization.

Organizational coaching primarily addresses these unique functions—functions that are often associated with critical moments of leadership. It is not primarily concerned with technical assistance nor is it primarily concerned with either fiscal management or the legal matters of the organization. Its primary concern is not the resolution of specific organizational problems, except to the extent that these organizational problems centrally influence or are impacted by the functioning of the person being coached. Organizational consultants are hired to focus on the resolution of a specific problem, whereas organizational coaches primarily focus on the client, not the problem. Neither does organizational coaching focus on the personal life and needs of the person being coached—except to the extent that life issues and needs impact on the organization. A counselor or therapist can better deal with this as a primary area of focus. The perspective of the organizational coach puts the working leader first, and the coaching engagement is usually long-term. An organizational coach typically looks beyond the immediate issues to help the client discover, explore and practice the most productive patterns of thought and behavior that will lead the person (and any team and organization he serves) to long-term success.

Focus on Distinctive Competencies and Strengths

From an appreciative perspective, organizational coaching concerns the identification of distinctive competencies and strengths. Organizational coaching does not focus, as do most training and development programs, on the deficits or weaknesses of the person being coached. We begin with the assumption that coaching clients have reached their level of success and have assumed their level of responsibility because of certain distinctive competencies of which they may or may not be fully aware. While these coaching clients also inevitably retain certain deficits and continue to exhibit certain weaknesses, these deficits and weaknesses are not central to their performance. We have discovered through our organizational coaching that in many instances, these weaknesses may be the very strengths of the client used too often, too exclusively or in inappropriate settings. Such framing helps coaching clients be more motivated and confident in embarking on the never-ending adventure of shifting to new habits or perspectives as their working lives require them. Appreciative organizational coaching focuses on the clear identification of a client's distinctive strengths and on the more productive and appropriate use of these strengths.

Focus on Building Strong Peer Relationships

An appreciative approach to organizational coaching has to result in coaching clients helping each other, since great coaches always endeavor to "work themselves out of a job". If we begin with the assumption that those seeking coaching support have distinctive skills and expertise, then we should also give them credit for the ability to assist one another. Counselors and therapists need not themselves have operated successfully in an organization in order to assist and to support their clients in addressing their own personal difficulties, for these difficulties are not confined to their clients but are instead inherent in the human condition. Neither do consultants need to have substantial organizational experience, for they are focusing not on the person but rather on a functional problem. Consultants typically are skilled in helping groups of people rather than just individual clients address a problem. But there is only one credible source for those who seek coaching—other men and women who have also faced organizational challenges first-hand. Thus, effective organizational coaching at its best is performed by internal or external coaches with strong organizational or leadership backgrounds. And at its most scalable, organizational coaching ultimately evolves to becoming peer-based. It involves a helping relationship established between two or more members of an organization.

> We begin with the assumption that coaching clients have reached their level of success and have assumed their level of responsibility because of certain distinctive competencies of which they may or may not be fully aware.

An appreciative approach to organizational coaching requires basic and mutual respect for and appreciation of a client's distinctive experiences and resources. As peers, a client and an organizational coach share similar expertise. Either of these participants in the organizational coaching process could serve in the role of coach and either could receive assistance from the other. While counselors and clients, or consultants and clients, never switch roles in the middle of counseling or a consulting process, this certainly could (and occasionally does) occur during an organizational coaching session. Colleagues benefit most from this process if they are given the opportunity to serve in both roles. Several studies have also found that executives who received coaching in turn embrace becoming coaches and mentors themselves to a higher extent and with greater success than other colleagues.

Conclusions

In the excitement and even glamour of new managerial techniques and strategies for motivating employees, of team building and conflict-management, of personal and interpersonal growth, one thing remains constant: men and women in an organization go to meet with and supervise subordinates, cooperate with colleagues, and influence superiors and customers on Monday morning. What happens in these daily meetings and informal encounters is crucial and central to the effective operations of any organization.

There is only one credible source for those who seek coaching—other men and women who have also faced organizational challenges first-hand.

This is, if you will, the true bottom line of contemporary organizations. Organizational coaching that is offered from an appreciative perspective provides one of the most powerful methodologies yet conceived for actual improvement in the daily practices of a manager, senior executive or technical specialist. Behavioral, Decisional and Aspirational coaching offer concrete assistance to productive and harried members of organizations. In whatever ways these coaching processes are further developed and modified to meet local needs and resources, they can and perhaps must be a central component of any program that seeks to support, improve and leverage the functioning of women and men in an organization as they face the complex, unpredictable and turbulent challenges of our times—the gaggle of black swans flying in circles around us. These hard working team members need and deserve the appreciative mixture of challenge and support that masterful organizational coaching can provide.

The internal and external professional coaches who take responsibility for relentlessly and passionately continuing to hone their craft earn the privilege of partnering and continuing to grow together with some of the most productive, admirable and inspiring people – their organizational clients.

Organizational Coaching Resources

Coaching Resource 1: The Forms of an Appreciative Approach to Coaching

This handout was developed to summarize the essential "basic" elements of an appreciative approach to coaching and is based on concepts offered by David Cooperrider. By seeking to integrate these elements into organizational coaching sessions, deeper levels of connection, exploration, and discovery can emerge.

This document might serve as a reminder to a coach when preparing for a coaching session—especially if this session might surface deficits of the leader or concern ways in which the coaching client has failed to meet certain deadlines or agreements set in earlier coaching sessions. It might also most usefully be handed out at a session that orients prospective clients and organizational sponsors to the appreciative model of Behavioral coaching.

The Forms of an Appreciative Approach to Coaching

Understanding

- Appreciating the context within which another person is operating *("walking in their shoes")*

- Seeking deeper levels of meaning in the messages given by other person *(what we focus on becomes our reality)*

- Finding compassion for, but not merging with, another's problems or identity

Valuing Another Point of View

- Looking at the world from the perspective of another person *(valuing differences)*

- Providing articulate admiration *(appraising worth from an outside point of reference)*

- Identifying the nature and power of alternative narratives *(the language we use to create our reality)*

Recognizing Contributions

- Acknowledging the distinctive, unacknowledged impact of another person

- Identifying and celebrating past efforts and achievement before undertaking new challenges *(we should bring along the best of the past when journeying into the future)*

- Establishing an ongoing mutuality of respect, including rituals of recognition and respect

Vision: A Compelling Image of the Future

- Investing oneself with a compelling sense of hope/optimism *(reality is created in the moment and there are multiple realities)*

- Balancing a concern for "what is" (reality) with attention to "what could be" (ideal)

- Identifying ways all parts of system can contribute to a compelling future

Recognizing Distinctive Strengths and Competencies

- Focusing on strengths rather than deficits *(we are more likely to change when we have been appreciated than when we have been criticized and told to change)*

- Focusing on lessons to be learned from mistakes and, in particular, the elements of competency and success within the mistake *(success-orientation versus failure avoidance)*

Uncovering Distinctive Strengths and Competencies

- Discover obscure strengths through the encouragement of feedback that focuses on moments of competency and success

- Realize potential and latent strengths through the provision of safe times and places for exploration, experimentation and learning *(sanctuaries)*

Recognizing the Value of Cooperation

- Integrating oneself through an appreciative culture

- Recognizing and uncovering the strengths and competencies of another as they seek to appreciate our distinctive strengths and competencies *(strategic advantages of cooperation and mutuality)*

Constructing Provocative Propositions

- A statement bridging the best of "what is" with a speculation or intuition of "what might be"

- Stretch the realm of the status quo, challenge assumptions or routines and suggest real/desired possibilities

Coaching Resource 2: Freeing and Binding Communication

We influence other people through our responses to them. If those responses are open and genuinely helpful, they can have the effect of freeing the other person to become more autonomous and self-directed. If, on the other hand, our responses diminish the other person's sense of autonomy by being closed and directive, we "bind" the other person, decrease his or her freedom and limit personal growth. The following exercise allows an organizational coach to examine the consequences of various responses and to explore her own most commonly used freeing and binding behaviors.

We are presenting this as a group exercise; however, it is evidently highly adaptable to a one-on-one coaching situation.

1. The coach either gives each participant a copy of "Freeing and Binding: The Interpersonal Effect of Various Responses" and asks them to read it over; or delivers a short lecture based on the handout.

2. Copies of "An Exercise on Freeing and Binding" are then distributed, and the participants work through the *First* Section either on their own or in small groups.

3. After each of the responses has been discussed, the participants complete Section *Two* of the exercise, which they may then share with each other in small groups.

Variations

1. A role play of an interview may be designed to demonstrate the concept of freeing and binding responses.

2. The twenty items in Section One of the exercise could be discussed by the entire group.

3. The participants could be asked to make up their own list of freeing and binding responses.

4. The participants could be asked in small groups to give each other feedback on the freeing and binding behaviors each has demonstrated during the workshop.

When Coaching One-on-One

1. The coach and client will reconstruct problematic or successful exchanges or conversations.

2. The coach and client will evaluate whether freeing or binding behaviors were used (potentially making use of the Freeing and Binding checklist as a guideline).

3. With the coach's assistance, the client will assess the impact of this freeing or binding behavior.

4. With the coach's assistance, the client will identify lessons to be learned from this analysis.

Freeing and Binding:
The Interpersonal Effect of Various Responses

I. Freeing Effects: Increase the other person's autonomy and creates a sense of equality.

Active attentive Listening: Responsive listening, not just silence.

Paraphrasing: Testing to insure that the message you got was the one that was sent.

Perception check: Showing your desire to relate to and understand the other person's inner state by showing your acceptance of his or her feelings.

Seeking information: Helping you understand the other person.

Questions: Directly relevant to what the other person has said.

Offering information: Relevant to the other person's concerns, that he or she may or may not use.

Offering new alternatives   As hypotheses to be tested.

II. Binding Effects: diminishes the other person's autonomy

Changing the subject:	Avoids the other person's concerns and feelings.
Interpreting the other person's behavior:	You do that because your mother always. . . ." Binds the other person to the past or may be seen as an attempt to get him or her to change.
Advice and persuasion:	"What you should do is. . . !"
Denying the other person's feelings:	"You don't really mean that!" "You don't feel that way."
Generalizations	"Everybody has problems like that."
Approval on personal grounds:	Praising the other for thinking, feeling, or acting in ways that you approve.
Disapproval on personal grounds:	Blaming or censuring the other person for thinking, acting, and feeling in waysyou do not approve.
Commands, orders:	Telling the other person what to do.

NOTE: The effect of any response depends upon the degree of trust in the relationship. The less trust, the less freeing effect from any response. The more trust, the less binding effect from any response.

An Exercise on Freeing and Binding

I. Which of the following behaviors bind the other person by controlling or manipulating his or her behavior?

1. Listening attentively.
2. Saying, "Do you really mean that?"
3. Saying, "That's a good thought."
4. Nodding in agreement.
5. Asking, "What do you think?"
6. Saying, "Everyone has problems like that."
7. Paraphrasing what someone has just said.
8. Asking, "Do you want to comment on this?"
9. Expressing vigorous agreement.
10. Saying, "I get the feeling that. . . ."
11. Changing the subject when someone is upset.
12. Saying, "You mean you would actually do that?"
13. Looking expectantly toward the quiet member.
14. Saying, "What you should do is. . . ."
15. Speaking at length.
16. Asking, "What should I do?"
17. Not participating in the discussion.
18. Shifting the topic of conversation to yourself.
19. Saying, "Tell me more about that."
20. Saying, "I don't understand why you felt that way."

II. List in one column several characteristic responses of your own that you consider to be freeing. In another column list several responses, phrases and expressions that you characteristically use which you feel are binding.

Coaching Resource 3: The Nature of Coaching Problems

Problems are complex issues that can be addressed from a variety of different perspectives. Problems usually require multiple strategies when being confronted. Furthermore, the level of success in confronting a problem is not easily accessed. An appreciative approach in organizational coaching is particularly appropriate given that most clients are facing problems not puzzles or mysteries.

This **handout** enables a coach and client to better understand the nature of the problem they are facing – once it is acknowledged that the issue being faced is something more than a readily solved puzzle.

An Organizational Coaching Challenge: The Nature of Problems and Dilemmas

Types of Problems

Complicated Problems

Issues that involve many factors and have multiple causes that operate essentially independent of one another

Example: Identify inaccuracies in a preliminary corporate financial statement; select test-market for new product

Appropriate Coaching Strategies: Reflective Coaching

Complex Problems

Interwoven issues whose causality chains are not easily disentangled.

Example: Reduce pollution in a production plant; increase productivity on assembly line

Appropriate Coaching Strategies: Reflective Coaching /Advocacy-Inviting-Inquiry

Cyclical Problems

Complex, multi-tiered issues that periodically reappear and never seem to get resolved.

Examples: Allocate assets in a savings portfolio, make adjustments in strategic plan based on economic cycles; balance corporate expansion against cost-savings.

Appropriate Coaching Strategy: Polarity Management

Types of Dilemmas

Polarities

Issues that are based on two or more equally valid but conflicting goals, such that the successful achievement of one goal reduces the chances that the other goal(s) can be fully achieved.

Example: Work-based accomplishments versus quality of family life; collaboration versus competition among peers

Appropriate Coaching Strategy: Paradox/Polarity Management

Nested Dilemmas

Multiple issues, one or more of which are embedded in another issue.

Example: Improving job performance through educational and training programs that build on existing skills and interests of current employees

Appropriate Coaching Strategy: Reflective Coaching

Nested Polarities

Multiple issues that represent conflicting goals and priorities (Polarities)). In each case, one or more of the issues are embedded in another issue (Nested Polarities).

Examples: *Position One*: (1) Globalize the company, (2) develop global talent, (3) require high job mobility
Position Two: (1) Empower local markets, (2) differing legal-political conditions, (3) local innovation.

Appropriate Coaching Strategies: Reflective Coaching and Polarity Management

Coaching Resource 4: Whose Problem is it?

The Ownership of Coaching Issues

We will examine the barriers to masterful coaching relationships that exist when ownership for the problems of the client inappropriately shift from the client to the coach in a manner that is usually unacknowledged.

Managing the Monkey

To solve a problem, someone must take responsibility for it. If the problem is particularly difficult to understand or solve, then no one may want to assume responsibility.

The Monkey is ignored. Difficult problems are often ignored, for to acknowledge that the problem exists suggests that someone must solve it.

The Monkey leaps up... or down: At other times, difficult problems are directed upward in the organization, each employee looking to a boss for the answer. Harry Truman placed a sign on his desk stating that "the buck stops here." He recognized that difficult and (sometimes) seemingly irresolvable problems were often bumped up in the federal government until they reached the president's office. The president had nowhere to send these problems and hence had to solve them himself

Sometimes the ownership of problems moves down in an organization. Administrators shift blame for a problem from themselves to their subordinates, defining the problem as one of poor work habits or lack of motivation. Those at the bottom of the hierarchy are forced to work harder and smarter, precisely because no one higher up in the organization has taken responsibility for the broader problem.

The Monkey goes external: Managers or supervisors who are faced with a difficult problem may be tempted to bring in an advisor, consultant or organizational coach in order to shift responsibility to this person. This shifting of responsibility usually is not conscious on the part of the person requesting advice or consultation. However, the manager or supervisor may leave the meeting with an advisor, consultant or coach feeling enormous relief. A burden has been lifted off the manager's shoulders and placed on the shoulders of some-one else. We propose that this shift in responsibility is a shift in problem ownership. The monkey often leaps from the shoulder of a client to the shoulder of her coach. A client enters a coaching session with the monkey on her shoulder and leaves with the monkey sitting on the shoulder of her coach.

How do you know when a monkey is present? It's not hard to tell when a monkey is present. Most of the time, when we are asked for advice from a member of our family, a friend or a colleague, it's clear that this person has a monkey on their shoulder. People in our society typically do not ask for help unless they have a monkey, for we value self-sufficiency and competence. While some people create *false monkeys* in order to get the attention of other people, most would rather not admit they have a monkey that won't depart.

More concretely, we know that a monkey exists whenever another person tells us one or more of three things:

- *Things aren't what I would like them to be* [recognition that a problem exists].

- *I want to do something about this situation* [assumes some responsibility for problem and is motivated to seek solution to problem]

- *I don't know what to do about this situation* [lack of clarity about nature of problem and/or lack of an adequate solution]

When someone makes one or more of these three statements to us (in whatever words are appropriate) then we know that a monkey is sitting on that person's shoulder.

How do you know when the monkey lands on your shoulder? This is also rather easy to detect. You will know the monkey is beginning to move to your shoulder:

- The moment you *focus more on the problem than on the person who is telling you about the problem* [you begin to lose track of what the person is saying, having begun to think about the problem and its solution].

- The moment you begin to *offer solutions to the problem while the person is still talking about the problem* [you are usually not testing to see if the person has a clear idea about the nature of the problem or if she has identified her own solution to this problem].

- The moment you begin to *worry about your own ability to solve the problem* [rather than focusing on the other person's ability to solve the problem].

Sometimes you are not aware that you have taken on the monkey until after the coaching session has concluded. You know that you have the monkey on your shoulder if you:

- Continue to *worry about the problem* long after the session is completed.

- Continue to *worry about your ability to solve the problem* long after the session is completed.

- *Expect your client to check with you* about the problem and about progress toward resolution of the problem. Your colleague may seek to gain your approval or permission regarding a certain action. You may grow resentful if you are left out of this process, even though it is not really your problem.

- *Have responsibility for next step* and realize that nothing is likely to happen unless you take some action and follow-up on any solutions generated regarding the problem.

- *Habitually feel ecstatic about client successes and defected by their misstep.* Ask yourself, who owns the client's results?

If any of these conditions exist during or after work with a client, then the monkey probably can be found sitting quite securely (and heavily) on the shoulder of her organizational coach.

What's wrong with having a monkey on your shoulder? There is nothing inherently wrong with monkeys in moderation. We accept a bit of a monkey on our shoulders whenever we offer help and support to a colleague for a problem that we have just helped identify. We assist our elderly parent as they prepare for an upcoming operation. We help our child prepare for a play at their school. We take over temporarily for a colleague when she is ill or overworked. Most of the time, however, it is inappropriate to take ownership for a problem that is not ours. It is particularly inappropriate to take ownership away from a colleague when they are seeking our assistance as an organizational coach.

- When we allow a monkey to leap to our shoulder, we have unduly and inappropriately burdened ourselves with someone else's problem (and reduced our capacity to address our own problems).

- Even more importantly, we have eliminated the opportunity for this other person to learn how to solve this problem (or a similar problem) in the future. We build client dependency rather than client independence. We exhibit little appreciation for our client's own strengths.

- We also increase the chances that our client in the future will once again attempt to move a monkey from her shoulder to our own.

- The key is to avoid the temptation of "owning" too much of either the success or the missteps of the project, making sure that all experiences become great sources of learning for the client.

Coaching Resource 5: Ensuring Understanding

Effective Listening

Effective communication in a coaching session involves the engagement of the coach and client in active listening. This is particularly the case with regard to the role played by the coach. There will be times when a coach will want to be sure that he has been understood, and that his client knows that she has been understood. In such cases, two basic communication skills, paraphrase and perception check, can express that sense of understanding. They can be both usefully role-modeled and explicitly reviewed during coaching sessions, so that the client may acquire the skills for their communication needs in the organization.

Paraphrasing

Tell people your phone number and they will usually repeat it to make sure they heard it correctly. However, if someone makes a complicated statement, most people will express agreement or disagreement without trying to ensure that they are responding to what you said.

How does a coach know that the leader's remark means the same to her as it does to him? Of course, he can get the other person to clarify the remark by asking, "What do you mean?" or by saying "I don't understand." However, after the other person has elaborated, the coach still faces the same question: "Am I understanding this idea as she intended it to be understood?" A feeling of certainty is no evidence that in fact understanding has taken place.

If coaches state in their own words what a client's remark conveys to them, their client can begin to determine whether her message is coming through as intended. Then, if there appears to have been a misunderstanding, the coach and client can directly address that specific problem. To paraphrase, therefore, is to show a client what her idea or suggestion means to us. It is a way of revealing an understanding of our colleague's comment in order to test that understanding. Paraphrasing has additional benefits.

- It lets our colleague know that we are interested in her; it is clear evidence that we want to understand what she has said.

- If we can satisfy our colleague that we really do understand the message, our colleague will be more willing to attempt to understand what we have to say as their coach.

- It can move the comprehension of the conversation along for both parties by highlighting the essence of what is being said.

The process of testing for understanding through the use of paraphrasing can take several different forms. To illustrate this point, we will begin with a simple statement: "Bill is certainly not doing what I expected him to do on this project."

o The paraphrase can be a restatement by the recipient in her own words: "I heard you say that you are disappointed with the quality of Bill's work on this project. Is this accurate?"

o A second approach is based on the use of past experiences or hypothetical situations. The recipient tests her understanding by offering an example: "Would Bill's delay in getting the report to you be an example of what you mean when you say that Bill isn't doing what you expected?"

o A third approach involves a somewhat provocative testing of limits: "Does this mean that you are ready to fire Bill from this project?" This third approach can be particularly clarifying for someone being coached, as they test the limits of their own thoughts and feelings. It also requires considerable trust between the coach and client, given that the coach is pushing the limit and must not seek to use this form of paraphrasing to indirectly offer advice or promote a specific agenda.

o The fourth approach can also be quite provocative and limit testing. It involves the use of negative examples: "Does this mean that Bill would be doing what you expected if he never complained or stirred things up?" Like the third, this fourth approach requires trust between the coach and client if it is to be constructive.

Perception Check

A paraphrase is only a check on the literal content of what the other person has said. If I paraphrase something you have said, I am attempting to understand the literal intended meaning of what you are trying to say to me. But many messages have meaning at both a *literal*, a *feeling* and a contextuallevel; in fact, in many cases, the literal content will be quite clear, while the feeling behind the content will be less clear but all the more important. A perception check (sometimes called paraphrasing-for-feeling) is a way of being sure that understanding has taken place at that emotional level.

The emotional content of most messages will be communicated non-verbally and, often, unconsciously, which makes that content particularly difficult to understand and describe.

- Just as a paraphrase puts into someone's own words their understanding of what the other has meant, a perception check can expresses their understanding of what the other person is feeling at the moment: "You seem to be feeling angry right now. Am I correct?"

- While a paraphrase may reveal a misunderstanding at the literal level ("No, that's not quite what I meant. What I intended to say was . . . ."), a perception check may reveal a similar misunderstanding at the emotional level ("No, I'm not really feeling angry right now, but I am a little confused.")

- Alternatively, the perception check can focus on how the client felt at some time in the past: "I would guess that when she did that you felt angry." The purported feeling, offered by the coach as a personal perception, with no strings attached, can – even if rejected - serve as a conversation opener and yield valuable additional insight into how the client processes similar events.

When used independently or together, paraphrasing and perception checking can ensure that the coach has fully understood the presenting concerns of the other person.

Coaching Resource 6: The Coaching Style Inventory

Each of us, obviously, approaches the process of coaching in our own way, using our own unique experiences and strengths. It is useful, therefore, to spend some time reflecting on our preferred style of coaching and even to share something about our style with those we are coaching. The Coaching Style Inventory invites us to respond to three brief case studies—indicating the way in which we are likely to respond in each case by rating and ranking four alternative responses on a seven point scale.

We have provided a **fact sheet, an instruction sheet, the inventory, a score sheet and a brief description** of the four coaching styles. Each of the styles relates to one of the three domains of coaching that we have emphasized throughout this book. The domain of information is prominent for those who prefer what we call a Golden Yellow style of coaching, while the domain of intentions is prominent for those who prefer an Azure Blue style of coaching. The third style of coaching (Ruby Red) is associated with the domain of ideas, whereas the fourth style (Rainbow) is associated with movement through all three domains.

Coaching Style Inventory

Coaching Style Inventory
Score Key

Overview:

This inventory consists of three questions that address your preferred way of working with other people in a Coaching relationship. Each question is accompanied by a set of responses that are in some instances quite characteristic of the answer you would probably give to the question and in other instances quite uncharacteristic of the answer you would give. You are to indicate the extent to which each of the alternative answers—when compared to the other three answers—is characteristic of your typical response. There are no answers that are right or wrong. The purpose of this inventory is to provide you with information about yourself as a coach, based on your own self-reflection. The information that this inventory provides is no better or worse than the care and honesty you provide in rating the answers to each question.

Instructions:

First, read the question and then the set of alternative answers to this question. The alternatives have been designated a, b, c, and/or d.

Next, select the answer from the alternatives which is *most* characteristic of you and place the latter which corresponds to that item on the scale provided (see the example below) at the point on the scale which most accurately reflects how characteristic that answer is of *you*.

Then select the alternative answer that is *least* characteristic of you and place the corresponding letter at the appropriate point on the scale.

Once you have found the *most* and *least* characteristic answer, enter the corresponding letters of the remaining alternatives within this range according to how characteristic each of these is of you. DO NOT place more than one letter per space.

For example, you might be given the following question:

How do you feel when you take an inventory like this?

    a.   Like a million dollars

    b.   Burdened

    c.   Afraid

    d.   Curious

If <u>curious</u> is the most characteristic answer for you, while <u>like a million dollars</u> is least characteristic, and <u>afraid</u> is next most characteristic, with <u>burdened</u> being slightly more characteristic than "like a million dollars," then your responses might be as follows:

Very
Uncharacteristic 1:__a__ 2:__b__ 3:_____ 4:_____ 5:_____ 6:__c__ 7:__d__ Very Characteristic

Once you have completed the first question, turn to the next question and proceed in this manner until you have responded to all three questions. Work rapidly and don't dwell on any one question. You are likely to find parts of some answers highly characteristic of you and other parts uncharacteristic—go with your immediate reaction and don't be too concerned about consistency or precision in your answers.

CASE NUMBER ONE

When you think about yourself as a coach in an organizational setting, what stands out as the typical way in which you operate? Obviously, your role as coach will shift from person to person—but what is most characteristic about the way in which you anticipate working with people who will look to you as a coach? What do people who look to you as a coach in the organization expect of you?

A. I am a strong, dependable coach. I tend to supply direction and am energetic about helping my coaching clients seize on an opportunity and make things happen. My coaching colleague is likely to see me as full of ambition and initiative.

B. I tend to be very pleasant when I am engaged in a Coaching relationship. My coaching clients can count on me to lend a helping hand. I tend to be a feeling person who is quick to respond to the needs that a coaching colleague expresses. My coaching colleague is likely to see me as trustworthy and full of compassion and interpersonal understanding.

C. I will work very hard as a coach. I will be actively engaged in the Coaching relationship, offering suggestions, making sure that my coaching colleague is engaged in the process. Coaching colleagues can count on me to provide energy in the Coaching relationship. At times I will even confront my coaching colleague to ensure that all views are being heard and considered by my coaching colleague. My coaching clients are likely to see me as engaged, interpersonally oriented and enthusiastic.

D. I will be very thoughtful when engaged in a Coaching relationship. I study things carefully before acting or providing advice. I am a very practical person who doesn't just leap into a discussion. My coaching colleagues will be able to count on me to be fair and to stand by what I believe is right. My coaching clients are likely to see me as reserved (even quiet), as practical, and as realistic.

Very
Uncharacteristic

Very
Characteristic

I:_____ 2:_____ 3:_____ 4:_____ 5:_____ 6:_____ 7:_____

CASE NUMBER TWO

Reflect back on a relationship with someone you have worked with as an informal coach or experienced co-worker in an organization that has been particularly gratifying. This is someone with whom you thoroughly enjoyed working. What are/were the characteristics of this relationship that you found most gratifying?

A. This person is a strong leader—someone I greatly admire. I have great faith in this person's competency and their intentions. We have/had a warm and personal working relationship. I has been a great honor for me to work with this person as their coach or experienced co-worker.

B. This person has greatly admired my own leadership and abilities. This person has readily followed my directions and has exhibited great loyalty in working with me. I can fully trust this person to get work done or make interpersonal changes that I have suggested.

C. Neither of us in this relationship is either the leader or follower. We worked together, but my co-worker was free to pursue his or her own independent interests. We respect differences in the ways we work with one another and interact with other people.

D. The two of us worked closely together. At times we struggled with one another, but we have always been able to resolve our conflicts and differences of opinion. We respect one another and are willing to be open about ideas, beliefs, and feelings.

Very
Uncharacteristic

Very
Characteristic

I:_____ 2:_____ 3:_____ 4:_____ 5:_____ 6:_____ 7:_____

CASE NUMBER THREE

Reflect back on a recent coaching or co-worker experience in which you were particularly effective. You were very skillful and were able to strongly influence your coaching colleague or co-worker in terms of a decision he or she made or action he or she took inan organization. What were the characteristics of the situation in which you found yourself that helped to make you effective and successful as an informal coach or experienced co-worker.

A. This was a wonderful opportunity for me. My coaching client or co-worker asked me to provide a clear directive and wished to report back when he or she had completed the specific task upon which we both agreed. I encouraged my coaching client or co-worker to work in a logical and systematic manner without a lot of interference

B. This was a situation that called for collaboration—a real joint effort between myself and my coaching client or co-worker. We each identified our distinctive strengths and potential sources of contribution, then worked together to achieve the goal. There were disagreements and even some arguments, but we found a way to get past the differences to be successful as cooperative co-workers.

C. The situation was such that my coaching client/co-worker was encouraged to turn to me for guidance. I was given adequate information by my coaching colleague/co-worker to guide me in making appropriate and accurate suggestions. I helped my coaching colleague/co-worker identify a clear sense of mission and purpose.

D. The situation was such that I was able to be direct and of immediate assistance to my coaching client/co-worker. My coaching client/co-worker wanted my help and I had sufficient support and resources to be of benefit to my coaching colleague/co-worker. My coaching colleague/co-worker trusted me. Furthermore, I was able to directly witness how my coaching colleague/co-worker benefited from what I was able to do for and with them.

Very
Uncharacteristic

Very
Characteristic

I:_____ 2:_____ 3:_____ 4:_____ 5:_____ 6:_____ 7:_____

Coaching Style Inventory
-Scoring Key-

Instructions: Enter the score assigned by rater for each of the following responses

Case #	Ruby Red	Azure Blue	Golden Yellow	Rainbow
1.	A=	B=	D=	C=
2.	B=	A=	C=	D=
3.	C=	D=	A=	B=
Total:				

COACHING STYLE INVENTORY

The Ruby Red Coach

This person is oriented toward helping her coaching client achieve specific, articulated goals. There is a strong emphasis in her coaching relationships on making decisions and getting the job done. This coach is likely to give considerable advice and is interested in monitoring her coaching client's tangible achievements. This person often gains credibility from her coaching client based on past experiences and accomplishments.

The Azure Blue Coach

This person is oriented toward providing caring and consistent support of his coaching client. There is a strong emphasis in his coaching relationships on inspiration and encouragement. This coach is likely to offer considerable assurance is interested in helping his coaching client identify safe and supportive environments in which to learn, take risks and realize personal dreams. This person often gains credibility from his coaching client based on careful and empathetic listening.

The Golden Yellow Coach

This person is oriented toward providing accurate information and thoughtful analysis to his coaching client. There is a strong emphasis in his coaching relationships on rational problem analysis and realism. This coach is likely to work very carefully, systematically and deliberatively with his coaching client. This person often gains credibility from his coaching client based on technical expertise and reasonableness.

The Rainbow Coach

This person is oriented toward providing a dynamic and highly interactive coaching relationship with her coaching client. There is a strong emphasis in her coaching relationship on open and collaborative interactions. This coach is likely to be confrontational at times with her coaching client, as well as being supportive, thoughtful or even assertive when appropriate. This person often gains credibility from her coaching client based on flexibility and a diverse organizational background.

Coaching Resource 7: Listening Habits

Primary Strategy: Behavioral Coaching
Primary Model: Engagement Coaching

This coaching resource introduces several questions that coaching clients (and coaches themselves!) can ask themselves when assessing their own listening habits. In focusing on interpersonal engagements the coach and client can begin by responding to the following questions.

How good a listener are you?

Question One: "During a meeting, do you take extensive notes?" Your motto is, 'there is no substitute for documentation.' Besides, it gives you something to do during boring meetings, helps you concentrate… and makes you appear interested." Note taking may be necessary, but it can also be a distraction to the speaker. It is possible to have a written record of a meeting without mentally comprehending what was said. If I am an obsessive note- taker, who focuses more on creating a correct record than picking up on the dynamics in the room, then I might learn to write less and listen more. A coach or a leader who is inclined to take many notes should be particularly alert to certain words that may trigger a reaction in him because they are easily overheard or dismissed in the writing process.

Some note-taking can also free the mind, on the other hand. If the coach has a "brilliant idea" while listening, it may be best to download it onto paper, and continue remaining engaged with the client, without worrying about losing that excellent train of thought..

Question Two: "Do you finish sentences for the person speaking to you?" Predicting or anticipating is caused by impatience and lack of sensitivity. Under the guise of understanding what the speaker is discussing, we "help them along." Interrupting, no matter what the intention, has the appearance of rudeness. Focus on listening, not talking.

Question Three: "To save time, do you hold a meeting while you are waiting for a cell phone call?" When the call comes through, it will be a distraction. In this type of environment, neither party can hold a quality interaction. If the speaker wants to talk about anything requiring your full attention, he or she will wait or find another listener. The leader who appears harried, no matter how much she wants to have positive impact on her staff, will isolate herself if she does not fight distractions. (Mobile phone protocol is a bone of severe contention in every contemporary team and needs to be decided by consensus, because it will determine the culture of the group.)

Question Four: "When a co-worker surprises you with a seemingly devastating problem, do you lose your cool?" Once you make the atmosphere emotional, listening becomes more difficult. Concentrating on delicate issues like employee under-performance or dissatisfaction is impossible when you are in the middle of expressing outrage. Be particularly aware of certain words that may trigger a reaction in you.

Question Five: "At a business presentation, if the subject is momentarily uninteresting or does not exactly pertain to you, will you use the time more constructively by secretly doing paperwork? Are you inclined to multi-task when the presentation is being made during a telephone conference call?" In good listening, the receiver assumes the role of staying interested. There is always something to be learned if you are open to it. Many meetings last longer than they need to because some of the potential participants are (temporarily) disengaged and therefore don't catch the opportunities when they can make a contribution for the benefit of the whole.

Coaching Resource 8: Active Listening

Primary Strategy: Behavioral Coaching
Primary Model: Engagement Coaching

In response to the questions posed in Coaching Resource Seven, a coaching-oriented leader might wish to reflect on his active listening skills and strategies. These skills and strategies (as the list below illustrates) is much more than just trying to "pay attention" to the speaker or, on occasion, offering a few words of encouragement. An active listener is someone who shares responsibility with the speaker regarding the clarity and mutual understanding of what the speaker is trying to convey. It is not enough for an active listener to be present when someone is trying to convey something, active listening requires the full engagement of both parties in the sending and receiving process. The following statements (actually we might call them "dictums") regarding active listening can prove quite helpful when reflecting on and engaging in active listening.

1. **Stop talking:** You can't listen while you're talking.

2. **One conversation (and task) at a time:** Don't try to engage yourself in two conversations or activities at once. You may *hear* two people at a time, but you can't effectively *listen* and *respond* to each.

3. **Seek out the speaker's perspective:** Put yourself in his or her place so you can better see where the speaker is going.

4. **Ask questions:** When you don't understand or when you need further elaboration or clarification, ask questions.

5. **Don't interrupt:** Give the speaker time to say what s/he has to say. *Then and not before,* ask your questions and/or take issue with the speaker has said.

6. **Show interest:** Look at the speaker's face, eyes, mouth, and hands. This effort will help the speaker be more effective and enable you to better concentrate.

7. **Concentrate on what's being said:** Actively focus your attention on the speaker's thoughts and feelings. Distinguish between irrelevant or insignificant data not central to the speaker's main thrust.

8. **Don't jump to conclusions:** Be fair to the speaker. By your swift climbing up the ladder of inference and reaching premature conclusion, you may be off base, and the speaker may not have the opportunity to correct your erroneous conclusion.

9. **Control your emotions and body language:** Take responsibility for not losing emotional control as a reaction to what the speaker says. Often your emotional reaction, such as anger, will prevent you from understanding the speaker's *true message.*

10. **React to ideas, not the speaker:** Don't allow gut reactions to the speaker to influence your interpretation of what s/he says. The speaker's ideas may be good even if you don't like the manner in which they are being presented.

11. **Listen for what is *not* being said:** Sometimes you can learn as much by determining what the other person leaves out or avoids as you can by listening to what is actually said.

12. **Share the responsibility for communications:** Only a part of the responsibility for ensuring the message is clearly communicated rests with the speaker—the other part depends on the listener. Ask questions for clarification.

13. **Organize the speaker's main thoughts and supporting ideas as the speaker proceeds:** Don't wait for the conclusion. Keep summarizing mentally, then articulate the essence and subject it to verification.

14. **Evaluate facts and evidence:** As you listen, identify the significant facts and evidence and see how they relate to the point the speaker is trying to make.

Some people find that active listening is very difficult. They want to say something and are waiting for a lull in the conversation. They are (apparently) way ahead of the speaker in their thought processes and want to leap to the conclusion. Several techniques have been found to be useful for those who struggle with the discipline of active listening. The first tool is quite obvious, yet it seems to fly in the face of a recommendation made earlier in this section (regarding note taking). While it is preferred that an active listener concentrate on the speaker and not take notes, anyone who finds it difficult to be active listener might decide that he should take notes and in this way focus on what the speaker is saying, rather than on what he, the note-taker, wants to say. If privately taken, these notes can even contain some of the active listener's own thoughts and reactions. Rather than interrupting the speaker, the listener records his own reactions in his notes. Notes can also be public—that is to say the listener can record them on a flip chart or on computer screens that are seen by both the speaker and listener. This public note-taking is particularly aligned with the twelfth (shared responsibility) and thirteenth (organize while the speaker proceeds) dictums listed above.

A second, even more radical, tool—often called "shadowing" or "echoing"—is used by actors as they prepare for a new play. When a person is speaking, the active listener silently repeats the words just spoken in his own head. In this way, the speaker remains focused on the speaker. He is distracted from his own thoughts and is less likely to interrupt. While this second tool tends to be closely aligned with many of the dictums listed above—particularly the seventh (concentrating on what's being said) and eight (not jumping to conclusions) dictums, it does make it more difficult to organize the speaker's thoughts (dictum thirteen) or to evaluate facts and evidence (dictum fourteen).

Regardless of the tool or set of techniques we use to become and remain active listeners, we must recognize that it is a skill-set and an attitude that is not easily acquired and that is readily lost in the midst of a conversation where there is a lot at stake and we feel time-constrained. t. Active listening is also frequently lost when the speaker is conveying something about which we believe we have the most expertise or experience, or something about which we don't believe the speaker is knowledgeable. Perhaps the most difficult interpersonal engagement (where active listening is readily lost) concerns biases: we believe the speaker approaches a topic with a definite bias and it is a bias with which we don't agree. Get out the note pad or begin echoing—and start listening! In the long run, you will find that the investment of time and attention pays off handsomely in avoiding confusion and misdirection.

Coaching Resource 9: Empathic Listening

Primary Strategy: Behavioral Coaching
Primary Model: Engagement Coaching

While active listening (Coaching Resource Eight) is critical to effective interpersonal engagements, there is also the need for a second skill-set and attitude. Empathy is the process of grasping or understanding the other person's point of view—putting oneself in the other person's shoes or viewing a situation or idea through his or her "filter." It is one of the most valuable, powerful characteristics one can develop to strengthen interpersonal engagements, communications and the ability to get things done through people—and it is directly aligned with the appreciative perspective we are emphasizing in this book. Everyone who has any association with anyone, which includes all of us, practices empathy to some degree, but our propensity varies by personality type and training (yes, this is both a natural and a learned skill) so most of us can very profitably extend its us to other areas of our lives and make it an increasingly automatic and more effective habit.

Empathy does not involve voluntary or involuntary acceptance of the other person's viewpoint, but rather the development of an increasingly clear understanding of the way that person is seeing the situation. In some cases it may be confused with *sympathy*, the acceptance and identification with the other person's idea or feeling, but these are two distinctly different processes. Either may be observed in isolation, or they may be (and often are to some degree) in action simultaneously.

There are three definite steps in the practice of empathy. As it becomes a more automatic habit, the three steps flow in a smooth fluid sequence, but it helps to recognize and understand each stage. The three steps are:

1. Recognize that every person in the world has a personal, unique, individual filter through which that person perceives reality. It is made up of certain hereditary factors, education, childhood training, attitudes, prejudices and countless experiences.

2. Embrace this fact as a useful and valid. Be willing to allow the other person the right to be one's own self and to see rea lity in their own way – thus enriching the

idea pool. This doesn't mean you should necessarily like the other person's point of view –just that you do not insist that everyone think exactly as you do and acknowledge that nobody ses the full spectrum of reality. While this is an easily espoused idea, it requires a lot of emotional and mental maturity to implement in the moment.

3. Only to be degree that the first two steps have been taken can one proceed to crawl behind another's filter and see how the world looks from in there. Of course, this can never be done perfectly because we can never completely set aside our own point of view. But the entire process of communication between human being can certainly be strengthened and enriched to the degree that those communicating do grasp or understand the various elements of the filter mechanisms with which they are dealing... first in themselves and then in their dialogue partner.

You will find that as empathy becomes a habit, your ability to relate effectively to other people will substantially increase, the decisions arrived at jointly will be of higher quality and more readily implemented and exhausting friction will be much reduced in the work-place.

Coaching Resource 10: Description of Feelings

Primary Strategy: Behavioral Coaching
Primary Model: Engagement Coaching

When we are working on our own interpersonal engagements—especially those that have been problematic—it is often helpful to explore ways in which we might effective describe our feelings as they relate to this interpersonal engagements. In exploring ways to convey our feelings, it is important to distinguish between the expression of feelings (which usually occurs at the moment of an emotion-filled interaction) and the description of feelings (which usually takes place at a slightly later time, when the two people engaged in the emotion-filled interaction seek to understand what occurred). Most people think of themselves as eminently logical, especially in work situations, often denying (to themselves and others) the emotional coloring of their statements and actions. However, because emotions can never be eliminated from intense interactions, it is critical that colleagues *identify and describe feelings* to a greater extent than acting them out, especially in a professional context, where decisions are often complex, impactful, time-pressed… and therefore stressful.

Any spoken statement can convey feelings. Even a factual report—"It's three o'clock"—can be said so that it expresses anger or disappointment. However, as we all know, it is not just the words that convey the feelings. What determines whether the statement is perceived as a factual report or as a message of anger or disappointment? The key factors are often the speaker's tone, emphasis, gestures, posture and facial expression. Nevertheless verbal statements can be used to communicate feelings—and are particularly important when we are involved in a complex, emotional or critical engagement with another person.

We all have experienced feelings being conveyed by words. We know what it is like to be the recipient of feelings conveyed by people who are: (1) *issuing commands* ("Get out!" "Shut up!"), (2) *asking indirect questions* ("Is it safe to drive this fast?"), (3) *making accusations* ("You only think about yourself!") and (4) *offering judgments* ("You're a wonderful person."

"You're too bossy"). Notice that although each of the examples conveys strong feeling, the statement does not say what the feeling is. In fact, none of the sentences even refers to the speaker or what he or she is feeling.

By contrast, the emotional state of the speaker is precisely the content of some sentences. Such sentences will be called "descriptions of feeling." They convey feeling by naming or identifying what the speaker feels. "I am disappointed." "I am furiously angry!" "I'm afraid of going this fast!" "I feel discouraged."

How do we go about discerning the difference between expression and description of feelings? When are we describing our feelings and when are we conveying feelings without describing them? Trying to verbally describe what you are feeling is a helpful way to become more aware of what it is you do feel. A description of feelings conveys maximum information about what you feel in a way that will also probably be less hurtful than commands, questions, accusations and judgments. Thus, when you want to communicate your feelings more accurately you will be able to do so.

To illustrate and provide a framework for discussing the differences between expression and description of feelings, we offer a few sentences sets that all convey feeling. Any of them could have been spoken by the same person in the same situation. Each sentence, however, illustrates different ways of communicating feelings by words.

1. Let's start with an obvious statement: "Shut up! Not another word out of you." Commands such as these convey strong emotion, but do not name what feeling prompted them. What about the following: "I'm really annoyed by what you just said." She is describing her feelings, rather than just expressing them—though we still don't know what is annoying or why she feels annoyed. The description of feelings, however, at least opens the door, to this further discussion.

2. What if we turn to three statements that seem to be conveying the same feeling: "Can't you see I'm busy? Don't you have eyes?" "I'm beginning to resent your frequent interruptions." and "You have no consideration for anybody else's feelings." The first of these statements (framed as questions) express a strong feeling without naming it. The second statement is a description: the speaker says he feels resentment. The third statement again is expressive but not descriptive. These accusations convey strong negative feelings; however, because the feelings are not named we do not know whether the accusations stemmed from anger, disappointment, hurt or some other feeling.

3. A third pair of statements concerns a different source of feelings: "I feel discouraged because of some things that happened today." and "This has been an awful day." In the first of these statements the speaker says she feels discouraged. While the second statement appears to describe what kind of day it was, it expresses, in fact, the speaker's negative feelings without saying whether she feels depressed, annoyed, lonely, humiliated, or rejected.

4. The fourth pair of statements concern more positive feelings: "You're a wonderful person." And "I really respect your opinions; you're so well read." The first of these statements represents a value judgment. It reveals positive feelings about the other person but does not describe what they are. Does the speaker like the other person? Is it a case of respect, enjoyment, admiration or perhaps love? By contrast, in the second statement, the speaker describes his positive feelings as respect.

5. Similarly, in a third set of statements we again can discern the difference between expression and description of positive feelings: "I feel comfortable and free to be myself when I'm around you." versus "We all feel you are a wonderful person." and "Everybody likes you." The first of these three statements is a clear description of how the speaker feels when with the other person. The second statement is an example of expression, not description. First, the speaker does not speak for himself but hides behind the phrase "We feel..." Second, "You're a wonderful person" is a value-judgment and not the name of a feeling. The third statement does name a feeling (likes), but the speaker attributes it to everybody and does not make clear that the feeling is her own. A description of feeling must contain "I," "me," "my," or "mine" to make clear that the feelings are the speaker's own—are within him or her. Does it seem more affectionate for a person to tell you "I like you" or "Everybody likes you"?

6. The sixth set of statements moves even further into the challenge associated with description rather than just expression of feelings: "If things don't improve here, I will look for a new job." "Did you ever hear of such a lousy place to work?" and "I'm afraid to admit that I need help with my work." The first of these statements conveys negative feelings by talking about the condition of things in this organization but does not describe the speaker's inner state. The second statement is a question that expresses a negative value judgment about the organization. It does not describe what the speaker is feeling. Only in the case of the third statement do we find a clear description of how the speaker feels in relation to his job. The first

two statements are criticisms of the organization that could come from the kind of fear described in the third statement. Negative criticisms and value judgments often sound like expressions of anger. In fact, negative value judgments and accusations often are the result of the speaker's fear, hurt feelings, disappointments or loneliness.

7. A seventh pairing of statements reveals a communication trick that we often play on ourselves and one another: "This is a very poor policy" versus "I feel this is a very poor policy." The first statement is clearly a negative value judgment that conveys negative feelings but does not say what kind they are. What about the second statement? Although the speaker begins by saying "I feel," she does not then name that feeling. Instead the speaker passes a negative value judgment on the exercise. Merely tacking the words "I feel" on the front of a statement does not make it a description of feeling. People often say "I feel" when they mean "I think" or "I believe." For example, "I feel the Yankees will win" or "I feel you don't like me." Many persons who say they are unaware of what they feel or who say they don't have any feelings about something habitually state value judgments without recognizing that this is the way their positive or negative feelings get expressed. The speaker could have said that she felt confused or frustrated or annoyed by the policy. She would then have been describing her feelings without evaluating the policy itself.

Many arguments could be avoided if we were careful to describe our feelings instead of expressing them through value-judgments. For example, if Joe says the policy is poor and Fred says it is good, they may argue about which it "really" is. However, if Joe says he was frustrated by the policy (and why) and Fred says he was interested and stimulated by it, no argument should follow. Each person's feelings are what they are. Of course, discussing what it means that each feels as he does may provide helpful information about each person and about the policy itself.

8. The eight pair of statements concern feelings conveyed in a group setting: "I feel inadequate to contribute anything in this group." and "I am inadequate to contribute anything in this group." In the first statement, the speaker clearly says he feels inadequate. We must be careful in categorizing the second statement. While this sounds much the same as the first statement, it says that the speaker actually *is* inadequate—not that he just feels that way. The speaker has passed a negative value judgment on himself. This subtle difference is introduced because many people confuse feeling and being. A person may *feel* inadequate to contribute in a group and yet make helpful contributions. Likewise, he may *feel* adequate and yet perform very

inadequately. A person may *feel* hopeless about a situation that turns out not to *be* hopeless. One sign of emotional maturity may be that a person does not confuse what he feels subjectively with the objective nature of the situation. Such a person knows that he can perform adequately *in spite of feeling* inadequate to the task. This person does not let feelings keep him from doing as well as possible because he knows the difference between feelings and performance, and that the two do not always match.

9. The ninth set of statements move us further along in understanding the important distinction between expression and description of feelings: "I am a failure—I'll never amount to anything." "My supervisor is awful—he hasn't helped me at all." and "I'm depressed because I did so poorly on that performance review." In the first of these statements, the speaker has evaluated herself a failure. In the second statement, the speaker has blamed her supervisor rather than sharing her feelings. This is another value judgment and not a description of feelings. It is only in the third statement that we hear the speaker say that she feels depressed. The first and second statements illustrate the important difference between passing judgment on oneself and describing one's feelings. Feelings can and do change. To say that I am now depressed does not imply that I will or must always feel the same. However, if I label myself as a failure—if I truly think of myself as a failure—I increase the probability that I will act like a failure. One woman stated this important insight for herself this way: "I have always thought I was a shy person. Many new things I really would have liked to do I avoided—I'd tell myself I was too shy. Now I have discovered that I am not shy although at times I *feel* shy." Many of us avoid trying new things by labeling ourselves. "I'm not artistic." "I'm not creative." "I'm not articulate." "I can't speak in groups." If we could recognize what our feeling is beneath such statements and that it does not need to determine our actions and behavior, maybe we would be more willing to risk doing things we are somewhat fearful of.

10. Finally, we turn again to statements about feelings that are generated in a group setting: "I feel lonely and isolated in my group." "For all the attention anybody pays to what I say I might as well not be in my group." And "I feel that nobody in my group cares whether I'm there or not." In the first statement, the speaker clearly is describing his feelings. He feels lonely and isolated. The second statement conveys negative feelings but does not say whether the speaker feels angry, lonely, disappointed, or hurt. In the third statement the speaker should have said "I believe" instead of "I feel" The last part of the statement really tells what the speaker believes that *other*

people feel about him and not what he feels. The first and third statements relate to each other as follows: "Because I believe that nobody in my group cares whether I am there or not, I feel lonely and isolated."

These examples suggest ways in which the description of feelings can be of great benefit in ensuring a constructive interpersonal engagement, as well as suggesting ways in which we sometimes deceive other people (and ourselves) in seeming to describe feelings, but in fact only expressing them. There is nothing wrong with the expression of feelings. This is part of what it means to be human and to be part of a dynamic interpersonal relationship. However, it is when we describe our feelings that a constructive dialogue can begin regarding the sources of these feelings and the ways in which our relationships with other people, with our job and with our life can be further enhanced. The coach whose own language is "clean" in this regard and who can help her client re-state his position and feelings both more specifically, descriptively and therefore more productively will have a transformative impact on that leader.

Coaching Resource 11: Characteristics of Constructive Feedback

Primary Strategy: Behavioral Coaching
Primary Model: Engagement Coaching

The process of providing another person with constructive feedback regarding their performance is often a compelling challenge for 21st Century leaders. An appreciative approach is particularly important to engender when we are preparing for a feedback-based engagement. This appreciative approach to the giving of feedback should be based on the goal of preserving the dignity, respect and independence of both parties. The following characteristics are particularly important for a coaching-oriented leader to keep in mind when preparing for the delivery of constructive feedback to a colleague:

1. It is *descriptive* rather than evaluative. By describing one's own reactions and interpretations, it leaves the individual free to use the information or not to use it as he sees fit. By avoiding evaluative language, it reduces the need for the individual to respond defensively.

2. It is *specific* rather than general. To be told that one is "dominating" will probably not be as useful as to be told that "in the conversation that just took place you did not appear engage with what others were saying and your repetitive, insistent statements seemed to force us to accept your arguments."

3. It is focused on *behavior* rather than on the person. It is important that we refer to what a person does rather than to what we think or imagine he is. Thus we might say that a person "talked more than anyone else in this meeting" rather than that he is a "loud-mouth!" The former allows for the possibility of change; the latter implies a fixed personality trait.

4. It takes into account the *needs of both the receiver and giver of feedback*. Feedback can be destructive when it serves only our own needs and fails to consider the needs of the person on the receiving end. It should be given to help, not to hurt. We too often give feedback because it makes us feel better or gives us a psychological advantage.

5. It is directed toward *behavior that the receiver can do something about.* Frustration is only increased when a person is reminded of some shortcoming over which he has no control.

6. It is *solicited* rather than imposed. Feedback is most useful when the receiver himself has formulated the kind of question that those observing him can answer or when he actively seeks feedback.

7. It is *well-timed.* In general, feedback is most useful at the earliest opportunity after the given behavior (depending, of course, on the person's readiness to hear it, support available from others, a private setting, and so forth). The reception and use of feedback involves many possible emotional reactions. Excellent feedback presented at an inappropriate time and place may do more harm than good.

8. It involves *sharing of information,* rather than giving advice. By sharing information, we leave a person free to decide for himself, in accordance with his own goals and needs. When we give advice we tell him what to do, and to some degree this takes away his freedom to decide for himself.

9. It involves the *amount of information the receiver can use* rather than the amount we would like to give. To overload a person with feedback is to reduce the possibility that he may be able to use what he receives effectively. When we give more than can be used, we are more often than not satisfying some need of our own rather than helping the other person.

10. It concerns *what is said and done,* or how, not why. The "why" takes us from the observable to the inferred and involves assumptions regarding motive or intent. Telling a person what his motivations or intentions are more often than not tends to alienate the person and contributes to a climate of resentment, suspicion, and distrust; it does not contribute to learning or development. It is dangerous to assume that we know why a person says or does something, or what he "really" means, or what he is "really" trying to accomplish. If we are uncertain of his motives or intent, this uncertainty itself is feedback, however, and should be revealed. If we feel we have to present our assumption of their motivation, we need to present that assumption as the impression they are creating in us.

11. It is *checked to ensure clear communication.* One way of doing this is to have the receiver try to rephrase the feedback he has received to see if it corresponds to what the sender had in mind. No matter what the intent, feedback is often threatening

and thus subject to considerable distortion or misinterpretation in that stressful moment.

12. It is *checked to determine degree of agreement from others.* On the hopefully rare occasions when feedback is given in the presence of other people, both giver and receiver have an opportunity to check with others in the group about the accuracy of the feedback. Is this one person's impression or is it an impression that is shared by others? Such "consensual validation" is of value to both sender and receiver.

13. It is followed by *attention to the consequences of the feedback.* The person who is giving feedback may greatly improve his helping skills by becoming acutely aware of the effects of his feedback. He can also be of continuing help to the recipient of the feedback, thus managing the (often stormy) "wake" her words have left in the recipient.

14. It is an important step toward *authenticity.* Constructive feedback opens the way to a relationship that is built on trust, honesty, and genuine concern. Through such a relationship, we will have achieved one of the most rewarding experiences that man can achieve and will have opened a very important door to personal learning and growth.

Coaching Resource 12: Helpful Statements, not Advice

Primary Strategy: Behavioral Coaching
Primary Model: Engagement Coaching

We usually think of helpfulness as being the giving of good, sound advice to another person. While the advice might be warranted and at times very appropriate, we are usually of greatest help to another person if we offer something other than advice. There are five different kinds of statements that can be helpful to another person. As you will note, the characteristics of these statements relate closely to those we identified in other coaching resource documents with regard to active (Coaching Resource Eight) and empathic listening (Coaching Recourse Nine), as well as more generally to the characteristics of an appreciative interpersonal perspective.

Encouraging statements are the first way in which we can be helpful. These statements tend to convey interest and encourage the speaker to keep talking. In providing this type of statement we should neither agree nor disagree with what the other person has said, but should instead use noncommittal words and varying intonations of our voice.

We can also be helpful when we offer *clarifying statements*. The primary purpose of these statements is to help both you and the speaker clarify what's being said, to gather more information and to help the speaker see other points of view. We provide clarifying statements when we ask questions and when we restate wrong interpretations that force the speaker to explain further.

A third way of being helpful is to be found in the *restating statement*. The primary purpose of this type of statement is to show that you're listening and understanding what's being said. It also enables you as the listener to check your meaning and interpretation with the speaker. To provide this type of help one needs to restate the speaker's basic ideas, premises, and facts.

A fourth type of helpfulness is found in the *reflecting statement*, the purpose of which is to show that you're listening and understanding what's being said. It also enables you to demonstrate that you understand how the speaker *feels*, and it helps the speaker evaluate her feelings after hearing them expressed by someone else. To engage in this type of helpful interpersonal engagement, one needs to use the description of feelings process that we described above.

Finally, there are *summarizing statements*. These statements enable you and the speaker to review progress, to pull important ideas and facts together, and to establish a basis for further discussion. Summarizing statements typically involve restatement of the major ideas that have been expressed by the speaker and reflect the speaker's basic feelings as conveyed through their statements and clarified through the active listening of the listener.

Coaching Resource 13: Setting the Stage for Feedback

Primary Strategy: Behavioral Coaching
Primary Model: Engagement Coaching

Keeping in mind the general principles about ways in which we can be helpful to another person (Coaching Resource Twleve), we turn specifically to the processes associated with giving constructive feedback. What do you say to start conversations with another person when you'd like to give them feedback? Following is a list of 21 specific questions you might use at various times to help you get the attention of another person for the purpose of giving feedback:

1. "Would you be interested in discussing how…?"

2. "May I share a few thoughts (feelings) with you about…?"

3. "How do you feel about…?"

4. "Would you be interested in the way I feel about…?"

5. "Do you have any questions (concerns) about…?"

6. "Are you aware that…?"

7. "Would you like some input (feedback) about…?"

8. "Is this a good time to ask you about…?"

9. "Do you have a few minutes to discuss…?"

10. "Would you like me to elaborate on…?"

11. "Does this information seem…?"

12. "Am I making sense about…?"

13. "Has anyone else expressed similar thoughts about…?"

14. "Do you have any idea why...?"

15. "Have you considered...?"

16. "Do you think it might help if...?"

17. "Would you prefer that I (or that I not)...?"

18. "Is it possible that...?"

19. "Have I said something that may have caused you to...?"

20. "Am I sensing that you feel...?"

21. "Would you like to think about what we've been discussing?"

We can also approach this stage-setting process by focusing on the other side of the table: what are the specific questions we might ask in order to get feedback from another person? What are some examples of wording used to get feedback from another person? Following is a list of 15 typical questions you might ask:

1. Would you share your observations (feelings) with me about ... ?

2. May I get your ideas on ... ?

3. Would you mind letting me know ... ?

4. Are you saying that ... ?

5. Do I understand that the point is ... ?

6. Could you help me understand ... ?

7. Is there anything else that ... ?

8. Do you think it would help if ... ?

9. Do you have any particular suggestions regarding ... ?

10. Is it likely that ... ?

11. Do you think this may be because I ... ?

12. How do you feel about ... ?

13. How do you think you (he/she/they) feel about ... ?

14. Would I sound defensive if I said (asked)...?

15. Would you like me to take some time to think about what we've been discussing?

There are several other strategies we can use in setting the stage for constructive and influential feedback. We can establish a "feedback contract" with the other person so she can expect routine feedback. For example, as the potential provider of feedback, one might make the following statement: "Since we are going to be working together over the year, it would be good to talk periodically about how things are going ... how does this sound as a way of working together?" It also makes sense to contract with the other person to give feedback in a timely fashion and in a private setting if possible. In addition, we can ask the recipient of the feedback to provide their own self-assessment. In this way, we can determine together what would be most relevant in our own feedback for the recipient.

Another very important ingredient in planning for and setting the stage for constructive feedback concerns something called the "feedback sandwich." We are inclined to surround the negative feedback we want to deliver (the "meat of the feedback") with positive (though usually diffuse and non-descriptive) feedback (the "bun")" "You are doing a wonderful job . . . I have just one area of concern . . . However, I want you to know that I am thankful every day that you are working in this organization." We should avoid a pattern of commenting on strengths before describing weaknesses. For example: "I thought you were careful and methodical in presenting information on that new project to the committee. I noticed, however, that you made very little eye contact with other committee members and didn't stay afterwards to answer their questions." The recipient of this feedback is likely to remember the second half of the statement (the weakness) and not the first half (the strength). In setting the stage for a feedback session, we should try to separate the two pieces of feedback.

It is also important to focus one's feedback on potential consequences of behavior. For example, rather than saying, "That was a stupid question to ask your customer," one can say, "I saw that when you asked the question in that way the customer seemed to get angry." Furthermore, in planning for a session where negative feedback will be given, one should identify concrete suggestions for improvement. We do not help our colleagues very much when we point out what is wrong, yet offer no suggestions concerning ways things can become right. For example, we might offer the following statement: "Since you had a hard time structuring this wandering interview, perhaps next time you have a job candidate like this you can focus on a series of prepared, sequential questions."

Overall, it is important in setting the stage for a feedback session, that we do some planning and that we use respectful, non-evaluative language in giving the feedback. We should strive to create a setting for the feedback that indicates: "I care about you."

Coaching Resource 14: Delivering Critical Feedback

Primary Strategy: Behavioral Coaching
Primary Model: Engagement Coaching

Behavioral Coaching and specifically Engagement-based Coaching is often most challenging when the client is preparing for the particularly difficult process of providing a subordinate with feedback regarding their inadequate performance and of countering the angry and often manipulative response of subordinates to this feedback. An appreciative approach is particularly hard to embrace in these situations. However, an appreciative approach does become part of the plan if the dignity, respect and independence of both parties are kept in mind when the feedback session is being designed.

An effective confrontation allows you to express your irritation with another person while minimizing his defensive response. An effective confrontation should: (1) produce willing cooperation, (2) preserve the self-esteem of both parties and (3) maintain the quality of the relationship. The "I" message is a specific formula for an effective confrontation. "I" messages consists of three parts and may be preceded by the statement, "I have a problem."

> ***"When you . . ."*** [Include the specific behavior that bothers you]
>
> ***"I feel . . ."***   [Include a description of the feeling that you have in relation to that behavior—see previous section of this chapter]
>
> ***"Because . . ."***   [Include the specific effect that this action has on you so the other person can see the connection between his/her behavior and its effect]

Example: "When you ask me to help you with your work, I feel anxious because then I can't get my own work done on time." The "I" message is a way of giving feedback and soliciting the willing cooperation of the other person. Let the other person decide what to do about the feedback. In that way you are jointly resolving the conflict.

Rehearse the engagement ahead of time. This will increase the probability that you will remain calm while you discuss the problem. If you can remain calm then you are more likely to be very clear in your communication and to hear and deal with the responses of the other person. You may need to repeat your basic message several times to ensure that your concerns are heard. In a difficult situation, you may need to write out a script prior to the engagement, including in this script the anticipated defenses the other party may put up, like the "broken record" and perhaps even "fogging" (see examples of these techniques in the next Resources below).

Following is a practice script that can help a coaching-oriented leader prepare for a particularly difficult—potentially confrontational—feedback session (a closely-related script is presented in the accompanying table). The leader will prepares complete statements in response to each of the following stems and then rehearse the presentation of these statements with the coach.

- I want . . .

- I am getting . . .

- I feel . . .

- Because . . .

- Let's work this out . . . etc. [Express desire for workable compromise, solution.]

- [Note: You should be ready to listen to the feelings, concerns, and reactions from the person I am confronting and to respond to their defensive detours. You should also be ready to use Broken Record (see discussion of this technique later in this chapter)]

- If you do it as I propose it [State positive consequences]

- If you don't . . . [State negative consequences.]

- "I hope you make the right decision for yourself.   I want to check progress on . . . [date, hour]."

When you feel dissatisfied with an employee's performance, you might also wish to consider the following four strategies:

Try This: "I want the monthly reports to me by the last day of every month." Be specific. Try to describe the behavior or result that you desire.
Not This: "You should be more conscientious." Avoid personality traits and generalizations.

Try This: "I'm getting the reports 3 to 7 days late. It's happened twice in the last three months." Be specific—even precise! Describe the actual behavior and/or results that you are getting from the employee.

Not This: "You're constantly late." Avoid references to the employee's personality traits.
Not This: "I think you're developing a poor attitude." Avoid judging, blaming, accusing.

Try This: "I feel dissatisfied with this aspect of your work." Disclose your feeling about the performance gap. (How you feel about the difference between what you want and what you are getting.)
Not This: "I'm disappointed in you." Avoid attacking the person. Deal with the performance.

Try This: "When your reports are late, I have to work overtime to get mine in on time." While you're not obliged to give an explanation, pointing out the impact of the employee's poor performance on you and others often leads to change.
Not This: "Everyone has to pull his weight around here." Avoid explanations that are vague or don't relate to you personally.

These strategies will usually help you to say what you want, how much, and why. It will also enable you to confront the employee without intentionally intimidating, putting-down, or judging.

A Sample Feedback Script
Clarify
I want to meet with you because there are some specific things I want to go over with you and I feel our meetings haven't been productive in the past.
Describe Specific Behavior
This is what I want from you... This is what I'm getting . . .
Use "I" Statements and Description of Feelings
I feel angry because when you do that it takes me away from my central job.
Try Mutual Problem-Solving
I am confident that we can resolve this. . . [Express a desire for workable compromise, solution.]
Point Out Consequences
If you do this, you'll stay in the program. If you don't, the long-term consequences may be that you won't be in the program.
Express Concern
You can choose not to do this. It's your decision. I'm not sure which decision is the right one for you now, but my wishes are for your success and your welfare.
Offer Coaching Support
If you are committed to making this change and feel you need additional resources, please count on my (or Mary's) support and coaching availability.
Establish a Check-In Time
Let's get back together at this same time next Thursday and see how you are doing.

Coaching Resource 15: Recognizing Avoidant Communication

Primary Strategy: Behavioral Coaching
Primary Model: Engagement Coaching

There are several common ways that a leader's staff or peers might defend, block, or ignore her assertions or directions. When she reacts aggressively or defensively to the other person's detour, she has lost control of the situation.

Do you recognize any of these detours that have been used around you? To which are you most vulnerable?

Put-Off Detours

> "Not now, I have to go do...."

Distracting Detours

> "I thought you were going to the budget meeting today. "How's that going by the way?"

Denying Detours

> "I did not ...... "

Blaming Detours

> "Why pick on me? What about the others? Everyone is doing it."

Verbal Abuse

> "You can just go to hell. I don't have to put up with this!"

Joking/Discounting Detours

> "Late again? Oh, well, win some, lose some. "

"Late again? Hey, better late than never."

Poor Me Detours

"I can't do anything right . . . I don't know what's wrong with me."

"This is really hard for me to hear. . . I've been having such a hard time with . ."

Negative Vibes

"You're still worried about that? Hard to believe!"

"I suppose this makes you feel a whole lot better!"

[Body language that expresses boredom, anger, dominance, defiance.]

Apologizing Detours

"I'm so sorry. I didn't mean to. I never should have...." (and other interruptions)

Debating Detours

"Why do you want that?"

"That doesn't make any sense!" [Followed by logical arguments against your position.]

Procrastinating Detours

Agrees but postpones action.

Non-Negotiating Detours

"I refuse!"

Co-Option Detour

"Yes, you're absolutely right, and you know this is the same problem I am having with several of the people reporting to me. You know, we should tackle this problem together. Here are some ideas on how we could start . . . ." [shifting the monkey at least in part to our shoulders – see discussion of monkey/problem ownership in Chapter Three]

Coaching Resource 16: Dealing with Avoidant Communication

Primary Strategy: Behavioral Coaching
Primary Model: Engagement Coaching

There are two effective strategies to use when helping a client deal with a difficult associate who is using avoidant communication strategies (see Coaching Resource Fifteen): fogging and broken record.

Fogging

Fogging has, rightly, very limited usage. It was developed as a communication tactic for addressing consumer complaints. It will only be useful to when one finds oneself under attack from a *manipulative use of criticism* by another person. It is useful to supervisors because they are so visible and often do things that dissatisfy employees. Thus handling un-gracious criticism often goes along with being a boss.

"Fogging" gives a leader an alternative to resisting or backing down in the face of an angry or manipulative person, when a straightforward discussion is not possible. When you are fogging, you take what the person says, calmly acknowledge that there may be some truth in what he or she is saying, and envelop the person in a fog by neither agreeing nor disagreeing. The goal of Fogging is to drain off the other's anger or emotionality, until his or her real message comes forth and a dialogue can begin. The fogger must be like a fog bank. Fog banks don't fight back, don't resist. They don't offer any hard striking surfaces. To fight back in the following example would very likely produce more heat and escalate negative feelings.

Example

> Pat [The Angry/Manipulative Person]: For a high-paid, experienced manager, you sure make off-the-wall decisions sometimes. What were you thinking of when you pulled that one off!

Susan [The Person Doing the Fogging]: Well, maybe I should make better decisions sometimes.

Pat: You big wheels never give a thought to how we feel.

Susan: Perhaps we could be more thoughtful sometimes.

Pat: I'm sorry I'm yelling at you, but you should see what your new system is doing to morale. [Opening to discuss the facts.]

Broken Record

The Broken Record enables a manager to be calm and effective in the face of manipulations or defensive detours used by the other person. As the name implies, this skill involves repeating over and over what you want until the other person "gives up" his or her strategy of avoidance.

What to Do: Politely acknowledge the other person's response, e.g., "I appreciate your concern about that issue. We can talk about it in another meeting, but in this meeting I'd like to talk about this." Repeat the "I want" portion of the original message

Example

Susan (Supervisor): Alice, I want you to arrive at **8:00**.

Alice: I don't see why you keep pointing the finger at me. I'm not the only one to be late.

Susan: (*Acknowledgement*) I know you feel picked on sometimes, but (BROKEN RECORD) I still want you to arrive at **8:00** in the morning.

Alice: I always get me work done and sometimes stay late, so what's the big deal?

Susan: (*Acknowledgement*) I understand that it doesn't seem important to you and (*Self Disclosure*) I appreciate you staying to get the work done, but (*Broken Record*) I still want you to arrive at **8:00**.

Alice: You have been late yourself before, so why can't the rest of us?

Susan: (*Acknowledgement*) I know it seems that way to you. Now, (*Broken Record*) I want you to start arriving at **8:00** as your schedule shows. It's important to me and to the others.

Alice: Well, okay, if I have to.

Coaching Resource 17: Team Functions

Primary Strategy: Behavioral Coaching
Primary Model: Empowerment Coaching

Task functions are those team activities that relate directly to the task, the project, or the problem the team is working on. *Maintenance functions* relate more directly to the process aspect of the team's operation, to the procedures and organizations the team is using to reach its goal.

Studies indicate that teams that successfully achieve goals over an extended period of time are those that have members performing both task and maintenance functions. The team is not only meeting its immediate work objectives but is also building its own resources and skills for working effectively together. Such a team is aware of its own process and can supply needed maintenance functions.

Teams that limit themselves only to task functions may be very effective for short periods of time but eventually can develop the kind of internal conflicts that tend to reduce their effectiveness and disrupt the team. A team that exercised only maintenance roles might develop at first a happy, country-clubbish feeling; but certainly such a team would not be very productive.

Finally, if a number of people were brought together for some purpose or project who exercised only *self-oriented functions*, either chaos or arbitrary action would result.

- Task, maintenance, and self-oriented functions express in a number of particular activities which are outlined on the **checklist** we have provided, which can be used in many ways:In one-on-one coaching, as a *self awareness* check-list for the manager who is working on becoming a more effective team member.

- As a feedback tool the coach can use when engaging in *observational* coaching and following a leader during his team activities.

- In team-building sessions, as a *self* or *group* diagnostic tool: Which activity types are over-used and which ones are under-represented on the team?

Task Functions

1. **Initiating, contributing**: suggesting or proposing new ideas or changed ways of looking at the problem or goal; suggesting a new goal for the team, a new definition of the problem, a possible solution or new way of handling difficulties or a new procedure or way of organizing the team.

2. **Information seeking**: asking for clarification of suggestions in terms of their factual adequacy; seeking information and facts pertinent to the problem or task.

3. **Opinion seeking**: asking for clarification of the values relevant to the team's task or of the values inherent in proposed solutions.

4. **Information giving**: supplying facts and information that are "authoritative;" relating personal experience relevant to the team's task.

5. **Opinion giving**: pertinently stating beliefs or opinions concerning suggestions or alternatives.

6. **Elaborating**: spelling out suggestions through examples or developed meanings; offering a rationale for previous suggestions; attempting to deduce how a suggestion might work out if adopted by the team.

7. **Coordinating**: showing or clarifying the relationship between ideas or suggestions; coordinating the activities of members and/or various subteams.

8. **Orienting**: defining the position of the team in relationship to its goals by summarizing what has taken place, pointing to departures from agreed upon directions or raising questions about the direction which the team discussion is taking.

9. **Evaluating**: subjecting the accomplishments of the team to some standard of operation in relationship to the team task; evaluating or questioning the "practicality," the "logic," the "facts," or the "procedure" of a suggestion or idea.

10. **Energizing**: prodding the team to action or decision; stimulating or arousing the team to "better" activity.

11. **Acting as procedure technician**: expediting team activity by performing routine tasks like distribution materials, arranging seating and so forth.

12. **Recording:** writing down suggestions, making a record of the team's activities and decisions.

Maintenance Functions

1. **Encouraging:** praising, agreeing, and accepting the contributions of others; indicating understanding and acceptance of other points of view, ideas, and suggestions.

2. **Harmonizing:** mediating the differences between other members; attempting to reconcile disagreements and relieve tensions

3. **Compromising:** operating from within a conflict in which his ideas or position is involved, the compromiser may yield status, admit error, or discipline himself to maintain team harmony.

4. **Gate keeping and expediting:** attempting to keep communication open by encouraging or facilitating the participation of others or by proposing regulation or limits on the flow of communication.

5. **Standard-setting:** expressing standards for the team in its functioning; applying standards in evaluating the team process.

6. **Observing and commenting:** keeping records of various aspects of team process; supplying this information, with interpretations, to the team's evaluation of its own procedures.

7. **Following:** going along with the movement of the team; accepting the ideas of others; serving as an audience in team discussion and decision.

Self-Oriented Functions

1. **Aggressing:** deflating others, expressing disapproval of other's values, acts, or feelings; attacking the team or the task; aggressively joking; trying to take credit for another's contributions and so forth.

2. **Blocking:** adopting a negative and stubborn stance; disagreeing and opposing without or beyond reason; attempting to maintain or bring back an issue after the team has rejected or bypassed it.

3. **Recognition-seeking**: calling attention to oneself through boasting, recounting personal achievements, acting in unusual ways, etc.

4. **Self-confessing:** using the team to express personal, non-team oriented, feeling, insight, ideas, and beliefs.

5. **Withdrawing, avoiding involvement:** making a display of a lack of involvement through cynicism, nonchalance, horseplay, or other more or less studied forms of behavior.

6. **Dominating:** attempting to assert authority or superiority in manipulating the team or certain members; flattering, asserting a superior status or right to attention, giving directions authoritatively, interrupting others, and so forth.

7. **Help-seeking:** attempting to call forth sympathy from other members or from the team as a whole.

8. **Pleading special interests:** speaking for a particular interest team; cloaking prejudices or biases in a stereotype position.

9. **Depending:** attempting to identify with a strong individual or sub-team.

Coaching Resource 18: Group Leadership Functions

Primary Strategy: Behavioral Coaching
Primary Model: Empowerment Coaching

Joan North (University of Wisconsin/Stevens Point) has suggested that most meetings can be more effectively run with three rather than one leader.

One of the leadership roles is defined as *coordinator*, the second being defined as *task facilitator* and the third as *team facilitator*.

Personal preferences and personality inclinations will cause leaders to run meetings from just one of these three focus areas, and that is acceptable - provided all three team needs are otherwise covered. Any of these tasks could be delegated to someone other than the team's titular leader, but she has the responsibility of ensuring that all these considerations are fulfilled, if the team is to meet effectively.

Group Leadership Functions

Coordinator

I. Logistics

Arrange time and space for meetings, keeping in mind the usual concern for convenience, but also remembering to combat boredom and the waste of unplanned time. Irregular time periods
Meeting by phone, video-conferencing
Meetings by mail, e-mail, computer conferencing
Meetings at home or hotels
Stand-up meetings

Arrange room preparation.
Flip chart or white board
Visual aids (overhead projector, slide projector, VGS for projection of computer-generated images)
Semicircle of chairs facing flip chart or board
Coffee, tea, refreshments

Think of ways to get work done without the whole group's meeting together.
Subcommittees
Individual assignments
Small group work at meetings

Start and end on time.

II Agenda

Prepare the agenda, ask for additional input by a dead-line, distribute it ahead of time, and specify results expected.
On the agenda allocate time to each topic proportional to its importance.
List important items first on agenda.
Be ready to suggest tools or structures for discussion; e.g., brainstorming.

III. Liaison

Serve as the person to receive or send information about the group and serve as spokesperson to outside groups.

Be responsible for considering the political implications and strategies for the group's work. If the group is "representative," be sure that constituencies are informed.

> Fishbowl meetings (asking some members of the group to observe the other members operating for a specific period of time and then reversing roles with the observers being the participants and the participants being the observers)
>
> Divide up constituency and assign members for consultation
>
> Attendance at departmental meetings
>
> Special guests
>
> Polling

IV. Chairing

Lead the meetings.

Be responsible for meeting improvement; use an evaluation checklist occasionally to see what aspects need work.

Task Facilitator

I. Group Memory

Serve as the group note taker on a flip chart, whiteboard or digital screen visible to all members. Record progress, options, or discussion. Cross off agenda items when they are completed.

Keep track of and review decisions made so that old ground is not re-plowed. Keep track of assignments to be done, by whom, when. Offer assistance when appropriate.

From flip chart, prepare minutes, and circulate them before the next meeting.

II. Traffic Cop

Help the group members agree to the agenda and its time frames at the beginning of the meeting and then serve as traffic cop by helping them manage the sequence and times.

Help the group members choose tools, rules, structures for discussion; and then help them stick to their rules. If the group has decided to brainstorm, the traffic cop will allow no evaluation of ideas during that process.

Help the group members become clear about how it will make decisions and then stick to those methods.

III. Commentator

Summarize where the discussion stands - in an attempt to get it moving along. Try to get closure on items, especially when there appears to be no great disagreement but a lot of need to talk. If there is disagreement, find points of agreement and work from there.

Synthesize so that the group can visualize the discussion and differing points.

Group Facilitator

I. Communication

Too much/ too little.

> Work for broad participation by bringing quiet members into the discussion. Silence does not mean agreement; it often means the opposite.

> Handle the rambler (the content facilitator will serve as traffic cop if person rambles off the topic) with delicate phrases: "Why don't we hear from some other people now?" "I'd like to hear some other opinions, and we only have five more minutes allocated to this topic." "It would be useful if you would briefly summarize your position on that."

Saying/ hearing

> Check for clear communication. Be sure that others understand what a person is saying; e.g., "Will you say more about that?" "Did everyone understand that point?"

> Make sure that members are listening to one another rather than behaving like radios talking to each other. If needed, try imposing a five-minute rule that each speaker must repeat the content of the previous speaker to the previous speaker's satisfaction before he can proceed.

> Protect minority views. In an effort to get things accomplished, groups often ignore or reject minority opinions without regard to the merit of the views. Also, the disliked person or the divergent thinker is seldom really heard by others.

II. Conflict/Agreement

> Encourage disagreement. Disagreements and doubts help make better decisions and yet there is a tendency, especially for those who dislike conflict, to muffle, ignore, or cover up disagreement. If everyone agrees too readily, that may mean that there are unexamined alternatives. While encouraging disagreement, remember to depersonalize the conflict: concentrate on ideas not egos.

> Move eventually to agreement. After sufficient disagreement has surfaced, help the content facilitator find points of agreement. Use continuum lines to ascertain how far apart views are. Ask the group to list aspects of the discussion which all could agree upon. Ask opposing forces if they can find arguments in favor of the other group's proposal.

III. Problem solving

Adopt a problem solving mindset. The purpose of group discourse is not winning points or pushing points of view but finding the best possible solutions. Help the group understand problem solving. Make sure that there is clarity about the problem before fighting over solutions. Concentrate on the problem, not the solutions.

Use consensus whenever possible. Since the group facilitator is focused on the morale of the group, she will be more drawn to decision-making techniques which leave no losers. Voting contributes neither to good group morale nor to good problem solving. Good problem solving requires inventing more and more creative solutions until one finally meets everyone's criteria. While voting on ultimate outcomes should be a choice of last resort, as a process tool it can help in prioritizing or selecting issues along the way.

IV. Tolerance

The group facilitator should help the group understand and accept each other's working styles.

Provide more information and offer varying perspectives. Some people need a lot of information; some need to think about things ahead of time; some need a lot of discussion.

V. Fun/Appreciation

Celebrate completion of steps or tasks.
Celebrate group, organizational and personal birthdays.
Begin meetings with riddles, jokes, cartoons. Lighten up!

Coaching Resource 19: The Situation-Target-Proposal Model for Problem Solving

Primary Strategy: Behavioral Coaching
Primary Model: Empowerment Coaching

Usually when confronted with a pressing problem, we attempt almost immediately to generate solutions to the problem. This is the classic *deficit-based model* of problem solving: discover the deficit and immediately try to reduce or eliminate it. While at times we have all experienced the gratifying feeling of rapidly producing a solution, we have also all undoubtedly experienced the frustration of repeated failure, or we find that our "solution" has created other unexpected problems that are even more difficult to solve.

One approach to problem analysis and solution that seems to avoid these pitfalls is to emphasize the concrete *specification of desired outcomes*. The management-by-objectives (MBO) approach to administrative problem solving, for instance, places great emphasis on the specification of outcomes or objectives. The assumption is that problems are often not fully understood, analyzed, or solved because they have not been formulated in terms of goals, objectives, or outcomes. Without such guidelines, proponents of MBO would argue: We have neither a direction for solution of the problem nor a basis for evaluating our actions.

However, this approach still lacks a full appreciation of the problem and of the current state in which the problem is being experienced. Therefore, any objective we might establish runs the risk of being unrealistic. Or, when achieved, the solution selected is the cause of yet another, unexpected problem. Furthermore, it is often difficult to establish a realistic objective without first understanding the *resources and resistance inherent in the current situation*.

John Wallen and Fred Fosmire offered a model of problem analysis (the S-T-P Model) many years ago that can be of great value to an organizational coach who is assisting a leader to empower her team. It models a dynamic process that allows the discovery of the current state, the image of the future as well as the solutions being considered to inform each other continuously during the discussion, while emerging ideas are still organized in a clear fashion.

The Situation-Target-Proposal (STP) Model

The STP Model is a method that serves the objective of *organizing information* to define a problem in a way that minimizes wasted time and the possible conflict that can occurs on the path to a group solution.

Information is organized into three interrelated dimensions:

> **The Situation (S) Dimension:** Information about the essential features of the current state.

> **The Target (T) Dimension:** The desired state. What we want to accomplish and to avoid. Targets are chosen because those working on the problem value and desire them.

> **The Proposal (P) Dimension:** Specific action proposals aimed at changing the current state into the desired state.

Following are some *common expressions* and terms that are associated with these three dimensions:

> **(S) Situation**: starting point, facts, opinions, explanations about the current state, predictions about change, the environment as perceived by the planners.

> **(T) Target**: terminating point, goals, aims, ends, purposes, objectives, desired outcomes, a description/picture of how the outcome will look and work.

> **(P) Proposal**: path from the situation to the target, means, plans, strategies, implementation procedures, possible actions.

Interdependence:

The following interrelationships among the three dimensions are common:

Interrelationships	Type of Interdependence
Situation-Target	Dissatisfaction with the situation implies a particular target as a standard of comparison
	Any suggested target implies by comparison what is unsatisfactory about the current situation

Target-Proposal	A target defines the results desired from any proposal
	Any proposal embodies assumptions about the nature of the desired target
Proposal-Situation	A proposal embodies assumptions about the causes of the unsatisfactory situation and implies resources and requirements for change
	The situation places limits on the effectiveness and feasibility of acceptable proposals

Practical application:

The information that is generated should be recorded in *three separate columns* if working alone, or on *three separate flip charts* if working in a group.

Entries can be made in the appropriate category as they occur and are accepted. Because these three dimensions are so clearly interrelated, all three dimensions should, however, be addressed at the same time rather than one at a time.

- When information is generated about the *situation, target* information can be elicited by such questions as:
  "If you could change the present situation, what would you want to accomplish?"
  "What's missing in the present situation that you want?"
  "What would be your goal in improving the situation?"

- *Proposal* information can be generated from that same situational statement by such questions as:
  "What might be done to improve that?"
  "What kind of action does that seem to require?"
  "What plan would use that resource?"

- When a *target* is identified, *situational* information can be elicited by questions as:
  "In what ways does the present situation fall short of that goal?"
  "Why does the present situation fall short of that goal?"
  "What forces for improvement are there for reaching that goal?"
  "What obstacles stand in the way of reaching that goal?"

- *Proposals* can be elicited from the same *target* statement by asking:
  "What might be a possible way to accomplish that?"
  "What steps might lead toward that goal?"

- In a similar manner, when a *proposal* presents itself, *situational* information can be elicited by asking:
  "What might that improve in the present situation?"
  "What part of the problem do you see that dealing with?"
  "What resources are there for doing that?"

- And, finally, *target* information can be elicited from that *proposal* by asking:
  "To accomplish what?"
  "In order to do what?"
  "What objective does that proposal aim at?"

Problem solving often seems to wander aimlessly from topic to topic without ever actually coming to grips with the problem at hand. By categorizing statements in visible columns according to *situation, target,* or *proposal* and by using statements in one dimension to bring forth information in other dimensions, an appreciative leader can become more effective and efficient in her team problem solving efforts.

Coaching Resource 20: The Task-Method-Relationship (TMR) Model for Groups

Primary Strategy: Behavioral Coaching
Primary Model: Empowerment Coaching

A group of individuals convened to accomplish a specific task must fully appreciative the complexity of their own dynamics. In addition to completing the task, group members must successfully address themselves to issues in the group that at first may seem unrelated to the task or decision at hand. These concerns may be seen as internal to the group's functioning, as distinct from those associated with accomplishing the task, and may seem unrelated to the task. Two kinds of issues may develop in a task group: those which focus on the method the group uses to work at the task, and those which emerge from and are related to group process and interpersonal relations. Proficiency in both is needed.

The Task-Method-Relationship Model

Task issues are directly related to accomplishing the goals mutually and explicitly defined by the group as its reason for being. Examples of task issues include:

1. Which of these proposals solves the problem most effectively?
2. Shall we approve this new course?
3. What will be our criteria for judging whether this project is successful?

Method issues focus specifically on the means by which the group will work at the task. Examples of method issues include:

1. How are we going to make decisions in this group?
2. How do we insure that the opinions of each member of the group are given an adequate hearing?
3. How long should this meeting last?

Relationship issues related to both the relationships developed through working on the convening task and relationships between members of the group and the total group itself, which members may have brought to the group or developed during its meetings. Examples of relationship issues include:

1. I feel isolated from the group and hurt by the apparent lack of concern of other members.
2. I really enjoy working with members of this group.
3. Jim and Susan never seem to be paying attention to me when I express an opinion they don't agree with.

Task, method, and relationship issues are closely interrelated and tend to stimulate one another. For example, a group may be having a great deal of trouble arriving at a satisfactory decision-making procedure; this looks like a method issue. However, if what is blocking the group is a contest for leadership and influence between two members of the group, the group is faced with a relationship issue and no amount of work at the method level will resolve the difficulty. Both method and relationship concerns may be disguised as task work, with the group struggling to reach a decision on a task issue while process difficulties build up and multiply.

Mechanistic Analogy: In many ways, the functioning of a decision-making group is comparable to the functioning of any other task-oriented system. A mechanical system, for instance, exhibits dynamics in many ways similar to those of task, method, and relationship. Like a group, a machine is designed initially to accomplish a specified task; for example, producing an automatic transmission. This design stage is similar to the state of group development in which methods are considered. The group must be designed to accomplish the assigned task.

Once a machine is designed and built, when it functions, should generate a minimum amount of friction- for in the short run, friction will reduce efficiency and in the long run, excessive friction will require considerable maintenance to keep the system operating. Similarly, a group must be designed in such a way as to accomplish its task with a minimum amount of disruptive inter-personal friction. Negative relationship issues, such as hurt feelings, anger, fear, mistrust, or poor communication, have been shown to reduce the immediate efficiency and, eventually, to necessitate costly, time-consuming maintenance.

Of course, a group, like any human system, differs significantly from a mechanical system in that it incorporates emotional components, memory, and the capacity to learn. These factors combine to make the specific functioning of a task group significantly less predictable than that of a well-designed machine. In practice, this means that the method or design issues must be approached in a tentative and experimental manner. What appears to be a satisfactory decision-making procedure at the first meeting may turn out by the third meeting to be inappropriate to the task.

For instance, the group members may decide initially to make all decisions by consensus, but discover as they work on their task that the task is just too large and the time too short to permit effective consensus decision-making. The group may use that information to revise its decision-making, subdivide the task, and form small task forces. Or, the initial method decision may generate process problems, like feelings of exclusion or not being heard; and the procedure may have to be adjusted to a more equitable one. The spirit of *tentativeness* that is recommended in dealing with method issues is less appropriate for task and relationship concerns.

Use of the T-M-R Model in a Decision-Making Group: An empowered decision-making group usually will begin its work at the method level. It will decide how it wants to decide. Consideration, in this appreciative context, also will be given to immediate relationship issues, although these may not surface until the group has moved into its "storming" stage. Very self-aware groups with high levels of previously gained trust may be able to deal early with personal goals related to the task, with interpersonal difficulties some members bring into the group from previous contact with the same people, and with issues of inclusion and influence. If method decisions are appropriate to the group and task; and once the relationship issues are dealt with, the group will spend most of its time working effectively at making decisions. Most decision-making groups, however, have a tendency to begin their work at the task level and to remain there until serious conflicts or break-downs (intense "storming") engenders a stop-action review.

As they emerge, method and relationship concerns are misinterpreted as disagreements over the decision, because people's thinking is limited to the task level. As a result, the response is frequently to push harder at trying to make the decision. As the group continues to beat its head against the task wall, process issues emerge in more or less undisguised form: "That's what you said the last time and look what happened!" "*You* guys just won't accept any idea from a woman, will you?" At this point, without rapid group attention to the neglected process and method issues, the group is dangerously near dissolution.

An effectively operating group will tend to work at all three levels at different times. They will learn to appreciate the need for work at each of the three levels. When issues cannot be resolved easily at the task level, the group will move rapidly to consideration of its methods, to determine if those methods and procedures are impeding making a decision. Inadequate problem resolution at this level may indicate a need for the group to shift its attention to the feelings, personal goals, and relationships in the group. This is what underscores the need for someone to always play the facilitator (process observer) role in the group – even if members take turns.

This moving through task, method, and relationship issues occurs during a period of several hours, days, or even years. Initially, this appreciative process is a self-conscious one and feels artificial to group members. Over time, as the group develops, the process becomes more natural and efficient; members acquire skills at diagnosing the level of group difficulty and in directing the group attention to their perceptions. In a decision-making group with a very long life, like a project team working together over several months or years, effective group methods become fairly stable so that unless the composition of the task or the group changes radically, there is less need for constant reexamination - and when it is needed, it is rapid and effective.

Coaching Resource 21: Decision-Making Choices for Groups

Primary Strategy: Behavioral Coaching
Primary Model: Empowerment Coaching

Decisions can be made and identified in a number of ways, each with inherent benefits and difficulties. There is no one right way to make decisions, though several commonly used decision-making processes are often detrimental to group empowerment, and to the creation of an appreciative climate in the group.

Perhaps the simplest way of evaluating decisions is to see if they are made by the minority or by the majority. In either case, though a differing proportion of the group membership participate in the formal decision-making process, all members of the group will have implicitly agreed or chosen not to disagree about how the decision is to be made (even when only one person is making the formal decision). Group dynamics researchers suggest that this process represents the "collusion" of all group members regarding how a decision is to be made. In many instances, this collusion is quite understandable given the cost associated with speaking up against the way a group (or leader) is making the decision. In other cases, the collusion may be a product of indifference, alienation or distorted communication. In those instances when everyone is aware of and fully committed to the process of decision-making being used, the group is not colluding. It is instead consciously and explicitly deciding how to decide. What then are the different ways in which groups make decisions, be they minority or majority forms of decision-making? We offer eight common ways group decide, as a starting point, as an **inventory** for the coach, as a **handout** for groups, or as an **observation guide** for a team coach or an observational coach .

How Groups Decide

1. *Self-Authorization: One Person-Decision to Do Something.* This occurs when a group member suggests a course of action and immediately proceeds upon that course, assuming that since no one disagreed, the group has given its approval. Such action

can lead a group down blind alleys. Even if the rest of the group agrees with the decision, they may resent the way it was made; and no one knows how much support the decision will receive from the other members of the group.

2. *Handclasp: Two Person Decision to Do Something.* A suggestion made by one member elicits a reaction of support and permission to proceed from another. The group is launched into action without adequate testing as to whether the proposal is acceptable to the group as a whole. The handclasp between two or three is evident in cliques that form within the group and is a powerful method of control of the group. It often results from the failure of some members to meet their responsibility to the group by speaking up, voicing their opinions, keeping the group on target, and insuring that alternatives are considered.

3. *Plop: One Person Decision Not To Do Something.* A plop results when a group member makes a suggestion that meets with no response from the group as a whole. It falls "plop." Not only is there no recognition or evaluation of the suggestion by the group, but the individual who offered the suggestion feels he has been ignored and possibly rejected. He feels that no one will listen to him. The result is that the decision making has not advanced.

4. *Kill: Two Person Decision Not To Do Something.* A suggestion offered by one member of the group is rejected at once, either by one or more of the powerful members of the group as a whole.

5. *Oligarchy: Multiple Person Decision To Do Or Not To Do Something.* A minority of the group ramrods a decision or suggestion into group action that the majority does not support but tolerates. This leads to little future support by the group as a whole for the action taken.

6. *Simple Majority.* A common method of determining a majority support decision is by voting. Many groups make the mistake of assuming that simply because a majority support the decision, the minority will come along *willingly*. Often they may appear to do so, but frequently they resent the action and give no more than token support.

7. *False Consensus.* Teams that really try to avoid the pitfalls associated with the plop, self-authorized, handclasp, kill, minority, and simple majority decisions often try to include every member in the final decision. All members may agree, but some may have serious reservations regarding the decision; and, although not disagreeing, often withdraw support at crucial times. This practice occurs when the leader fails

to elicit explicit verbal commitment from the team members, (mis-)interpreting silence as commitment.

8. *True Consensus.* All members have contributed to the decision or feel that their contributions have been given a fair hearing and are more satisfied with it than with any of the other alternatives that were considered. Even if there are alternatives they would personally prefer, they have arrived at the conclusion that the team's chosen path is the one they are willing to commit to. True consensus is tested after the meeting: team members don't later second guess the conclusions reached by the team publicly, nor look for ways to avoid implementation.

Coaching Resource 22: Balancing Leadership Preferences

Coaching Strategy: Decisional Coaching
Coaching Model: Reflective Coaching

Reflective coaching takes place in three interrelated dimensions: (1) information (the essential features of the current state), (2) intentions (the desired state; what we intend to accomplish and/or avoid) and (3) ideas (specific ideas and subsequent actions taken to change the current state into the desired state). Effective coaching blends attention to information, intentions and ideas.

Effective coaching also balances phases of reflection and action. Frequently, coaching clients will spend too much time in reflection and never move beyond untested ideas, or they will move precipitously toward action with insufficient attention to either information or intentions. The personality preferences of individual leaders will cause them to favor some of these domains over others, requiring that the coach help restore balance, if the leader is to be successful and well-rounded.

The Activist

The "activist" is to be found among many clients. The activist dwells in a world of ideas that lead directly to action. Things are to be done immediately: "Why put off till tomorrow what we can do today!" For the activist, cautious deliberations are frustrating and demoralizing: "Let's get on with it!" The activist tends to define the world in terms of leadership and risk-taking: "Nothing ventured, nothing gained." He or she often suspects that the real problem of those who urge more deliberation is an unwillingness to take risks. The activist believes that action must be taken even though not all the information is in and even though the proposed solution is not perfect—"Something is better than nothing."

The Realist

By contrast, those people who tend to dwell more on reflection than action are oriented either toward "realism" or "idealism." Whereas the "activist" tends to dwell in the domain of actionable ideas, the "realist" prefers the domain of information and the "idealist" the domain of intentions. The activists perceive the overly analytical realist as an immobile, often obsessive person. . Similarly, activist views the idealist as hopelessly romantic—a person who would rather build castles in the air then build a durable bungalow on earth The realist, while very "well-informed", may never lift up his or her head long enough or far enough to see what is actually happening in the world beyond the data.

Coaching clients are often pulled not only between reflection and action, but also between realism and idealism. The realist is careful and cautious, because of concern that problems may appear to be "solved" through wishful thinking (the failure of idealism) or without anticipating the consequences (the failure of activism). Too many people, according to the realist, go off half-cocked, with very little sense of the resources needed to solve a problem and without a clear understanding of the current situation to anticipate all of the consequences associated with a particular solution.

The Idealist

The idealist is someone who can envision rapidly how things could be and should be better. Within minutes of arriving on a new job, entering a new relationship, purchasing a new home or formulating a new program, the idealist is imagining and "seeing" how things could be improved. He or she challenges the mundane reasoning of the realist and notes that new perspectives are needed on old problems if the activist is to be successful in generating proposals to solve these problems.

Like the realist, the idealist is reflective—but in a big-picture sense, not because he has a great interest in adequate information. The idealist is concerned about those who ponder the means too heavily and lose sight of the ends—concerned about losing the war while seeming to win individual battles through expedience. The idealist confronts the realist with her lack of courage: if bold vision is lacking then when will risks be taken and progress made? Without courage and vision where is the capacity to endure against adversity?

The Pragmatist

The pragmatist, in the extreme, is only interested in what is immediately useful or applicable. Idealists are too abstract for her, realists too slow and data-bound and activists too reckless. But a pragmatist's lens on utilitarian decision-making and action short changes an organization when it needs a broader vision or longer term perspective. Such a longer view may require investments before the pragmatist can be convinced of their utility, or research that slows down what seem to be working, tried-and-true activities.

The Balanced Leader

Effective leadership requires a balance between, or even an integration of, these different perspectives. This requires that pragmatism, realism, idealism and activism be combined or used in turn, situationally. Effective problem solving—especially when enhanced by skillful coaching—will shift between the domains of information, intentions and ideas. When confronted with a new, unpredictable situation, a balanced problem-solver will tend to become realistic by attempting to assimilate this new reality. When confronted with an old, unchanging environment, the balanced problem-solver will tend to become more of a daydreamer, creating images of how this environment might be transformed. When confronted with the press of time and events, the balanced leader will tend to mobilize his or her activism, creating proposals to meet these challenges. He will side with the pragmatists when expediency would save the day and would gain the organization some time and money to regroup and redirect its efforts.

The balanced leader is someone who will adapt to changing conditions by moving through all three domains. By contrast, the extreme realist will attempt to collect information even when the environment is unchanging and in this way will contribute to the resistance of this environment to change. Similarly, the extreme idealist will daydream not only under conditions of relative stability, where a shake-up would be beneficial, but also under conditions of rapid change and instability, and in this way will add to the instability of the environment and to its unpredictability. The idealist under stress retreats to another, safer world, when he or she should be confronting the current situation. The extreme activist will respond with hasty actions even when there is no press of time or events. He will even create crises where there are none in order to justify precipitous action. The failure in the activist's haste may in turn produce a new crisis that makes activism appear to be appropriate, thereby initiating a self-reinforcing crisis-management mentality.

Put quite simply, all four of these extreme preferences tend to be ineffective in some settings and to create more problems than they solve. Reflection must be balanced against action. Furthermore, the period of reflection in a coaching session must provide opportunities for both the collection of new information and the clarification of intentions. An effective balancing and integration of reflection and action requires that action produce and be based on information, that action inform and clarify intentions, and that reflection lead to decision and action. The successful organizational coaching process inevitably involves movement between the domains of information, intentions and ideas, and a balancing between reflection and action.

Coaching Resource 23:
The Clearness Process

Coaching Strategy: Decisional Coaching
Coaching Model: Reflective Coaching

In the Quaker tradition, an assumption is made that consensus exists in any group when it convenes and that the process of finding consensus is one of uncovering this underlying agreement rather than somehow creating a consensus among constituencies who are inherently in a state of disagreement. Similarly, the Quaker tradition suggests that individuals hold the answers to the problems that they face and need only uncover these answers. They don't need assistance because of an absence of a solution to the problems they face; rather they need assistance in gaining greater clarity regarding the nature of this problem and the solution(s) they already possess that will solve this problem. Ralph Waldo Emerson—the great American essayist—asked when greeting an old friend or acquaintance he had not seen for a while: "What's become clear for you since we last met?" In the deeply-embedded American tradition of blending optimism, pragmatism and individualism, Emerson believed strongly that each individual possesses the capacity to solve his or her own problem, provided there is clarity.

The clearness process, like the consensus process, engages a community of people who are committed to a specific set of norms about how they will relate to one another. Specifically, in the case of the clearness process, a person who faces a problem convenes a group of people to do nothing more than (and nothing less than) asking probing questions regarding the problem over a two to three hour period. Members of this clearness committee are not to give advice nor are they to ask leading questions that subtly (or not so subtly) imply a specific definition of the problem or a specific solution.

Though the clearness process has most often been used in small groups, it is equally appropriate when used in an appreciative and reflective coaching process. First, the clearness process begins with an appreciative assumption that the person with the problem also holds the solution to this problem is in keeping with the Decisional coaching focus on strengths rather than weaknesses. Second, the clearness process is a wonderful way in which to encourage reflection on the part of the coaching client. The problem remains with the client, rather than being transferred to either a consultant or counselor who begins with the assumption that their client or patient cannot herself come up with an appropriate solution.

Third, the clearness process offers a gentle way in which an Decisional coach can encourage increasingly deeper reflection on the part of their client, without violating the basic premise of this peer-based approach that one need not be an expert or authority to be helpful to another person in an organization. All one has to do is be an active listener and provide a balance between challenge and support. The clearness process encourages active listening and provides both challenge (the questionnaire process) and support (offering help to a client who faces a difficult problem).

Steps:

The reflective coach first explains the purpose and conditions of the clearness process, emphasizing the basic assumption that a clear sense of the problem and viable solutions to the problem reside with the client(s). Their role as an organizational coach is to help their client discover this inherent sense of the problem and solutions.

A coach then asks their client to describe the problem as they now see it, as well as identify any solutions that already come to mind. The reflective coach should remain relatively inactive during this initial problem description—asking questions only to help him/her (the coach) better understand the situation.

Finally, the reflective coach begins to ask questions that help their client clarify the nature of the problem they face. In keeping with the analysis we offered in the main text, these questions usually touch on three domains: (1) the desired state (the domain of intentions), (2) the current state (the domain of information) and (3) the nature of the gap between the current and desired states (the problem).

Following are several general kind of probing questions in each of these three domains:

The Domain of Intentions [The Desired State]

- How would you know if you have been successful in this endeavor?
- What would make you happy?
- Who else has an investment in this project and what do they want to happen?
- What would happen if you did not achieve this goal?
- What would happen if you did achieve this goal?

- What scares you most about not achieving this goal?
- What scares you most about achieving this goal?

The Domain of Information [Current State]

- What are the most salient facts with regard to the circumstance in which you now find yourself?
- What are the "facts" about which you are most uncertain at the present time? How could you check on the validity of these facts?
- What are alternative ways in which you could interpret the meaning or implications of the facts that you do believe to be valid?

The Problem [Gap between Current and Desired State]

- How do you know that there is a problem here?
- To what extent do other people see this as a problem? If they don't, why don't they?
- How long has this problem existed? How big is it? Is there any pattern with regard to its increase or decrease in magnitude?
- What are the primary cause(s) of the problem? What is different when the problem does and does not exist? What remains the same whether or not the problem exists?
- Who benefits from the continuing existence of the problem? In what ways do you benefit (even indirectly) from the continuing existence of this problem?
- What will you miss if and when this problem is resolved?

The clearness process will then tend to shift toward the uncovering of solutions. This uncovering may occur while the problem is being described and explored—or it may even precede the exploration of the problem. It is not for the reflective coach to control the flow of the clearness process. Rather the reflective coach continues asking questions that move with rather than impede the client's own "natural" way of exploring the problem.

When exploring solutions to the client's problem, the coach and client move into a third domain—the domain of ideas. One or more of the following questions may be appropriate to ask:

The Domain of Ideas [Solution(s)]

- What have you already tried to do in solving this problem and what did you learn from these efforts?
- What actions have you taken that somehow reduced the scope or impact of the problem—even if this action was not intended to address this problem? What did you learn from this serendipitous impact?

- How might other people help you solve this problem—especially those who have not previously been involved with this problem? What other resources which have not previously been used might you direct to this problem?
- What would happen if you just ignored this problem? What would happen if you devoted all of your time and resources to solving this problem?
- What is the most unusual idea that you have about solving this problem? What solutions have you dreamed of or thought about at a moment when you were particularly tired or frustrated?
- What would you do if you had much more time to solve this problem?
- What would you do if you had very little time to solve this problem?
- If you were "king" or "queen" what solution(s) would you impose to solve this problem? If you were a "fool" or had nothing to lose in trying something out, what would you do in attempting to solve this problem?

These questions all encourage a fresh look at solutions to the problem and encourage one's client to probe deeper into his or her own ideas regarding potential solutions. Coaching clients often limit themselves in considering nontraditional ideas, in part because they have been "right" so often in their life that it is hard to risk being "wrong." The reflective coach provides a safe and supportive environment in which to articulate and explore these "wrong" and crazy ideas and in which to consider parameters of the problem and solution (time, resources, authority, approaches) which have always been on "the back burner" for this harried client.

More generally, the clearness process provides a safe setting—a sanctuary—in which a coaching client can reflect with his or her coach regarding the nature of a problem and its solutions. It is safe not only because the coach is accepting and supportive, but also because the coach is not intruding with his own ideas. When we impose our ideas as colleagues, then the recipient of these ideas must acknowledge them, find something good about them (so that our feelings aren't hurt), and—if we have been particularly helpful (in terms of giving our client considerable time and attention)—plan some way in which to make use of these ideas (even if it means that the solution is unsuccessful). All of this distracts our client from the real task at hand which is to find a solution to his or her problem, not to the newly created problem (making us feel good about our assistance, etc.). The clearness process is simple, straightforward and often very a valuable tool for a coach who works in an organizational setting.

Coaching Resource 24: The Convergent Questioning Process [Asking "Why?"]

Coaching Strategy: Decisional Coaching
Coaching Model: Reflective Coaching

Peter Senge and his associates have offered a variety of wonderful suggestions in showing the readers of their *Fifth Discipline Fieldbook* how they might more effectively think in a systematic manner. One of the simplest and most effective of these suggestions is the process of asking five "why questions." If we repeatedly ask someone "why" then they are likely to move closer to the core of their problem and to a deeper and more systemic appreciation of the situation in which they find themselves. They are also likely to move closer to the solution(s) that might effectively address this more clearly articulated problem.

The Five Whys can be used in a somewhat modified form by reflective coaches when they are working with someone who has to make difficult decisions. We suggest a modified form, for the five Whys can become quite tedious and predictable. After a few minutes, the coaching client can ask his or her own "why" question. The key is not just in asking "why" but also in asking a variety of "why" questions that can help to move one's client deeper into the central issue.

In general, a reflective coach should ask the "why" question at least five times, provided this question is not repeated in exactly the same way each time. The following, for instance, is an inappropriate use of the five Whys:

Client: I hate to fire Susan for this one small mistake.
Coach: Why do you hate to fire her?
Client: Because it will hurt her feelings.
Coach: Why will it hurt her feelings?
Client: Because she will have to find a new job.
Coach: Why must she find a new job?
Client: I don't know, I assume she needs one.

In this case, the coach simply picked up the second half of the client's statement and made it into a why question. As a result, the coach's client was led off the topic and ended up being asked a why question about something that was not central to the issue and about which the client had no information. The why questions might have instead been as follows:

> Client: I hate to fire Susan for this one small mistake.
> Coach: Why do you hate to fire her?
> Client: Because it will hurt her feelings.
> Client: Why are you concerned about her feelings being hurt?

Alternatively, the why questioning might have proceeded as follows:

> Client: I hate to fire Susan for this one small mistake.
> Coach: Why do you hate to fire her?
> Client: Because it will hurt her feelings.
> Coach: Why do you believe that her feelings will be hurt?

Or:

> Client: I hate to fire Susan for this one small mistake.
> Coach: Why are you firing her?

The first of these series of "why" questions focus on the client's feelings: "Why are you concerned about her feelings being hurt?" This parallels the discussion in the main text about reframing goals. We ask "why" questions that encourage clients to reflect more deeply on their own intentions and values.

The second series of questions focused on the way in which one's client is defining and interpreting present conditions: "Why do you believe that her feelings will be hurt?" This parallels our discussion of reframing a current situation.

By contrast, the third series of questions immediately pushes a coaching client deeper into a consideration of the actions to be taken: "Why are you firing her?" This parallels our discussion of reframed solutions. Typically, an effective series of "why" questions often moves across all three domains, encouraging a client to reflect on his or her desired state as well as current state, and to consider more fully and critically the initial solutions that have been identified. Our client's reflection on the decision to fire Susan might have proceeded as follows:

Client: I hate to fire Susan for this one small mistake.

Coach: Why are you firing her? [Why question regarding initial solution]

Client: Because it is the latest in a series of incidents suggesting that Susan doesn't care about her job.

Coach: Why does this incident suggest that she doesn't care about her job? ["Why" question regarding interpretation of current state]

Client: She showed no remorse and became very defensive when I brought this mistake to her attention. She is more interested in being right than in doing a good job.

Coach: Why is an expression of remorse a sign of wanting to do a good job? ["Why" question regarding interpretation of current state]

Client: Because I want people who work with me to be open to criticism.

Coach: Why do you want people who work with you to be open to criticism? ["Why" question that concerns desired state]

Client: I want them to be able to learn from their mistakes.

Coach: "How do you know that Susan can't learn from her mistake even if she shows no remorse and is defensive? ["Why" question regarding initial solution]

Client: "I don't exactly know that, but I've had other past employees who behaved this way and never improved."

Coach: "How and when would you be able to evaluate whether Susan has really learned or not from your feedback?"

Each question need not start with "why," though by starting with a "why" we are likely to refrain more often than not from giving a chunk of advice, when we should just be asking questions and listening. Even with a why question, we can still slip in a little advice giving. The coach in the above example, for instance, could have moved close to giving advice by asking: "Why can't Susan learn from this mistake—even if she shows no remorse and is defensive?" This coach has gotten away from a "why" question, instead asking: "How do you know that Susan can't learn from her mistake?" This is a less leading question, though it still is leading if the coach is trying to push toward a conclusion that Susan should get a second chance. The Five Whys must be asked with a genuinely open mind—otherwise, they can seem (rightfully) quite manipulative and insincere.

A variation on the Five Why's has been offered by Will Schutz, who encourages us to identify first what we know *is not* the problem—what is it that we absolutely know is not what we are struggling with. Then, what do we know for sure would never work in terms of a solution to the problem we face? Schutz's approach then uses a single "why": "Why is this a stupid (silly, unacceptable, absurd, unimaginable, awful, unthinkable) idea?" This type of "why" question is asked when a client dismisses a perception, desired outcome or proposal without any reflection.

If the unacceptable notion was offered by the coach, then it should be left alone—otherwise, the coach is pushing his or her own notions and a win-lose scenario is established. Schutz's approach should only be taken when a coaching client has dismissed his or her own thoughts or those of an associate—for these thoughts often contain the germ of a wonderful idea or are only stupid because they reframe the current state, the desired state, an accepted definition of the problem or potential solutions to the problem. The reflective coaching process is in essence a means of shaking up settled thoughts and feelings (challenge) while also offering the client being coached a sympathetic and encouraging setting (support) in which to explore alternative perspectives, values and proposals.

The "Why" Questioning Process

Domain of Intentions: The Desired State

- **Why** is success in resolving this problem important?

Domain of Information: The Current State

- **Why** do you think you have an accurate and unbiased perspective regarding the current reality surrounding this problem?

Defining the Problem: Gap between Current and Desired State

- **Why** do you think your current assessment of the problem is valid?

Domain of Ideas: Reducing Gap between Current and Desired State

- **Why** do you think the idea(s) you have generated is (are) likely to be effective in resolving this problem?

Coaching Resource 25: The Divergent Questioning Process [Asking "If"]

Coaching Strategy: Decisional Coaching
Coaching Model: Reflective Coaching

As in the case of the "why" questions, a series of "if" questions can be asked to help a coaching client better understand his current and desired state, and in particular become more open to his own "wild" ideas regarding how to achieve the desired state. The "if" questioning process is essentially one of inviting a coaching client to imagine that the desired state has already been reached and to consider what it would be like to dwell in this desired state and to look back on how this state was achieved. This is a wonderful tool, especially for the visual, visionary client who is open to dreaming a bit in the presence of his or her coach regarding a desired state.

The questions asked in the "If" process should be reviewed and modified (as necessary) by the coach before being given to a client. The client can respond to these questions in writing and then talk about them with the coach. Alternatively, the client can reflect on these questions in the presence of the coach. This **coaching tool** is usually most appropriate when utilized after some trust has been established between the coach and client. It is usually not appropriate as either an opening or closing exercise in a coaching process.

The "IF" Questioning Process

If . . . you could have been given one piece of advice by a wise leader when you entered your current position, what would this advice have been?

If . . . you could spend a week with any person who has served in a leadership role (whether or not this person is still living), who would you choose?

If . . . you could only address one type of problem in your organization for the rest of your life what would it be?

If . . . you could only work with one colleague in your current organization for the rest of your life who would this person be?

If . . . you could either:

(a) make a great deal of money as a leader, but have very little autonomy (working for a very large and high-pressure organization), **OR**

(b) make a relatively small amount of money (enough to live on) but have substantial autonomy (working for yourself or in a small organization), which would you choose?

If . . . you could revise one decision you have made regarding your career, what would this decision be?

If . . . you were to achieve one major goal in your career, what would this goal be?

If . . . an obituary were to be written about you at the end of your life, what would you like it to say?

Coaching Resource 26: The Left-Hand and Right-Hand Column Exercise

Coaching Strategy: Decisional Coaching
Coaching Model: Reflective Coaching

This exercise represents an appreciative approach to exploring underlying assumptions, self-fulfilling predictions and self-sealing beliefs. It isbased on ideas first presented by Chris Argyris and Donald Schoen, and later expanded and adapted by Peter Senge, and is founded on several central principles:

- Coaching clients hold thoughts, feelings, assumptions, predictions and beliefs that are often unacknowledged by themselves, that are rarely communicated to others, and that have great influence over their actions and learning.

- These unacknowledged components are often neither chosen by our client, nor particularly appreciated. Embarrassment often accompanies the acknowledgment and articulation of these components.

- Coaching clients usually assume that it is inappropriate to express the content of these components; furthermore, they are correct in that the norms of our society do not support this expression.

- Coaching clients usually recognize that these components get them in trouble at times and that they would be more effective if they could somehow express these components at critical moments to those people with whom they are experiencing some difficulty.

This exercise helps coaching clients find a way and a space in which to examine these components in both an appreciative/reflective coaching context and in the "real" world.

This exercise involves seven steps and is built around a key analysis of one's "right column"—which are the behaviors and statements that are made in a public, observable manner— and one's "left" column which are the unarticulated beliefs, thoughts, feelings and assumptions that one has in this specific situation. The central task is to identify, discuss and find ways to effectively express the content of the left column.

Step One: Identifying the Critical Moment

A coaching client chooses a critical moment from a recent and important relationship in her life. Coaching Resource Twenty Eight (The Critical Incident) briefly describes and offers a rationale for focusing on critical moments. This **handout** should be distributed to the client at the start of this first step. "In focusing on a critical moment the person being coached picks a moment of interaction in which there was a "gap" between her initial intention and the consequences of the conversation—there were unintended or unsatisfactory outcomes.

Step Two: Right Hand Column

The client will first write the actual dialogue between herself and the other person on the *right* side of the Left/Right Hand Column Chart that accompanies this exercise. Five to six actual statements are more than adequate. You may wish to reassure the client that she does not have to recall the exact words that were stated. The client should, however, identify each of the key words or phrases that triggered some of her own assumptions, feelings, predictions or beliefs. Instruct the client to place a number next to each statement and indicate who made the statement.

Step Three: Left Hand Column

The client next turns to the *left* column on the chart and writes her own unexpressed thoughts and feelings in response to each statement that was made either by herself or by the other person. The client should be encouraged to write the words that she would have liked to have said, as well as identifying the assumptions, feelings, predictions and/or beliefs that were solicited by this interaction.

Step Four: Description of Left and Right Hand Columns

At this point the client completes the following assignments, which should take about five minutes. (The coach might assist here client if needed and appropriate):

- Provide a brief story regarding this critical moment (who was involved, events and interactions leading up to critical moment, consequences of the interaction)

- Describe the interaction as it actually took place (read and talk about the right hand column)

- Describe the interaction as it actually took place in conjunction with the unacknowledged and undisclosed thoughts, feelings, assumptions, predictions and beliefs (left hand column)

Step Five: Appreciative Coaching

The coach then asks the following questions with regard to the client's left and right hand columns:

- What did you want to have happen at the outset of the conversation?

- Identify a time when a similar outcome was successfully achieved in interaction with this person.

- What were the differences between these two interactions? Why were you able to accomplish the outcome in one interaction but not in the other?

- Were there differences in the two interactions between what existed in your left hand column?

- Were there differences in the two interactions between what you disclosed from the left hand column?

- What would you guess was in the left-hand column of the other person during and at the end of these two interactions?

Step Six: Experimentation

The client then returns to the critical moment for five minutes and replicates the interaction, but in a manner that is more likely to yield the desired outcome and that leads to an even richer dialogue regarding the content of the left-hand column. The reflective coach might play the role of the other person in the interaction, responding in a manner that seems appropriate, given the context and history of the interaction. (If the client is working with a partner then the two partners reverse roles at the end of the five minute invention and a five minute feedback session -see step seven.)

<u>Step Seven: Feedback</u>

Following the experimentation (role play), the coach provides feedback regarding the nature of the interaction, the likely content of the other person's left hand column, and the specific moments when the interaction was most successful.

The Left-Hand and Right-Hand Column Guidelines:

Recommended Ground-Rules

- "Own" your opinions.

- Ground your facts in observable, verifiable data.

- Make your reasoning explicit: identify intermediate assumptions, beliefs, predictions, feelings that influence the direction and/or outcome of your reasoning process.

- Clarify and articulate your desired outcome for this activity.

- Advocate, and then invite inquiry: be frank and explicit about your own opinions and facts, and then invite other person to challenge your opinions and facts and to be explicit about their own reasoning.

The Left-Hand and Right-Hand Columns: Unacknowledged/Undisclosed Information

Left-Hand Column	Right-Hand Column

Coaching Resource 27: The Critical Incident

Coaching Strategy: Decisional Coaching
Coaching Model: Reflective and Instrumented Coaching

The Left-hand/right-hand column exercise (Coaching Resource Twenty Six) is most useful when we confront a critical incident. What are these? In recent years, attention has been directed toward a very controversial book titled *The Black Swan* that was written by Nassim Nicholas Taleb. Taleb notes that we believe all swans to be white—but what happens when we discover a black swan? He believes that we encounter many black swans in our individual and collective life—highly improbably and usually disturbing events for which we are not prepared. In our collective life, we have face such black swans as the emergence of the Internet during the 1990s, the attack on the World Trade Center on September 11, 2001, the collapse of the American stock market in 2008 and the assassination of many world leaders during the past forty years. These are the *critical incidents* that define who we really are in terms of our skills, knowledge and attitudes.

Ninety to ninety five percent of the time we are doing the "usual thing" in our job. We are doing what we were originally paid to do and what we have learned to do in a routine but skillful manner over many years of work. As managers, we hold regular weekly meetings with our subordinates and prepare budgets for the next fiscal year. In staff support functions, we provide recommendations to other people in the organization regarding policies and procedures. Yet five to ten percent of time we are doing the "unusual thing" in our job—we are faced with a black swan that is significant yet unpredictable.

This is the exceptional work that no one could have anticipated when our job description was being prepared. This is that one-time challenge we have encountered or the very difficult circumstance that requires a unique response. As a new global coordinator we are faced with the prospect of preparing an extended visit by a foreign dignitary who is about to make a substantial investment in our company. Where do we find someone to culturally prepare us for the protocols of this high-stakes visit? As a manager, we are suddenly faced with the challenge of handling the first large layoffs the company has ever faced, or with the challenge of informing team members that one of their colleagues is terminally ill. We are asked by the foreign financier to exaggerate a bit in preparing a prospectus that goes back to his partners. Is there a company policy on how to treat differing value systems in other countries? In a complicated matrix organization, we are reporting to two bosses who are in overt conflict. How do we navigate such a situation when we first encounter it? As organizational leaders we are confronted with black swans. We face a very difficult personnel problem that seems to be beyond our usual scope of work or expertise.

It is in these unusual circumstances—when confronting these black swans—that our skills as a colleague, manager or leader are being fully tested. We all know how to do our "normal" 90-95% job—especially after we have been doing this job for several months. Furthermore, the 90-95% is usually rather easy to teach and can be clearly described and documented in a personnel policy handbook. If an employee can't do or is unwilling to do the 90% job, then he or she should be looking for different work.

By contrast, the unusual, 5-10% circumstance often demands knowledge, skills and attitudes that are acquired slowly over time. The black swans are not easily understood by new employees and are not readily captured in either a job description or personnel manual. They are critical not only because they are significant and unpredictable and because they pose very difficult (sometimes insurmountable) challenges for those involved, but also because they are opportunities that help define and manifest the central character and quality of an organization.

When we think of the character of an organization, we are focusing on its unique or distinctive features. Distinctive features appear when members of an organization are confronted with black swans—with special problems or opportunities. The founding of any organization is itself a special opportunity (a critical moment) that forges the initial distinctive character of an organization. This character is further tempered through subsequent critical incidents in the life of the organization. A small bank's management team decides not to mark to market all its outstanding mortgages in order not to have to foreclose on many of its customers; the decision costs them the ownership, as they get taken over by the FDIC. Our personal and organizational values, in particular, are evident in the ways in which we choose to confront these critical incidents—these black swans.

Organizational quality is also directly a product of our success in confronting critical incidents. Organizations of high quality prepare their employees for potential critical incidents by encouraging resourceful, out-of-the box thinking, by rewarding informed risk-taking and failed experiments that can be learned from, by doing post-action reviews, by coaching and feedback - thus preparing people for the unexpected.

Coaching Resource 28:
Advocacy Inviting Inquiry

Coaching Strategy: Decisional Coaching
Coaching Model: Reflective Coaching

The use of "advice-giving" in organizational coaching is usually considered inappropriate and even counter-productive. Actually, it can be quite effective if coupled with the request for joint inquiry. When framed as *advocacy-inviting-inquiry* (a strategy first proposed by Chris Argyris and Don Schön), advice from a coach becomes the precipitate for dialogue, which is the key feature in effective coaching. One can even move beyond advice-giving to the presentation of brief case studies, analogies, summarizations and even more radical insertions from the coach—provided these insertions are followed by an invitation to joint inquiry on the part of the coach and client. This document contains six suggestions regarding ways in which to structure advocacy-inviting-inquiry, as well as offering a distinction between "easing-in" and advocacy-inviting-inquiry.

Advocacy Inviting Inquiry

Questioning Strategies

Type One: Advice-Giving

- "Here is an idea that I would like to offer: xxxxx. Let's explore the positive and negative aspects of this idea." *Spectrum analysis*: finding the seed of a good idea in every proposal]

Type Two: Case Study

- "I had the following experience that seems to be similar in some ways to what you are experiencing. Here is what happened: xxxx. Here is how I felt/reacted: xxxx. Let's explore the ways in which this experience is similar to and different from what you have experienced." *Objectifying* a subjective experience]

Type Three: Co-Learner

- "This is what I've learned from what you just said (what we've discussed/the events you just described to me). What have you learned?"

Type Four: Absurd Suggestion

- "Here is an idea that is off-the-wall, weird, irrelevant: xxxx. Let's explore the positive and negative aspects of this idea." [*Spectrum analysis*: finding the seed of a good idea in every proposal]

Type Five: Analogy/Metaphor

- "Your situation reminds me of the following: xxxx. Let's explore the ways in which this analogy/metaphor relates to and doesn't relate to your situation."

Type Six: Clarification/Summarization

- "This seems to be what you have said/Let me summarize what I heard you say: xxxx. In what ways is this statement accurate and in what ways would you like to correct or add to this statement?" [*Paraphrase*]

Comparison between Easing-In and Advocacy-Inviting-Inquiry

Easing In [Potentially Loaded Questions]

- What do you think of this idea?

- Do you think that maybe this is the issue?

- Is my experience relevant here?

- Do you think this analogy/metaphor is accurate?

- Do you think this accurately summarizes your statement?

Advocacy Inviting Inquiry

- *Advocacy:* "Here is an idea/experience/analogy/summarization that I would like to present to you (and perhaps why I want to present this idea.)" [Option: check on colleague's understanding of the idea being presented]

- *Inviting Inquiry:* "Let's explore the strengths and weaknesses associated with this idea/experience/analogy/summarization (and perhaps why this exploration might be of benefit to you.)" [Option: "and I will go first, suggesting some of the weaknesses associated with this idea as it related to your situation/issue."]

Coaching Resource 29: Organizational Coaching Instruments and Assessments

Coaching Strategy: Decisional Coaching
Coaching Model: Instrumented Coaching

It is important to note that the list of instruments in this document is **not** intended to be definitive or exhaustive in any way. It has been presented to *illustrate* the broad range of resources that are available for instrument-based coaching and to point to several places where an organizational coach might begin building a library of appropriate instruments for use in their instrumented coaching.

Selection Criteria

The following criteria were used for selecting the instruments included on this list:

1. The company producing the instrument is stable and unlikely to go out of existence in the near future.

2. The company producing the instrument provides satisfactory or excellent customer service.

3. The instrument has been used by the authors of this book and found to be of value in various organizational settings.

4. The instrument is reasonably priced.

5. The instrument measures a dimension of organizational functioning that has been found to be of interest to many clients.

6. The instrument can be administered and interpreted without a professional license (though in some cases, formal training and certification is required to use the instrument, or certain data from the instrument can only be interpreted by a licensed professional).

7. In some instances the instrument was chosen in part because of the interesting format of the questions or scoring form.

Many of the instruments are available directly from the **Professional Coaching Library** (with link to the specific instrument) or from the **Center for Personal and Organizational Assessment** (P. O. Box 70, Harpswell, Maine 04079). In most cases, however, they must be ordered from the company listed with the instrument.

Organizational Coaching Instruments

1. Normative Instruments

Assessment instruments that generate scores regarding the extent to which specific **competencies** are evident in a specific person as determined by the person themselves [Self] or by other people [Other]

360-Degree Assessment

- **Leadership Behaviors**

Executive Dimensions®
    Center for Creative Leadership
    www.ccl.org

LEA 360™
    Management Research Group
    www.mrg.com

Campbell™ Leadership Index
    PEARL™ Solutions
    www.pearl-solutions.com

Legacy Leadership Competency Inventory
    Coachworks
    www.coachworks.com/pub-overview.lasso
    www.info@coachworks.com

- **Managerial Skills**

SKILLSCOPE®
    Center for Creative Leadership
    www.ccl.org

- **Developmental Skills Critical for Success**

Benchmarks®
    Center for Creative Leadership
    www.ccl.org

Hogan Development Survey
Hogan Assessment Systems
http://www.hoganassessments.com

- **Learning and Reasoning Skills**

Prospector®
Center for Creative Leadership
www.ccl.org

Business Reasoning Inventory
Hogan Assessment Systems
http://www.hoganassessments.com

- **Competencies Important to the Organization: Tailor-Made Assessments**

LEA™
Management Research Group
http://www.mrg.com

360 BY DESIGN®
Center for Creative Leadership
www.ccl.org

- **Developmental Needs Analysis**

Development Needs Inventory
Teleometrics International
www.teleometrics.com

- **Organizational Culture**

The Denison Organizational Culture Survey
Denison
www.denisonconsulting.com

Organizational Culture Inventory
Human Synergistics
www.humansynergistics.com

<u>Self/Co-Worker Assessment</u>

- **Employee Involvement**

Access Management Survey/Survey of Employee Access
    Teleometrics International
    www.teleometrics.com

- **Productive Practices**

Productive Practices Survey/Survey of Management Practices
    Teleometrics International
    www.teleometrics.com

<u>Team Assessment</u>

- **Team Readiness**

Teamness Index
    Teleometrics International
    www.teleometrics.com

2.   Descriptive Instruments

Assessment instruments that generate scores regarding **personal preferences** as assessed by the person completing the survey about themselves [Self] or by another person [Other]

Career and Personal Values

- **Achievement Orientation** [Self/Other]

Managerial Philosophy Scale
   Teleometrics International.
   www.teleometrics.com

- **Career Needs** [Self]

Career Anchors [Schein]
   Pfeiffer and Co., now subsidiary of Jossey-Bass Publishers,
   350 Sansome St., 5th Floor, San Francisco, CA 94104
   800/274-4434 or 415/433-1740
   www.pfeiffer.com

- **Career Report** [Self]

The Birkman Method
   Birkman International.
   3040 Post Oak Blvd., Suite 1425,
   Houston TX 77056.
   800/215-2760. FAX: 713/963-9142
   www.birkman.com

- **Personal Motivations and Life Interests [Self]**

Personal Directions®
   Management Research Group
   www.mrg.com

Motives, Values, Preferences Inventory
   Hogan Assessment Systems
   www.hoganassessments.com

Personal Interests, Attitudes and Values
  TTI
  Www.ttiinc.com

Change

- **Rate of Organizational Change** [Self]

Organizational Change Inventory [Bergquist]
  Center for Personal and Organizational Assessment

- **Rate of Personal Change** [Self]

Life Change Inventory [Holmes and Rahe]
  TheLibrary of Professional Coaching
  www.libraryofprofessionalcoaching.com

- **Style of Change Agentry** [Self]

Change Agent Questionnaire
  Teleometrics International
  www.teleometrics.com

Coaching/Mentoring Styles

- **Mentoring** [Self]

Mentoring Style Inventory
  Center for Personal and Organizational Assessment

- **Personal Coaching** [Self]

Personal Coaching Styles Inventory
  Corporate Coach U
  www.coachingwell.com

Conflict Management

- **Style of Conflict Management** [Self/Other]

Conflict Management Survey
   Teleometrics International
   www.teleometrics.com

Conflict Dynamics Profile
   Center for Conflict Dynamics at Eckerd College
   www.conflictdynamics.org

Thomas Kilmann Conflict Mode Instrument
   Xicom. Woods Road, Tuxedo, NY 10987.
   914/351-4735 800/759-4266
   www.store.kilmann.com

Decision-Making

- **Styles of Decision-Making** [Self/Other]

Styles of Teamwork Inventory [Hall]
   Teleometrics International.
   1755 Woodstead Court. The Woodlands, TX 77380. 713/367-0060
   www.teleometrics.com

Interpersonal Styles and Needs

- **Communications** [Self/Other]

Personnel Relations Survey [Johari Window]
   Teleometrics International.
   1755 Woodstead Court. The Woodlands, TX 77380. 713/367-0060
   www.teleometrics.com

- **Interpersonal Needs** [Self/Other]

Fundamental Interpersonal Relations Orientation—Element B
(Behavior)/Element F (Feelings)/ Element J (Job) [Schutz]
Will Schutz Associates. P. O. Box 1339. Mill Valley, CA.
94942-1339. 800/INCLUSION. FAX: 415/389-1630.
www.cpp.com

*   **Interpersonal Strengths and Needs** [Self]

The Birkman Method
Birkman International. 3040 Post Oak Blvd., suite 1425,
Houston TX 77056.
800/215-2760. FAX: 713/963-9142
www.birkman.com

*   **Interpersonal Style and Strengths** [Self/Other]

Strength Deployment Inventory [Porter]
Personal Strengths Publishing. P. O. Box 2605 Carlsbad,
CA, 92018-2605
www.personalstrengths.com

DISC: Personal profile [Self/Other]
Carlson Learning Company www.carlsonlearning.com
or Target Training International www.ttidisc.com

*   **Listening Styles** [Self]

Listening Styles Profile [Watson and Barker]
Pfeiffer and Co. [now subsidiary of Jossey-Bass Publishers,
350 Sansome St., 5th Floor, San Francisco, CA 94104 :
800/274-4434 or 415/433-1740
www.josseybass.com

Leadership

*   **Contextual Leadership** [Self/Other/Culture]

Leadership Style Questionnaires [Bergquist]
The Center for Personal and Organizational Assessment

- **Leadership Change** [Self/Other]

Leadership Practices Inventory—Delta [Kouzes and Posner]
Pfeiffer and Co. [now subsidiary of Jossey-Bass Publishers,
350 Sansome St., 5th Floor, San Francisco, CA 94104
800/274-4434 or 415/433-1740
www.josseybass.com

- **Leadership Competencies** [Self/Other]

Leadership Competency Inventory [McBer]
Hay/McBer.116 Huntington Ave. Boston, MA 02116.
800/729-8074. FAX: 617/425-0073
www.haygroup.com

Legacy Leadership Competency Inventory
Coachworks
www.coachworks.com/pub-overview.lasso
www.info@coachworks.com

- **Leadership Practices** [Self/Other]

Leadership Practices Inventory (LPI) [Kouzes and Posner]
Pfeiffer and Co. [now subsidiary of Jossey-Bass Publishers,
350 Sansome St., 5th Floor, San Francisco, CA 94104]
800/274-4434 or 415/433-1740
www.josseybass.com

- **Situational Leadership** [Self/Other]

Leader Effectiveness and Adaptability Description (LEAD)
[Hersey and Blanchard]
Pfeiffer and Co. [now subsidiary of Jossey-Bass Publishers,
350 Sansome St., 5th Floor, San Francisco, CA 94104
800/274-4434 or 415/433-1740
www.josseybass.com

- **Styles of Leadership** [Self/Other]

Styles of Leadership Survey [Teleometrics]
  Teleometrics International
  www.teleometrics.com

Learning

- **Cognitive Adaptability** [Self]

Adaptive Style Inventory [Kolb]
  Hay/McBer.116 Huntington Ave. Boston, MA 02116.
  800/729-8074. FAX: 617/425-0073.
  www.haygroup.com

- **Cognitive Style** [Self]

The Learning Style Inventory [Kolb]
  Hay/McBer.116 Huntington Ave. Boston, MA 02116.
  800/729-8074. FAX: 617/425-0073.
  www.haygroup.com

- **Interpersonal** [Self]

Student Learning Styles Questionnaire [Grasha and Reichmann]
  The Center for Personal and Organizational Assessment

- **Media**

Cognitive Mapping Inventory [Hill]
  The Center for Personal and Organizational Assessment

Management

- **Blake and Mouton's Managerial and Leadership Style Grid** [Self and Other]

Styles of Leadership Survey
  Teleometrics International
  www.teleometrics.com

Style of Management Inventory
   Teleometrics International
   www.teleometrics.com

- **Coaching** [Self]

The Birkman Method
   Birkman International. 3040 Post Oak Blvd., suite 1425,
   Houston TX 77056.
   800/215-2760. FAX: 713/963-9142
   www.birkman.com

- **Coaching and Management** [Self/Other]

Coaching Process Questionnaire [McBer]
   Hay/McBer.116 Huntington Ave. Boston, MA 02116.
   800/729-8074. FAX: 617/425-0073.
   www.haygroup.com

- **Empowerment and Management** [Self/Other]

Power Management Inventory [Teleometrics]
   Teleometrics International
   www.teleometrics.com

- **Hall's Style Parallax Model** [Self/Other]

Management Styles Inventory [Hall]
   Teleometrics International
   www.teleometrics.com

- **Management Competencies** [Self/Other]

Management Competency Inventory [McBer]
   Hay/McBer.116 Huntington Ave. Boston, MA 02116.
   800/729-8074. FAX: 617/425-0073.
   www.haygroup.com

- **McBer's Management Style** [Self/Environment]

Managerial Style Questionnaire [McBer]
Hay/McBer.116 Huntington Ave. Boston, MA 02116.
800/729-8074. FAX: 617/425-0073.
www.haygroup.com

- **Participation and Management** [Self/Other]

Participative Management Survey [Teleometrics]
Teleometrics International
www.teleometrics.com

- **Productive Management** [Self/Other]

Productive Practices Survey [Teleometrics]
Teleometrics International
www.teleometrics.com

- **Socio-Technical Management** [Self/Other]

Access Management Survey [Teleometrics]
Teleometrics International
www.teleometrics.com

Motivation

- **Work-Related Motivations** [Self/Other]

Management of Motives [Maslow/Herzberg]
Teleometrics International
www.teleometrics.com

Organizational Culture

- **Clarity/Standards/Responsibility/Flexibility/Rewards/Team Commitment**

Organizational Climate Exercise II [McBer]
Hay/McBer.116 Huntington Ave. Boston, MA 02116.
800/729-8074. FAX: 617/425-0073
www.haygroup.com

- **Inclusion/Control/ Openness/Significance/Competence/Likability**

Element O: Organizational Climate [Schutz]
  Will Schutz Associates. P. O. Box 1339.
  Mill Valley, CA. 94942-1339.
  800/INCLUSION. FAX: 415/389-1630
  www.cpp.com

- **Organizational Climate, General**

Organizational Climate Survey [Bergquist]
  The Center for Personal and Organizational Assessment

- **Power/Role/Achievement/Support**

Diagnosing Organizational Culture [Harrison]
  Pfeiffer and Co. [now subsidiary of Jossey-Bass Publishers,
  350 Sansome St., 5th Floor, San Francisco, CA 94104
  800/274-4434 or 415/433-1740
  www.josseybass.com

- **Readiness for Total Quality**

Total Quality Management Readiness Index [McBer]
  Hay/McBer. 116 Huntington Ave. Boston, MA 02116.
  800/729-8074. FAX: 617/425-0073
  www.haygroup.com

Personality

- **Birkman, Personality and Perspective** [Self]

The Birkman Method
  Birkman International. 3040 Post Oak Blvd., suite 1425,
  Houston TX 77056.
  800/215-2760. FAX: 713/963-9142
  www.birkman.com

- **Hogan Five Factor Model [Self]**

Hogan Personality Inventory
  Hogan Assessment Systems
  www.hoganassessments.com

- **Cattell's Sixteen Personality Factors** [Self]

16 PF [Cattell]
  IPAT. P. O. BOX 1188 Champaign IL 61824-1188

- **Enneagram** [Self]

Inventory and Profile [Aspell and Aspell]
  Pfeiffer and Co. [now subsidiary of Jossey-Bass Publishers,
  350 Sansome St., 5th Floor, San Francisco, CA 94104 :
  800/274-4434 or 415/433-1740   http://www.josseybass.com

- **Energy Patterns [Self]**

The Focus Leadership Balance Indicator (body-mind)
  www.focusleadership.com

- **Erikson's Eight Stages of Personality Development** [Self]

Measures of Psychosocial Development [Hawley]
  Psychological Assessment Resources. P. O. Box 998.
  Odessa, FL 33556. 813/968-3003

- **Jungian Behavioral Styles—Keirsey** [Self]

Keirsey Temperament Sorter
  www.matrixbooksinc.com/index.html

- **Jungian Personality Styles—Myers-Briggs Version** [Self]

Myers-Briggs Type Indicator
  Consulting Psychologists Press. 577 College Ave. Palo Alto
  CA 94306.
  www.cpp.com

- **Jungian Personality Styles—Singer-Loomis Version** [Self]

The Singer-Loomis Type Deployment Inventory
Moving Boundaries, Inc. 1375 SW Blaine Ct.
Gresham, OR 97030, 1-888-661-4433
www.movingboundaries.com

- **Jungian Personality Styles – Grey-Wheelwright [Self]**

The Gray-Wheelwright-Winer 4-Letter Type Indicator Test [Available at no cost]
Neurocare
www.neurocareusa.com

- **Personal Values** [Self]

Personal Values Questionnaire {McClelland]
    Hay/McBer.116 Huntington Ave. Boston, MA 02116.
    800/729-8074. FAX: 617/425-0073
    www.haygroup.com

- **Self-Concept/Self-Esteem** [Self]

Element S (Self Concept)/ Element E (Self Esteem) [Schutz]
    Will Schutz Associates. P. O. Box 1339. Mill Valley, CA.
    94942-1339.
    800/INCLUSION. FAX: 415/389-1630.

Power

- **Empowerment and Use of Power [Self/Other]**

Power Management Inventory
    Teleometrics International
    www.teleometrics.com

Problem-Solving

- **Style of Creative Problem-Solving** [Self]

Creative Style Inventory [McCarthy]
Hay/McBer.116 Huntington Ave. Boston, MA 02116.
[800/729-8074. FAX: 617/425-0073]
www.haygroup.com

- **Style of Problem-Solving** [Self]

Problem Domain Preference Scale [Phillips and Bergquist]
HRD Press, Inc. 22 Amherst Rd. Amherst MA 01002
800/822-2801. FAX: 413/253-3490
www.hrdpress.com

Teamwork

- **Team Dynamics** [Self and Others]

Styles of Teamwork Inventory/Teamwork Appraisal Survey
Teleometrics International
www.teleometrics.com

Values/Philosophy

- **Management & Leadership** [Self and Others]

Managerial Philosophy Scale/Reality Check Survey
Teleometrics International
www.teleometrics.com

Coaching Resource 30: Questions about Ethics

Primary Strategy: Aspirational Coaching

Ethics has always played a major role in organizational life. Some would say that ethics is the compass that should guide the direction in which an organization is moving; others would use the metaphor of the keel of a boat, providing orientation for the boat as it moves through the sea. Coaches can play a critical role in helping a client identify their ethical compass or keel. Thomas Friedman has recently suggested that ethical behavior is particularly important in a world that is populated by people who are increasingly interdependent (it is a "flat" world). This interdependency can't be fully prescribed or regulated by some rigid code-of-conduct. Rather, in a world of great complexity, unpredictability and turbulence (as well as increased interdependence), thoughtful (and ethical) men and women must base their conduct—and in particular their decisions—on a flexible, situation-dependent process of deliberation.

Ethics-based coaching can provide invaluable assistance to a client who is facing these challenging decisions. A coach and client operating within an organizational context enter the domain of intentions (rather than the domain of information or domain of ideas) when delving into ethical issues. They are collaboratively reflecting on what the client (and his/her organization) wants to accomplish (the desired outcome) and the way(s) in which we want to accomplish the desired outcomes (the desired processes).

The domain of intentions is comprised of four major sub-units: (1) rights and responsibilities, (2) implications, (3) process and identity and (4) connections and culture. We have identified several general questions in each of these sub-units of intention that a coach and client might want to consider.

Questions Regarding *Rights and Responsibilities*

All societies (and organizations) must continually provide a balance between the legitimate rights of all members of the society (or organization) and the individual and collective responsibilities to be assumed by all (or at least most) members of this society (or organization). While this balance between rights and responsibilities is always in need of some adjustment, it is our ethical responsibility to identify those who do have rights and responsibilities relevant to this decision.

- Who has the right to be concerned about this decision? Why do they have this right? Why are they potential "stakeholders" regarding this decision?

- Who is responsible directly for the outcomes of this decision? Why are they directly responsible? How is this responsibility assigned and how is it monitored?

- Who is responsible indirectly for the outcomes of this decision? Why are they indirectly responsible? How is this responsibility assigned and how is it monitored?

Questions Regarding *Implications*

Every significant decision that is made by members of an organization under conditions of complexity, unpredictability and turbulence has both anticipated and unanticipated outcomes. While we can never fully anticipate all of these possible outcomes, it is our ethical responsibility to at least reflect on and seek to discern at least some of the potential outcomes – both positive and negative.

- What are the potential positive outcomes associated with this decision? What are the most likely positive outcomes associated with this decision? Why do you assess these outcomes as positive? Can they also be negative?

- What are the potential negative outcomes associated with this decision? What are the most likely negatives outcomes associated with this decision? Why do you assess these outcomes as negative? Can they also be positive?

- Who is likely to be effected directly by the potentially positive outcomes of this decision?

- Who is likely to be effected indirectly by the potentially positive outcomes of this decision?

- Who is likely to be effected directly by the potentially negative outcomes of this decision?

- Who is likely to be effected indirectly by the potentially negative outcomes of this decision?

Questions Regarding *Process and Identity*

Important decisions are more likely to yield positive outcomes and to be accepted by all (or most) members of an organization if processes associated with this decision-making process are aligned with the personal values of those involved in these processes. While every decision-making process must be tailored to the unique nature of the organization and the decision being made, it is our ethical responsibility to embrace and engage a process that is consistent with our own best selves and the best practices of our organization.

- Which aspects of myself (or this organization) do I most like (appreciate) with regard to the way(s) in which this decision is being made?

- Which aspects of this organization do I most like with regard to the way(s) in which this decision is being made? Which aspects of this organization's process do I most appreciate regarding this decision?

- Which aspects of myself do I least like as it influences the way(s) in which this decision is being made? Which aspects of myself tend to depreciate the work I do regarding this decision?

- Which aspects of this organization do I least like (depreciate) as it influences the way(s) in which this decision is being made? Which aspects of this organization's process tend to depreciate the work being done regarding this decision?

- How might this decision change the way in which I view myself (especially as a decision-maker)?

- How might this decision change the way in which I view my organization and my role in this organization?

Questions Regarding *Connections and Culture*

Every organization is ultimately nothing more (or less) than a congregation of human beings who wish to engage with one another in a pleasing and growth-enhancing manner. The culture of the organization can sustain (or hinder) the creation and maintenance of an environment of connectedness. While all organizational cultures are inevitably in flux and interpersonal relationships are always complex, it is our ethical responsibility to reflect on and articulate the ways in which the decision to be made enhances or disrupts significant relationships and contributes to or distracts the creation of a culture of connectedness within the organization.

- How might my relationships with significant people in my life be impacted by this decision?

- In what way(s) does this decision reflect something about the way I relate to other people in my life?

- In what way(s) does this decision reflect something about the culture of this organization?

- How might this decision impact on the future culture of this organization?

Coaching Resource 31: Managing Life Transitions

Primary Strategy: Aspirational Coaching

An inventory, a series of coaching questions and some concepts are provided that can be of use when a coach is assisting his/her client in reflecting on past transitions, as well as preparing for future transitions. The inventory is an update of one prepared by Richard Rahe and his colleagues during the late 1960. The focus of this Life Change Scale is on the transitions that we all experience in our lives and the stress that is associated with these transitions. Coaching clients are asked to reflect on current changes in their lives, to explore past and future transitions and to consider the ways in which these transitions are managed —successfully or unsuccessfully.

The coach should begin by briefly discussing the concept of transitions. In a study of the effects which various human relations training programs have had on organizations, Charles Seashore found that participants, whether individuals or organizations, are unlikely to alter the directions in which they are currently moving simply as a result of the training. A program or a coaching intervention can, however, enable them to manage more effectively the rate of change; major transitions in life can thus be either accelerated or decelerated. Seashore concluded that the effective management of transitions is a valuable skill, especially in a world that seems to be changing at an increasingly rapid rate.

The work of Thomas H. Holmes and Richard H. Rahe also seems relevant here. In a 1967 study these two physicians found that specific changes or life transitions are directly correlated with the occurrence of physical illness and emotional disturbance (findings that have only become more relevant and have been further substantiated by later studies). The greater the number and magnitude of major life changes in a one year period, the more likely it is that physical and emotional problems will occur during the subsequent year. The effective management of transitions is something we can work on and vitally affects our lives, both physically and emotionally.

After this introduction, the coaching client should be given the Life-Change Scale. After the client has completed the scale and has calculated his/her own life-change score, the coach and client swill reflect together on the implications of the total score. In general, a score of 200 or more reflects a high level of transitions, though among faculty and college administrators scores of 200 are rather common. A score of 300 or more indicates that the respondent has experienced exceptional life transitions during the past year and might want to give serious consideration to the physical and emotional costs of these transitions. A score of less than 100 can reflect either contentment or a protected situation.

The coach and client should then move to an even more detailed and individualized assessment of the rate of change experienced by the client. The coach will ask:

- Have there been any other important transitions in your life this past year that were not included on this list? What score would you give these changes for yourself?

- Relative to the assigned scores, which of the transitions do you think have been most difficult for you? Which have been easiest? Why?

- If you were to relive this past year, which of these transitions would you like to avoid? Which transitions would you like to have experienced which did not occur?

- Some of the transitions on the original list are generally quite positive for most people. Which of the transitions that have occurred for you this past year have been most positive? Which have been most negative? Have both types of transitions been stressful for you? Which type was most stressful?

Pattern of Life Transitions

The coaching client might then be instructed to place his/her current transitions score on the Life Transition Grid (see **template** below). The leader can record either the score he obtained from the scale or an estimated score if the scale score seems inaccurate. The client's current stress score is to be recorded at the appropriate point of intersection between his current age (horizontal axis) and his life-change score (vertical axis).The client is then asked to plot probable transitions scores for his past and future. The leader should begin by identifying those points in his past when major transitions occurred, then those points when life was particularly stable. Similarly, the client should be encouraged to identify probable time periods in the future when major transitions are likely to occur and when relative stability will prevail. The client then draws a line from birth to death that connects these points, perhaps portraying other, less significant periods of transition and stability as well.

The coaching client is now encouraged to discuss ways in which he has handled or hopes to handle major life transitions:

- Have the transitions tended to be too fast or too slow? Why?

- Have certain types of events tended to precede or even precipitate major transitions?

- What have been the typical consequences of major life transitions? Immediate impact? Impact after one year? Physical illness? Health? Depression? Exhilaration? New relationships? The termination of old relationships?

- Have you consistently and consciously taken any specific actions to make these transitions more satisfying? What actions?

Either before or during this coaching discussion, the coach may wish to review briefly several of the different ways in which people manage transitions and might ask their client for his/her own ideas about the most effective ways to manage these changes. The concepts offered below regarding managing transitions might be considered at this point.

Some Strategies for Managing Major Life Transitions

One must acknowledge first of all that transitions are stressful. Furthermore, positive transitions — marriage, promotion, an award — may be as stressful as negative ones. A U-shaped curve seems to accompany most major life transitions. At first, after the transition has been initiated, the mood of the person or organization that is undergoing the transition will tend to turn from optimism to pessimism; excitement may give way to disillusionment. Production will fall off until the bugs are worked out in the system; the change will proceed slower than expected; advocates of the change will discover negative consequences or side effects that were not anticipated. Only at a later point, after the person or organization has traveled through this "valley of despair" will transitions begin to reap some benefits — if they have been successful. The planner of a personal or organizational transition must anticipate this period of stress and introduce ways to reduce its negative impact. Perhaps the simple anticipation of stress is itself one such way; several other more specific suggestions follow.

- *Ceremonies:* Every culture creates specific events that signal major life transitions for a member of the group. For example, in most societies, entrance into puberty, marriage, birth of a child, divorce and the death of a loved one are made the focus of a ceremony. Similarly, many organizations acknowledge the entry of new people into the organization by means of initiations, orientation programs, social gatherings and so forth. Most organizations also have some type of a ceremony to acknowledge the promotion, move or exit of individuals from the organization.

  Ceremony serves two important functions in helping people manage transitions. First, it helps anticipate the stress that is associated with the transition. The ceremony serves as a signal, formally telling us that some intensive times are immediately ahead. Second, the ceremony indicates that other people care about this transition and are available for support in this endeavor.

  In a society which seems to be increasingly less ceremonial, we must plan for our own ceremonies and provide ceremonies for significant other people; remember that the marriage ceremony may be more important to the transitional processes of the parents than to those of the newlyweds. Perhaps the practice of some couples, who periodically renew and update their marriage vows as a means of acknowledging the changes that have continued to occur in their relationship, is as important for them as the initial ceremony. Similarly, team off-sites serve to maintain and deepened the personal relationships tested during the year, especially for dispersed teams.

- *Support Group:* Most people who successfully manage a major life transition describe the critical role played by several people who served them in a variety of functions: the *nurturer* helped them feel better or stronger; the *friend* empathized with their predicament and often provided a humorous perspective; the *expert* provided important information to help them implement, accelerate or slow down a transition; the *clarifier* helped them better understand the current and probable future nature of the transition; the *client,* someone whom they were currently serving, was willing to let them know what the consequences would be if certain decisions were made about the transition; and the *challenger* forced them to reexamine their actions, values or expectations. Usually, people are more in need of the nurturer if the transition is particularly rapid and in need of the challenger if the transition is too slow.

A support group consists of people who fill one or more of these roles. It is critical that the departing coach leave the client with such resources at the end of the coaching assignment. Members of such a group need not know each other; they may never even have been in the same room together. Yet they all have one thing in common: they all know and in some way are willing to provide support to the individual going through the transition. It is the responsibility of that individual to integrate the different perspectives of the members of his group and to be sure he is not asking only one or two people to fill all of these roles.

- *Incremental Change:* Change should be planned from a long-term, wide-range perspective, rather than from a short-range or piecemeal point of view. In planning for change, however, it is often essential that the desired change be broken up into small, manageable units that have short-term and rather modest goals. A series of small change curves is usually preferable to a single large one. Furthermore, if a series of small change projects are identified, it is possible to initiate a second project when the first encounters significant resistance. Small projects can also be sequenced in a way that will meet current needs and concerns, while also being responsive over the long run to more basic and far reaching problems.

- *Diffusion of Interests and Activities:* If any one change absorbs all or most of a person's or organization's attention, then this transition is likely to be stressful, for the person or organization has no other interest or activity that can provide stability or variety. In preparation for a transition, one should ensure that other areas of interest in one's life do not get set aside during the change process. Given the tendency of many people who are experiencing stressful transitions to focus intensely on the change, it is essential that other roles, goals and activities be reinforced as salient features of the person's or organization's life.

Life-Change Scale

Each of the events listed below represent a significant change or transition in the lives of most people. Each change also has a certain amount of stress associated with it, regardless of whether the change is positive or negative. Please examine each of the changes listed below to determine if this change has occurred in your life *during the past twelve months*. If the change has occurred then record the given stress score that is associated with the change in the space located to the right of the event. After you have examined the entire list, you might want to add one or two life changes to the list (space is provided at end of list and assign your own stress score to this/these item(s). Then add up all the stress scores that you have recorded in the right hand column. Record this total at the bottom of the score sheet and discuss your insights with the coach.

Life Event	Stress Score	Your Score
1. Death of a significant other	100	
2. Divorce	73	
3. Separation from significant other	65	
4. Jail term	63	
5. Death of close family member	63	
6. Personal injury or illness	53	
7. Marriage	50	
8. Fired at work	47	
9. Marital reconciliation	45	
10. Retirement	45	
11. Change in health of family member	44	
12. Pregnancy	40	
13. Sex difficulties	39	
14. Gain of new family member	39	
15. Business readjustment	39	
16. Change in financial state	38	
17. Death of close friend	37	

18. Change to different line of work	36	
19. Change in number of arguments with significant other	35	
20. Mortgage over $100,000	31	
21. Foreclosure of mortgage or loan	30	
22. Change in responsibilities at work	29	
23. Son or daughter leaving home	29	
24. Trouble with in-laws	29	
25. Outstanding personal achievement	28	
26. Significant other beginning or stopping work	26	
27. Beginning or ending school	26	
28. Change in living conditions	25	
29. Revision of personal habits	24	
30. Trouble with boss	23	
31. Change in work hours or conditions	20	
32. Change in residence	20	
33. Change in schools	20	
34. Change in recreational activities	19	
35. Change in religious or spiritual activities	19	
36. Change in social activities	18	
37. Mortgage or loan less than $100,000	17	
38. Change in sleeping habits	16	
39. Change in number of family get-together	15	
40. Change in eating habits	15	
41. Vacation	13	
42. Celebration of major religious holiday	12	
43. Minor violations of the law	11	

TOTAL SCORE _____

Life Transition Grid

Life Change Score/ Age	0-15 Years Old	15-30 Years Old	30-45 Years Old	45-60 Years Old	60-75 Years Old	76 Years Old+
450-525						
375-449						
300-374						
225-299						
150-224						
75-149						
0-74						

Coaching Resource 32: Managing the Stress

Primary Strategy: Aspirational Coaching

We establish "stress ruts" when exposed repeatedly to real or imagined threats. Unlike the zebra living on the savannah of Africa, we not only respond to the threat of "real lions" (such as threatened attack by another person or the potential of job loss), but also the threat of "imagined lions" (such as feeling insulted by an email we have received or imagining the potential impact of a revenue shortfall in our organization) These ruts are grooved deeper with each stressful event and lead to permanent structural changes in our nervous/hormonal systems. We become increasingly vulnerable ("trigger happy") to stress. How might a coach assist her client in identifying and even seeking to avoid or reduce the impact of these stress ruts? Below are five tactics and four coaching strategies.

Tactics

Stress can be reduced in some tactical ways:

1. Avoid the stressful situation in the future.

2. Engage in activities that reduce stress once it has occurred, like practicing mindfulness, centering and slower, even breathing.

3. Identify "sanctuaries": settings and times when and where one can relax and "recreate" (allowing the body to recover from the stress and resulting physiological impact).

4. Obtain a good night sleep (restorative stages of sleep take place only under conditions of deep and sustained relaxation).

5. Avoid excessive use of substances (including alcohol) that may temporarily elevate mood but can soon lead to depression.

As a coach we can not only point to these five tactics, but also help our clients identify ways in which they can modify their habits and patterns of behavior in ways that are aligned with these five tactics. An appreciative approach can be engaged by helping our clients identify ways in which, times during which, and places in which they are already operating in a manner that is aligned with these five tactics.

Strategies

- *Awareness:* Point out to our clients that stress ruts continue to grow deeper with each stressful event. We become increasingly "trigger-happy" and these ruts are permanent. They don't go away when we finally decide to lead a less stressful life. They are enduring neuro-physiological "wounds" that do not heal. When these stress-ruts are established in our bodies, they can only be countered and thwarted by either the complete removal of stress from our life (very difficult in the 21st Century) or by the use of medications that moderate the stress (and place us in the vulnerable position of being drug-dependent and often less vigilant and alert). The third alternative—which is most often taken—is the moderation of the stress through the heavy consumption of alcohol, cigarettes, or over-the-counter drugs. Stress-reduction can't wait until tomorrow. It is a critical issue to be addressed by our clients (and ourselves) today!

- *Sunlight:* Recently, it has been widely acknowledged that "lumens" (light from the sun) trigger neurotransmitters in our brain that are very calming and uplifting. The absence of sunlight can contribute to depression, anxiety and related mood disorders (often identified as "seasonal" disorders). We should try to expose ourselves to at least 15 minutes of sunlight each day. This exposure should come through our eyes (no sunglasses), though obviously we should not look directly toward the sun and should wear appropriate clothing (including a hat) and sun-block lotion. When our coaching client is preparing for an event that could be quite stressful, we should encourage a brief walk outdoors—it helps to reduce the stress and can be very calming (especially if the setting is beautiful and peaceful, and if fresh air is abundant). If a walk outdoors is not feasible or appropriate, then we should encourage our clients to consider using a "light box" (which provides full-spectrum light), or at the very least find ways to work in a room with natural lighting or full-spectrum lighting. Coaching itself can often be enhanced if the coach and client walk around outside during the coaching session. The client is likely to feel less stressed (because of the lumens, as well as the exercise), and will be inclined to find the coaching relationship itself more satisfying.

- *Exercise:* Exercise is also widely accepted as a practice that can significantly reduce stress, and as the top long-term preventive health-measure. Most animals avoid or reduce stress because they engage in physical activities to escape from or fight with the source of the stress (the proverbial lion). We can similarly reduce the physiological arousal associated with preparation for flight or fight by engaging in physical activities (exercise). While we have known about this fight/flight dynamic for many years, recent research suggests that humans are much more inclined to engage in a third activity (or inactivity) when faced with a threat—this is "freeze." Like other animals that are not very fast and not very strong, human beings living on the Savannah tried to remain very quiet when confronting a real or imagined lion. This is a smart stance to take for a short period of time—the lion will soon move on and we can once again be active (and "burn off" the stress-related neural and hormonal stimulants that accumulated when we were frightened by the lion). Unfortunately, we often stay "frozen" for a lengthy period of time when confronting imaginary lions, given that these mental lions don't leave us, but linger in our thoughts and feelings. As a result, our bodies "burn up" with the excessive chemicals that don't get burned off when we remain frozen. As coaches we can help educate our clients about the destructive effect of "frozen behavior" and can encourage them to get some exercise—especially after being exposed to real, potential or imagined threats.

- *Socializing:* Finally, we have become increasingly aware that stress can be reduced through the establishment of (and active engagement in) social networks. Several neurotransmitters that are activated by "bonding" activities serve (like lumens and exercise) as stress-reducers. This does not mean that the social network must be extensive (there can be too much of a good thing), but it does mean that stress is rarely reduced by long term social isolation. We all need to "cocoon" sometimes and bow out of the social "rat race." However, sustained isolation produces depression and increases stress. Computer networking doesn't seem to be sufficient (in fact, extensive time on the computer can actually increase depression). There must be some face-to-face interaction (or at least audio interaction via phone, Skype, etc.) As coaches, we can help our clients identify those interpersonal relationships that are most gratifying and stress-reducing. How do our clients further cultivate these relationships? How do our clients diversify these relationships, so that they find "bonding" experiences at work, at home and in their neighborhood? Many years ago, Robert Bellah and his colleagues wrote about "life style enclaves" which are the new communities in 21st Century societies. These are social networks made up of people with similar hobbies, interests, values and life purposes (ranging from a Polka club to a Porsche car club and from a poker club to a support group for children of alcoholics). As a coach, we can assist our clients in identifying "enclaves" that they would like to join. As appreciative coaches, we can encourage our clients to participate without "guilt" in the enclaves that already bring them pleasure and that help to reduce the stress they inevitably encounter in their busy lives.

References

Adams, James (1974) *Conceptual Blockbusting.* New York: Norton.

Argyris, Chris (1990) *Overcoming Organizational Defenses.* Boston: Allyn and Bacon, 1990.

Argyris, Chris (1982) *Reason, Learning and Action: Individual and Organization.* San Francisco: Jossey-Bass.

Argyris, Chris & Donald Schön (1974) *Theory in Practice.* San Francisco: Jossey-Bass.

Bandler, Richard & Grinder, John (1979) *Frogs into Princes.* Moab, Utah: Real People Press.

Bandler, Richard & Grinder, John (1982) *Reframing.* Moab, Utah: Real People Press.

Bateson, Gregory (1961) The Biosocial Integration of the Schizophrenic Family in Nathan W. Ackerman, Frances L. Beatman and Sanford N. Sherman (Eds.), *Exploring the Base for Family Therapy,* New York: Family Service Association, pp. 116-22.

Bateson, Gregory (1972) *Steps to an Ecology of Mind.* New York: Ballantine.

Belenky, M. & Associates (1986) *Women's Ways of Knowing.* New York: Basic Books.

Bennis, Warren & Slater, Phillip (1968) *The Temporary Society.* New York: Harper.

Bergquist, William (1993) *The Postmodern Organization: Mastering the Art of Irreversible Change.* San Francisco: Jossey-Bass.

Bergquist, William (2003) The Future of Executive Coaching: Coaching with Appreciation through a 360 Degree Feedback Process. *International Journal of Coaching in Organizations,* v. 1, no. 2, pp. 12-22.

Bergquist, William, Julie Betwee & David Meuel (1995) *Building Strategic Relationships.* San Francisco: Jossey-Bass.

Bergquist, William, Kenneth Merritt & Steven Phillips (1999) *Executive Coaching.* Sacramento, CA: Pacific Soundings Press.

Bergquist, William & Mura, Agnes (2005) *Ten Themes and Variations for Postmodern Leaders and Their Coaches.* Sacramento, CA: Pacific Soundings Press.

Blanchard, Ken, John Carlos & Alan Randolph (1999) *The Three Keys to Empowerment.* San Francisco: Berrett-Koehler.

Blanchard, Ken, Susan Fowler & Laurence Hawkins (2005) *Self Leadership and the One Minute Manager.* New York: William Morrow.

Blanchard, Ken, Patricia Zigarmi & Drea Zigarmi (1999) *Leadership and the One Minute Manager.* New York: William Morrow.

Brutus, S., & Derayah, M. (2002). Multi-source assessment programs in organizations: An insider's perspective. *Human Resource Development Quarterly,* 13, 187-201.

Clark, Charles (1958) *Brainstorming.* Garden City, New York: Doubleday.

Cooperrider, David (1990) Positive Image, Positive Action: The Affirmative Basis of Organizing in Suresh Srivastva, David Cooperrider and Associates. *Appreciative Management and Leadership: The Power of Positive Thought and Action in Organizations.* San Francisco: Jossey-Bass, pp. 91-125.

Cummings, L. L. & Anton, Ronald J. (1990) The Logical and Appreciative Dimensions of Accountability. in Suresh Srivastva, David Cooperrider and Associates, *Appreciative Management and Leadership: The Power of Positive Thought and Action in Organizations.* San Francisco: Jossey-Bass, pp. 257- 286.

Durkheim, Emile (1933) *The Division of Labor in Society.* New York: Free Press.

Fiedler, Fred (1967) *A Theory of Leadership Effectiveness.* New York: McGraw-Hill.

Fortgang, Laura (2005) *Now What? 90 Days to a New Life Direction.* New York: Tarcher.

Fromm, Erich (1941) *Escape from Freedom.* New York: Rinehart.

Fromm, Erich (1947) *Man for Himself.* New York: Holt, Rinehart & Winston.

Frost, Peter & Carolyn Egri (1990) Appreciating Executive Action. in Suresh Srivastva, David Cooperrider and Associates, *Appreciative Management and Leadership: The Power of Positive Thought and Action in Organizations.* San Francisco: Jossey-Bass, pp. 289-322.

Gilligan, Carol (1982) *In a Different Voice*. Cambridge, MA: Harvard University Press.

Gladwell, Malcolm (2000) *The Tipping Point*. Boston: Little, Brown.

Goleman, Daniel (2006) *Emotional Intelligence* (10th Anniversary Ed.) New York: Bantam Books.

Goleman, Daniel, Richard Boyatzis and Annie McKee. (2004) *Primal Leadership*. Cambridge, MA: Harvard Business Press.

Goldsmith, Marshall (2000) *Learning Journeys*. London, England: Intercultural Press/Nicholas Brealey Publishing.

Gordon, William (1961) *Synectics*. New York: Collier.

Goss, Tracy. (1996) *The Last Word on Power*. New York: Crown Business.

Hamilton, Kendall (1996) Need a Life? Get a Coach. *Newsweek*. February 5, p. 48.

Handy, Charles (1994) *The Age of Paradox*. Cambridge: Harvard Busienss School Press.

Harmon, Willis (1990) Shifting Context for Executive Behavior: Signs of Change and Revolution. in Suresh Srivastva, David Cooperrider and Associates, *Appreciative Management and Leadership: The Power of Positive Thought and Action in Organizations*. San Francisco: Jossey-Bass, pp. 37-54.

Hill, Sandra & Joel Rothaizer (2007) A multidimensional approach to organizational effectiveness. *International Journal of Coaching in Organizations, 4(2),* 6-29.

Kanter, Rosabeth (1977) *Men and Women of the Corporation*. New York: Basic Books.

Kegan, Robert (1994) *In Over Our Heads: The Mental Demands of Modern Life*. Cambridge, MA: Harvard University Press.

Kolb, David (1983) *Experiential Learning: Experience as the Source of Learning and Development*. Englewood Cliffs, NJ: Prentice-Hall.

Kuhn, Thomas (1962) *The Structure of Scientific Revolution*. Chicago: University of Chicago Press.

Lawrence, Paul and Lorsch, Jay (1969) *Organizations and Environment*. Homewood, IL: Irwin.

Lazar, John & Bergquist, William (2003) Alignment Coaching: The Missing Element in Business Coaching. *International Journal of Coaching in Organizations*, v. 1, no. 1, pp. 14-27.

Lewin, Kurt. (1947) Frontiers in group dynamics. *Human Relations*, v. 1, pp. 5-42.

Likert. Rensis (1961) *New Patterns of Management.* New York: McGraw-Hill.

Lippitt, Ronald, Watson Jeanne & Westley, Bruce (1958) *The Dynamics of Planned Change.* New York: Harcourt, Brace and World.

Luft, Joseph (1969) *Of Human Interaction.* Palo Alto, CA: National Press Books.

McGregor, Douglas (1960) *The Human Side of Enterprise.* New York: McGraw-Hill.

Mezirow, Jack and Associates (2000) *Learning as Transformation.* San Francisco: Jossey-Bass.

Miles, Matthew (1964) On Temporary Systems. in Matthew Miles (Ed.) *Innovation in Education.* New York: Teachers College Press, pp. 437-490.

Miller, John & Scott Page (2007) *Complex Adaptive Systems.* Princeton, NJ: Princeton University Press.

Moreno, Jacob & Jonathan Fox (1987) *Essential Moreno: Writings in Psychodrama, Group Methods and Spontaneity.* New York: Springer Publishing Co.

Novak, William & Moshe Waldoks (1981) *The Big Book of Jewish Humor.* New York: Harper Collins.

Olalla, Julio (2008) Interview with Julio Olalla [Interview conducted by William Bergquist]. *International Journal of Coaching in Organizations.* v. 5, n. 1, pp. 6-33.

O'Neill, Mary Beth. (2007) *Executive Coaching with Backbone and Heart.* San Francisco: Jossey-Bass.

Phillips, Steven (1991) *Creating Effective Relationships: A Basic Guide to Relationship Awareness Theory.* Pacific Palisades, CA: Personal Strengths Publishing.

Phillips, Steven & William Bergquist (1987) *Solutions: A Guide to Better Problem Solving.* San Diego, CA: University Associates.

Porter, Elias (1976) On the Development of Relationship Awareness Theory: A Personal Note, *Group and Organization Studies*, 1, 302-309.

Prince, George (1970) *The Practice of Creativity.* New York: Harper and Row.

Raths, Louis, Merrill Harmin and Sidney Simon (1966) *Values and Teaching.* Columbus, OH: Merrill.

Rogers, Carl (1961) *On Becoming a Person.* Boston, MA: Houghton Mifflin.

Rosenblatt, Roger (1997) The Admiration of Others. *Modern Maturity.* January/February, pp. 22-23.

Rosenthal, Robert (1966) *Experimental Effects in Behavioral Research.* New York: Appleton-Century-Crofts.

Rothaizer, Joel & Sandra Hill. (2010) What is an Adequate Knowledge Base for Executive Coaching? *International Journal of Coaching in Organizations, 7(1).*

Rosinski, Philippe (2010) *Global Coaching.* Boston: Nicholas Brealey.

Sarason, Seymour (1973) *The Creation of Settings and the Future Societies.* San Francisco: Jossey-Bass.

Schön, Donald (1971) *Beyond the Stable State.* New York: Random House.

Schön, Donald (1983) *The Reflective Practitioner: How Professionals Think in Action.* New York: Basic Books.

Scott, Cynthia and Dennis Jaffe (1991) *Empowerment: A Practical Guide for Success.* Menlo Park, CA: Crisp Publications.

Senge, Peter (1990) *The Fifth Discipline.* New York: Doubleday.

Senge, Peter and Associates (1994) *The Fifth Discipline Field Book.* New York: Doubleday.

Sheerer, Robin (1999) *No More Blue Mondays: Four Keys to Finding Fulfillment at Work.* Mountain View, CA: Davies-Black Publishing.

Sperry, Len (1993) Working With Executives: Consulting, Counseling, and Coaching, *Individual Psychology,* v. 49, no. 2, June, p. 257.

Srivastva, S., Cooperrider, D., & Associates (1990) *Appreciative Management and Leadership.* San Francisco: Jossey-Bass.

Stacey, Ralph (1996) *Complexity and Creativity in Organizations.* San Francisco: Berrett-Koehler.

Taleb, Nassim Nicholas (2010) *The Black Swan.* New York: Random House.

Tillich, Paul (1957) *The Dynamics of Faith.* New York: HarperCollins.

Tuchman, Bruce (1965) Developmental Sequence in Small Groups, *Psychological Bulletin*, v. 63, pp. 384-399.

Vaill, Peter (1989) *Managing as a Performing Art*. San Francisco: Jossey-Bass.

Vaill, Peter (1990) Executive development as spiritual development. In Srivastva, S., Cooperrider, D., & Associates. *Appreciative management and leadership*. San Francisco: Jossey-Bass.

Watson, Goodwin & David Johnson (1972) *Social Psychology: Issues and Insights* (2nd Ed.) Philadelphia, PA: Lippincott.

Watzlawick, Paul, Janet Beavin & Don Jackson (1967) *Pragmatics of Human Communication*. New York: Norton.

Watzlawick, Paul, John Weakland & Richard Fisch (1974) *Change*. New York: W.W. Norton.

Wheatley, Margaret (1992) *Leadership and the New Science*. San Francisco: Berrett-Koehler.

Wheeler, Carol (1995) Could Your Career Use a Coach? *Executive Female*, v. 18, no. 5, September, pp. 49-51, 81.

Whitehead, Alfred & Bertrand Russell (1910/1913) *Principia Mathematica*. [Three Volumes, 2nd Ed]. Cambridge, England: Cambridge University Press.

Whitmore, John. (2009) *Coaching for Performance*. (4th Ed.) London, England: Nicholas Brealey Publishing.

Whitworth, Laura, Henry Kimsey-House & Phil Sandahl (2007) *Coactive Coaching*. Mountain View, CA: Davies-Black Publishing.

Index

15531342R00183

Made in the USA
Lexington, KY
03 June 2012